Jet Li

For my mother, Luo Yuanhui
and my father, Yu Hanhao

Jet Li

Chinese Masculinity and Transnational Film Stardom

Sabrina Qiong Yu

EDINBURGH
University Press

© Sabrina Qiong Yu, 2012, 2015
This paperback edition 2015

Edinburgh University Press Ltd
The Tun – Holyrood Road
12 (2f) Jackson's Entry
Edinburgh EH8 8PJ
www.euppublishing.com

First published in hardback by Edinburgh University Press 2012

Typeset in Monotype Ehrhardt by
Servis Filmsetting Ltd, Stockport, Cheshire

A CIP record for this book is available from the British Library

ISBN 978 1 4744 0280 4 (paperback)
ISBN 978 0 7486 8955 2 (epub)
ISBN 978 0 7486 4548 0 (webready PDF)

The right of Sabrina Qiong Yu
to be identified as authors of this work
has been asserted in accordance with the Copyright, Designs
and Patents Act 1988 and the Copyright and Related Rights
Regulations 2003 (SI No. 2498).

Contents

Illustrations vi
Acknowledgements vii

Introduction: Jet Li and transnational kung fu stardom 1

Part I Jet Li as Chinese *wuxia* hero

1 Jet Li and the new *wuxia* cinema in the 1990s 33
2 Kung fu master: martial arts and acting in *Once Upon a Time in China* (1991) 47
3 Gay lover? Gender trouble and male identification in *Swordsman II* (1992) 65
4 Mother's boy: adolescent hero and male masquerade in *Fong Sai-yuk* (1993) 83

Part II Jet Li as transnational kung fu star

5 Villain/killer/child: crossover images and Orientalist imagination 105
6 Asexual Romeo? Male sexuality and cultural perspectives 127
7 National hero/spectacular body: national and transnational identities 146
8 Borderless icon: star construction and Internet fandom 167

Conclusion 185

Bibliography 192
Index 210

Illustrations

All images are courtesy of the Kobal Collection.

1   Jet Li as semi-villainous General Pang in *The Warlords* (Peter Chan, 2007). 10
2   Jet Li as Wong Fei-hung in *Once Upon a Time in China II* (Tsui Hark, 1992). 55
3   Jet Li as Ling Hucong in *Swordsman II* (Ching Siu-tung, 1992). 70
4   Jet Li as Fong Sai-yuk and Josephine Siao as Fong's mother Miao Cuihua in *Fong Sai-yuk* (Corey Yuen, 1993). 87
5   Jet Li as Gabe Law in *The One* (James Wong, 2001). 112
6   Jet Li as Danny and Morgan Freeman as the piano tuner, Sam, in *Danny the Dog* (Louis Leterrier, 2005). 121
7   Jet Li as Liu Jian and Bridget Fonda as Jessica Kamen in *Kiss of the Dragon* (Chris Nahon, 2001). 133
8   Jet Li as Han Sing and Aaliyah Haughton as Trish O'Day in *Romeo Must Die* (Andrzej Bartkowiak, 2000). 140
9   Jet Li as Nameless in *Hero* (Zhang Yimou, 2002). 154
10 Jet Li as legendary Chinese martial artist Huo Yuanjia in *Fearless* (Ronny Yu, 2006). 179

Acknowledgements

The completion of this project, first as my PhD thesis, then developed into the current book, has witnessed my research journey from China to the UK in the past decade. This journey has been accompanied by the help, support, kindness and friendship of numerous people to whom I would like to express my sincere gratitude. I thank Julian Stringer for being a superb research mentor. Without his encouragement and guidance, this book might never have existed. My heartfelt thanks to everyone who has read and commented on individual chapters: Guy Austin, Mark Gallagher, Paul Grainge, Leon Hunt, Sarah Leahy, Eve Richards, Jacob Smith, Lisa Odham Stokes, Yvonne Tasker and Yingjin Zhang. I am also grateful to the colleagues who helped with this project at different stages and in different ways: Elizabeth Andersen, Martin Dusinberre, Mark Jancovich and Florence Myles.

I very much appreciate the help of librarians during my collection of data for this research from the British Film Institute National Library, Hong Kong Film Archive and Shanghai Film and Television Archive. I also wish to thank all the people who agreed to be interviewed by me. I am particularly grateful to Caroline Mason for proofreading my manuscript. Special thanks go to everyone at Edinburgh University Press who was involved in the publication of this book, in particular my editors Gillian Leslie and Donald Vicki, for their efficiency, professionalism and understanding.

My friends in both China and the UK have provided me with invaluable emotional support during the writing of my thesis and the process of reshaping it into this book. Among them, I especially thank Soojeong Ahn, Antoniya Aytova, Nandana Bose, Chen Qinghua, Kevin Dare, Mary Ellis, Fang Song, Jude Grundy, Jia Jing, Jiang Yuanlun, He Qun, Siti Hajar, Serene Oon Miller, Lynne Reast, Pan Qin, Wang Chenglin, Wang Hucheng, Xie Zhengfang and Zhou Min.

Finally, I would like to express my wholehearted gratitude to my family, in particular my mother Luo Yuanhui, my father Yu Hanhao and my husband Zhou Hongsheng, for their unfailing love, patience and support throughout these years. Most loving thanks belong to my daughters,

Felicia and Joya, who were both born during the time I was working on this project. People might think that your arrivals halfway through would make my writing more difficult, but only I know how much courage, strength and inspiration you have brought to me.

I thank the editors and publishers for allowing me to include in my book revised versions of previously published essays. An earlier version of Chapter 2 appears in *EnterText*, 6: 1, Autumn 2006. A small portion of an article I co-authored with Julian Stringer, which is included in Paul Cooke (ed.), 2007, *World Cinema's 'Dialogues' with Hollywood*, Palgrave Macmillan, is reproduced here with permission of Palgrave Macmillan. A shorter version of Chapter 8 appears in Mary Farquhar and Yingjin Zhang (eds) (2010), *Stars in Chinese Cinema*, Routledge, pp. 225–36.

Finally, all translations from Chinese are mine unless otherwise indicated.

Introduction: Jet Li and transnational kung fu stardom

The magic of cinema lies in its capacity for transmitting human experiences and emotions translocally and transnationally. While the contribution of stars to the universal appeal of film has been frequently investigated in scholarly writing over the past three decades, most of such work focuses on Hollywood stars. To a great extent, the field of star studies pioneered by Richard Dyer thirty years ago has been based on the discussion of Hollywood stars and stardom. Non-Hollywood stars are mostly discussed in the context of national cinemas (Vincendeau 2000; Sieglohr 2000; Babington 2001; Austin 2003; Perriam 2003; Hayward 2004; Stoila 2009; Farquhar and Zhang 2010). As I argue elsewhere (Yu 2012), the existing study of film stardom in different national cinemas often looks like a study of variations on the theme of Hollywood stardom, and national stardom needs to be defined in a more distinctive and definitive way. The subject of this book, however, is transnational stardom.

Stars' transnational mobility has been in evidence since the early days of cinema, and is becoming increasingly visible in contemporary times. Yet, the term 'transnational star' is often used within critical discourse as a self-evident term, and 'transnational stardom' remains an under-discussed area. There is some valuable research on 'imported' ethnic stars in Hollywood (Roberts 1993; Negra 2001; Phillips and Vincendeau 2006; Miyao 2007), but discussion in these works mainly focuses on these stars' Hollywood careers, and the transnational nature of their stardom is rarely explored. In fact, I cannot recall any serious effort to define the term, even in a book or article with 'transnational stardom' in its title.[1] Among the reasons for this scholarly omission, the most important one, in my view, is the failure to answer a basic but tricky question – what makes a transnational star?

It would be helpful to look at another term that is often used interchangeably with 'transnational star' but which has a wider connotation, namely, 'international star'. 'International star' refers to a star who achieves international recognition and fame, even if he or she never makes a film outside his or her own country. Many Hollywood stars fall into this category. By comparison, a transnational star needs to physically transfer from one film industry to another to make films, often in a different language from his or her own. Although any star who makes films in another country may be called a transnational star, being able to make films in a different language is one of the defining features of transnational stardom. For example, Penelope Cruz and Juliette Binoche are more likely to be regarded as transnational stars than Nicole Kidman and Kate Winslet, as the latter two, while crossing the national boundaries, appear in films in the same language – English.

It is worth noting that, while theoretically speaking the transfer of stars between film industries is central to the notion of transnational stardom, this transfer is almost always in one direction, that is, stars move from other countries to Hollywood, not vice versa. In most cases, if a non-Hollywood actor wants to become a transnational star, he or she has to move to Hollywood to make English-language films.[2] A typical career trajectory for a transnational star involves gaining fame in one's own country, attracting the attention of American producers and then being invited to make films in Hollywood. Hollywood has a long history of importing foreign stars but does not usually export its stars. It is, of course, not uncommon for a Hollywood star occasionally to appear in a film made in another country, for example, Andie MacDowell in *Four Weddings and a Funeral* (Mike Newell, 1994) and Renée Zellweger in *Bridget Jones's Diary* (Sharon Maguire, 2001), both British films, but this does not transform MacDowell and Zellweger into transnational stars.[3] This one-way traffic reminds us of the power relationship inherent in transnational stardom – Hollywood's assimilation of and control over foreign talents.

The emergence of transnational stardom is made possible by Hollywood's need to boost its domestic market whilst also expanding its global market. As Diane Negra argues, by recruiting stars from other countries and by packaging and selling such international stars, US cultural industries aim to establish 'American global reach and power' (2001: 60). Ninety years after Hollywood imported the first foreign star, Pola Negri, Hollywood has become a symbol of cultural hegemony and its global strategy has never looked so ambitious. Accordingly, contemporary transnational stardom is different from early transnational stardom in at least three aspects. First, while early crossover stars are exclusively European, the ethnic background of contemporary transnational stars is more diverse, and includes stars from Asia, for instance. This might attest to what Kwai-cheung Lo means when he remarks that 'today's

Hollywood, besides becoming more globalised in the economy of scale, has become more multicultural and more politically correct as a result of catering to the increasingly diversified tastes of the world market' (2005: 133). Second, many early transnational stars, such as Ingrid Bergman and Greta Garbo, had not fully established their stardom in their own country before being taken to Hollywood. It was their Hollywood work that made them stars. By comparison, a contemporary transnational star is usually already a big star in his or her home country and has gained some international fame prior to making films in Hollywood. This indicates a subtle change in Hollywood's global recruitment strategy, that is, to bring in established stars instead of 'raw talents' from other countries, so as to shorten the process of star-making and secure existing overseas markets.

Third, while most early crossover stars eventually remained in Hollywood and became Hollywood stars, contemporary trans-border stars often choose to travel between their home countries and Hollywood and make films in both industries. Consequently, they are recognised both as national stars and as Hollywood stars, for example, Antonio Banderas as a Spanish-Hollywood star and Jackie Chan as a Hong Kong-Hollywood star. In this sense, contemporary transnational stars seem to have more international mobility and freedom in their career choice. To better illustrate what transnational stars really are, applying a 'best-case scenario' as envisioned by Steve Fore in his discussion of Hollywood's Hong Kong film émigrés, they are 'oscillating semi-permanently between hemispheres, working on a range of projects with different geolinguistic emphases' (1997: 135). But from another perspective, this newly-gained mobility might also indicate that it is more difficult for foreign talents to be assimilated into (or accepted by?) Hollywood now than it was in the past. Contemporary transnational stars cannot afford to lose their home markets, so their images need to be 'constantly adjusted to cater for different market specifications' (Feng 2011: 78).

After a brief examination of transnational stardom from early cinema to the present, we may conclude that the term 'transnational star', in its most common connotation, refers to a non-Hollywood star who either rebuilds his or her career in Hollywood, or more often in contemporary times, constantly travels between his or her home country and Hollywood to make films, often in different languages. This definition does not exclude those stars who do not go to Hollywood but whose careers do go beyond national boundaries, such as pan-European or pan-Asian stars. While stars in this category can also be seen as transnational stars, they usually have less global visibility and face very different issues from those who cross over to Hollywood, and thus require discussion in a different framework.

In an increasingly globalising cinema world, transnational stars, in addition to embodying Hollywood's global ambition, function as an effective currency for cultural exchange at both production and reception level. Like national stardom, transnational stardom also deserves close academic scrutiny, to complement and develop the field of star studies dominated by the discussion of Hollywood stardom. This book hopes to contribute to such a development by examining transnational kung fu stardom. More specifically, this book is about the trans-border kung fu body – Jet Li – and the meanings this body contains. First of all, who is Jet Li? And why does he deserve a book-length treatment?

Jet Li: from Shaolin Temple to Hollywood

At the beginning of the 1980s, *Shaolin Temple*, which had been filmed over three years, created the spectacle of 'all the people in the city going to one film'. The film won countless fans, from children to the elderly, from the Mainland, Hong Kong and Korea to Japan. At a time when tickets cost 0.1 RMB each, the film achieved the box office miracle of grossing over 100 million RMB in mainland China. This film was so influential that it turned an obsolete monastery into a tourist attraction and sparked the first kung fu craze in mainland China. The leading actor Li Lianjie became a household name overnight and the idol of all Asian youth. (Phoenix Television: Interview with Lu Yu, 2007)

Jet Li has broken the record as the highest earning actor in a Chinese-language film after raking in 100m yuan (£6.5m) for his latest movie [*The Warlords*] ... He also held the previous salary record for his role in the 2002 film *Hero*, where he earned 70m (£4.6m). Director Peter Chan said Li was a 'guarantee' for global sales. 'Without Jet Li, we would not dare to invest 300m yuan in a Chinese-language film', he told Xinhua news agency. (BBC News, 26 November 2007)

The first quotation above is from the introductory remarks of a well-known talk show on Phoenix Television, one of the most popular television channels in China. Li Lianjie is Jet Li's Chinese name. This quotation tells us where Li started out. Nobody can talk about Li's career without mentioning *Shaolin Temple* (Zhang Xinyan, 1982). It was this very film that introduced the 19-year-old, Beijing-born Li to the world stage and presaged the arrival of a new kung fu superstar to follow Bruce Lee and Jackie Chan. The second quotation, from BBC news, tells us where Li was in 2007. In 25 years, he had not only risen to the top of the Chinese film industry, but had also achieved international fame as a kung fu/action star and received the attention of the global media, which referred to him as 'the best screen martial artist', 'Hollywood's new Bruce Lee', 'the Gene Kelly of the action film', and so on. Li's career thus stands in relation to a series of significant issues which will be discussed throughout this book: issues such as the national/transnational, genre and stardom.

Li is one of the most flexible and adaptable Chinese stars because his career has crossed numerous cultural and geographic boundaries, from mainland China to Hong Kong, from the East to the West and from Hollywood to Europe. After the huge success of his film debut, Li made several sequels, none, however, as successful as *Shaolin Temple*. Li also made his directorial debut with *Born to Defense* (Jet Li, 1986) which proved a box office disaster and precluded Li from any further attempts at directing. He experienced the first setback of his career and left for the US in 1987. During his short stay in the US, Li starred in two émigré films, *Dragon Fight* (Billy Hin-sing Tang, 1989) and *The Master* (Tsui Hark, 1992), both of which were Hong Kong productions and filmed in the US. The former did nothing to restore his reputation and the latter was shelved for three years due to its perceived 'dullness' and the fact that it was 'full of continuity flaws' (Parish 2002: 66). Li's declining career was revitalised by *Once Upon a Time in China* (Tsui Hark, 1991), a breakthrough film which teamed Li with Tsui Hark, a successful combination in 1990s' Hong Kong cinema. Li rapidly rose to superstardom in Hong Kong after a series of box office triumphs and maintained his popularity in East and South-East Asia throughout the first half of the 1990s. As the first Mainland actor to become a star in Hong Kong, Li later became one of the first Hong Kong stars to cross over to Western films.

In 1998, Li made his Hollywood debut playing a villain in *Lethal Weapon 4* (Richard Donner, 1998) and relocated to the West to pursue a global career. He has since starred in a number of English-language action films, such as *Romeo Must Die* (Andrzej Bartkowiak, 2000), *Kiss of the Dragon* (Chris Nahon, 2001), *Danny the Dog* (Louis Leterrier, 2005) and *The Forbidden Kingdom* (Rob Minkoff, 2008), working with well-known American and French producers such as Joel Silver and Luc Besson, and has established himself in Hollywood as a reliable action star. Since the beginning of the new century, while Li has continued to make films in the West, he has also periodically returned to the Chinese film studios to make so-called transnational martial art-house blockbusters such as *Hero* (Zhang Yimou, 2002), *Fearless* (Ronny Yu, 2006) and *The Warlords* (Peter Chan, 2007). In recent years, Li seems to have shifted his emphasis back to Asia by making more Chinese-language films than Hollywood films.

Li's career vividly illustrates the transformation of Chinese cinema from national to transnational (in terms of both production and consumption) in the last three decades: *Shaolin Temple* initiated the trend of Hong Kong-PRC (People's Republic of China) co-productions in the 1980s and became a pan-Asian hit; *Fong Sai-yuk* (Corey Yuen, 1993) and its sequel *Fong Sai-yuk II* (Corey Yuen, 1993), the first two films produced by Li's Eastern Productions, represent one of the earliest attempts to integrate Taiwanese investment, Hong Kong efficiency and the resources of mainland China into a successful pan-Chinese film product; Li attracted international attention with his Hong Kong work, subsequently relocating to Hollywood and starring in a number of B action movies, and then successfully bringing Chinese projects into mainstream cinemas in the West (*Hero, Fearless, The Warlords*). Li's film journey across borders therefore offers a perfect site from which to explore the challenges, achievements and difficulties associated with the transnationalisation of Chinese-language cinema, and martial arts film in particular.

Arguably the best martial arts actor in the world at present, Li's greatest contribution to Chinese/world cinema may lie in his irreplaceable role in the development and dissemination of Chinese *wuxia*[4] (martial chivalry) films over the past thirty years. With a number of *wuxia* classics, Li revived the genre three times, in the 1980s, the 1990s and at the beginning of the twenty-first century. As a five-times national martial arts champion and star of *Shaolin Temple*, Li established a martial artist-turned-actor tradition for the genre; many Mainland-trained martial artists, such as Ji Chunhua, Zhao Wenzhuo and Wu Jing, followed Li's footsteps and entered the film industry. The *Shaolin Temple* series also stimulated the first *wuxia* film trend since 1949 in the mainland Chinese film industry, an industry which has usually downplayed entertaining genre films. In Hong Kong, after a long dearth of *wuxia* films in the 1980s, Li's two sensational hits in the early 1990s, *Once Upon a Time in China* and *Swordsman II* (Ching Siu-tung, 1992), respectively signalled the renewal of the kung fu and swordplay subgenres and inaugurated a golden age in the history of *wuxia* film.

When the genre declined again after the mid-1990s, Li transferred to the domain of action films but never lost his strength as a martial arts star. Not only did he continue his graceful physical performances in contemporary settings, but the chivalrous spirit which defines his *wuxia* heroes also characterises many of his action roles (*The Bodyguard from Beijing* [Corey Yuen, 1994]; *Black Mask* [Tsui Hark, 1996]; *Kiss of the Dragon*). To some extent, the action films he made in Hong Kong can be seen as modernised versions of *wuxia* films, and his Hollywood action work may be called Westernised versions of *wuxia* films. It is instructive to consider how Li is actively involved in and accelerates the interaction between *wuxia* films and action films. At the beginning of the new century, Li came back to the genre by starring in several *wuxia* epics, which were both critically acclaimed and commercially successful. Li, together with others, appears to have initiated another ongoing *wuxia* film trend, which, on the one hand, brings the genre to a new height by incorporating elements of art-house cinema, epic and melodrama, and, on the other, further deepens the transnationalisation of the genre.

Jet Li is a star with multiple and ambiguous identities. For many mainland Chinese audiences, Li is a Mainland star since he was trained as a martial artist in Beijing from an early age and first became famous in mainland China. As well as winning national *wushu*[5] competitions as an adolescent between 1974 and 1979, Li also functioned as China's ambassador by performing on the international stage, most famously for President Richard Nixon at the White House in 1974. It is in precisely such a sense that Li is seen as a 'national treasure' (Hong Kong Film Archive 1999: 64). Xiao Zi (1984) even dubs Li the first film star of the PRC. This claim is valid if we consider that in the first six months after the release of *Shaolin Temple*, Li received 100,000 letters from fans (Li, 17 June 1999). In the heavily politicised circumstances of the early 1980s in the Mainland, it was quite unusual for an actor to be admired by a large group of people. In this respect, Li mirrors the emergence of stardom and popular culture in mainland China after the Cultural Revolution. However, after nearly twenty years away from his home country making films elsewhere, Li's identity as a mainland Chinese star has become blurred, especially for a new generation of Mainland audiences.

Meanwhile, Li's status as a Hong Kong star is even more questionable. As one of the first mainland Chinese actors to pursue a career in the Hong Kong film industry, Li's Hong Kong career bears many similarities to his later crossover to the West, in terms of his struggles in a strange and often hostile new land. While the discrimination against Mainlanders in Hong Kong society prior to the 1997 handover was probably more obvious[6] than racism in contemporary Western society, Mainland stereotypes in Hong Kong films, such as country bumpkins,[7] are no less biased and unpleasant than Asian stereotypes on Western screens. Moreover, Li's inability to speak Cantonese in a Cantonese-speaking film industry (his voice is dubbed in all his Hong Kong films) interestingly parallels his perceived inadequate English skills in his English-language films. Unsurprisingly, Li's Mainland background has often been recalled and highlighted in his Hong Kong career, as can be seen from entertainment reports and the film roles he plays. His identity as an 'outsider' is further reinforced by local researchers' neglect of him. Despite the fact that he was a guarantee of box office success and an indisputable leading actor in Hong Kong in the early 1990s,[8] Li is astonishingly absent from academic writing on Hong Kong stars and Hong Kong cinema. For example, Li is not seen as one of the local icons by Stephen Chan (2005) in his discussion of Hong Kong action heroes; Steve Fore (2004) even excludes Li from the list of Hong Kong talents who have 'gone Hollywood' since the mid-1990s.

Ironically, Li is probably more often labelled a Hong Kong star in the West. After all, it was his Hong Kong films such as *Once upon a Time in China* and *Fist of Legend* (Gordon Chan, 1994) that attracted Western attention, won him a cult following in the West, and later led to his crossover to Hollywood. Since Li started making English-language films in 1998, his identity has changed yet again. For Western audiences, he is simply an imported Chinese/Asian star, and whether he is from Hong Kong or mainland China is less important; for Chinese audiences, he is both a Chinese star and a Hollywood star. Like other crossover stars, Li in his Western career has been surrounded by debates such as: is he successful or unsuccessful in the West? Is he selling himself out in order to satisfy a 'Western gaze'? Have his talents been misused or wasted in Hollywood? Audiences who are familiar with Li's Chinese-language films are usually dissatisfied with his Western performances. They either lament that Hollywood is wasting, even destroying this former Chinese screen hero, or feel disappointed that Li has submitted to Hollywood's exploitation. This kind of criticism is very typical for a transnational star and reveals some common issues contemporary transnational stars have to face.

One such issue is how to negotiate with their old star persona and readjust to their Hollywood career. Lo's observation concerning overseas Hong Kong film talent is applicable to transnational stardom in general: 'Their past reputation in Hong Kong or in Asia upon which their cultural identity is built becomes relatively negligible since they are now workers looking for a new career in a different market' (2001: 469). It is unlikely that a transnational star can maintain the same star persona in Hollywood as in his or her home country. The newly acquired persona is often disappointing, especially for their home audiences, probably due to the fact that ethnic stars in today's Hollywood are still subjected to prejudice and constraints, but also because, as Julian Stringer rightly points out, ethnic stars are 'obliged to bear the burden of a minority's hopes and dreams' (2003: 236). It is therefore not surprising to see that the careers of transnational stars are always accompanied by the criticism that they are selling out and losing their identities. Compared to transnational European stars, stars from Asia like Li probably struggle more in Hollywood, not only because of a bigger discrepancy in terms of language and culture, but also because Asian stereotypes in Hollywood cinema seem to be more negative, and more difficult to break. As Jun Xing sympathetically observes,

'Asian-American actors and actresses have to confront the moral dilemma between reinforcing stereotypes of their people and maintaining their own professional and sometimes economic survival' (1998: 78).

However, this division – between a previous star image built up in one's home country as positive or authentic and the current one constructed in one's Hollywood films as negative or false – not only shows a tendency to create a new kind of power relationship and myth in cultural translation, but precludes us from further exploration of the issues surrounding the transnational journeys of Hollywood film émigrés. Is it true that their Hollywood performances can only end up reasserting racial stereotypes? Can transnational stars take advantage of the multiple possibilities in the global sphere to build new kinds of transnational representations, correct Hollywood stereotypes and thus reconstitute the discursive formations of race, class, and gender? In the past decade, by transferring from one film industry to another (the US, France, mainland China, Hong Kong), Li has been trying to dispel the doubts about him and consolidate his reputation as a transnational Chinese star. With his large-scale project *The Warlords*, Li became the most expensive actor in Asia at the time. It seems that negative opinions of Li's Hollywood adventures have not damaged his stardom in China/Asia, but instead have somehow boosted it. An examination of Li's transnational career can therefore help to deepen our understanding of the challenges and opportunities facing a transnational star.

Despite Li's significance in terms of genre, stardom and the transnationalisation of Chinese-language cinema, as elaborated above, there has been long-term neglect of Li in both Chinese-language and English-language academic writing. The limited amount of literature on Li is mostly written by Western scholars (Major 2000; Stringer 2003; Hunt 2003; Farquhar 2010a).[9] By comparison, the other two transnational kung fu stars, Bruce Lee and Jackie Chan, have received much more scholarly attention. Among other reasons, Li's ambiguous identity might have contributed to this critical omission. If Lee's stardom often epitomises Asian-American experiences, and Chan functions as a cultural symbol of Hong Kong, Li's career, characterised as it is by constant border crossing, makes it difficult to theorise his stardom. This book proposes to read Li as a transnational icon with a flexible identity; from Chinese kung fu master to Asian-American gangster, from ancient swordsman to anti-Japanese patriot, from a martial arts champion to an international star, Li does not belong to one particular cultural and geographic location, but crosses between many different ones. This book is not intended to be a biography of Jet Li, to repeat or compete with such work as *Jet Li: A Biography* (Parish 2002). It will not discuss in detail Li's life and career,

Figure 1 Jet Li as semi-villainous General Pang in *The Warlords* (Peter Chan, 2007). (Source: Kobal Collection.)

but will instead focus on his star image as constructed in selected films and audience reception. The fundamental purpose of this book is to use Jet Li as a case study to address some intriguing but under-examined issues surrounding transnational stardom in general and transnational kung fu stardom in particular.

It is noticeable that most Chinese stars who have had the opportunity to relocate to Hollywood work in the domain of action/martial arts film. Kung fu superstars – Bruce Lee, Jackie Chan and Jet Li – are among the few Chinese stars who have attracted a wide and solid international fandom. As Chinese cinema's most widely acknowledged contribution to world cinema, transnational kung fu stardom deserves careful investigation as a whole, alongside the study of individual stars. This book, while focusing on Li, tries to relate the investigation of Li to a broader discussion of transnational kung fu stardom by making frequent comparisons between Li and the other two stars: Bruce Lee and Jackie Chan. In the following sections, I examine the two most enduring critical assumptions/ clichés in existing scholarship on transnational kung fu stardom: firstly that Hong Kong martial arts cinema is chopsocky and, secondly, that it concerns the remasculinisation of the Chinese male body. By so doing, I wish to locate the discussion of Li's stardom within the debates on transnational action and Chinese masculinity.

Transnational Hong Kong action

Transnational kung fu stardom is made possible by the transnationalisation of Hong Kong action. Action is probably the only Chinese film form that has successfully crossed national and cultural boundaries and become truly transnational, whether it be kung fu films popularised by Bruce Lee in the 1970s, John Woo's gangster films, which have gained cult status in the West, Jackie Chan's globally successful action comedies, or pan-Chinese 'martial art-house' blockbusters from prestigious Chinese directors in the new century. Prior to recent heavy critical investment in transnational martial art-house epics such as *Crouching Tiger, Hidden Dragon* (Ang Lee, 2000) and *Hero*,[10] the scholarship on transnational Chinese action focused almost exclusively on Hong Kong action genres. Generally speaking, three main approaches can be discerned within the discussion on transnational Hong Kong action, respectively highlighting star bodies, the trans-border appeal of Hong Kong action and its global impact.

Although the roles played by a couple of directors in the internationalisation of Hong Kong action have been addressed (Bordwell 2000; Ciecko 1997; Lo 2005; Magnan-Park 2007) – in particular, King Hu and his stylised swordplay films that 'graced the screens of Western art cinema in the mid-70s' (Teo 1997: 87), and the influence of John Woo, the first Asian director to work in the Hollywood mainstream cinema, and his aesthetics of violence – the academic writing on transnational Hong Kong action is predominantly star-oriented. Two kung fu superstars Bruce Lee and Jackie Chan have aroused a great deal of interest in English-language scholarship and have thus become the symbols of the transnationalisation of Hong Kong action. On the one hand, Lee's widely circulated kung fu films and Chan's US-released kung fu/action comedies have been studied extensively, either in terms of their provision of a distinctive mode of action cinema and a fresh action hero image, outside Hollywood action traditions (Gallagher 1997; Fore 1997), or in terms of the discourses of class, race, gender, anticolonialism, postcolonialism and national identity (Ryan 1984; Tasker 1997; Teo 1997; Chan 2000; Fore 2001). On the other hand, the two stars' crossover English-language films have stirred the debate over Hollywood's (often disappointing) appropriation of Hong Kong action traditions in line with its commercial pursuits and racial politics (Marchetti 2001; Lo 2005; Chan 2009; Holmlund 2010). In his well-informed book *Kung Fu Cult Masters*, Leon Hunt (2003) offers a more comprehensive investigation of kung fu stars' transnational careers by looking at the transnational performance of Bruce Lee, Jackie Chan and Jet Li, as well as that of some less well-known kung fu stars such as Wang Yu.

The second approach to transnational Hong Kong action is what I call 'appeal studies'. The global appeal of Hong Kong action has been explored at both the aesthetic and ideological levels. David Bordwell's work is representative in proposing the 'kinaesthetic artistry' of Hong Kong action as its major appeal to audiences around the world. By closely analysing such tactics as 'constructive editing', 'slow motion' and the 'pattern of pause/burst/pause', Bordwell (1997, 2000) detects a strategy of 'expressive amplification' that endows Hong Kong action with physical or emotional qualities. According to Bordwell, instead of an impassive, restrained realism, Hong Kong filmmakers present a fight or chase which is 'given a distinct, vivid emotional profile' and aims to carry the spectator away (2000: 232). Similarly, Aaron Anderson (2001), employing a kinaesthesia-oriented analysis, reads Jackie Chan's choreographed fight sequences in his action comedies as dance rather than violence, and his masterly use of space as a type of art.

As well as visual spectacle and physical sensation, the 'ghetto' attraction of Hong Kong martial arts/action films has been elaborated by different authors. From Stuart Kaminsky's article 'Kung fu film as ghetto myth' (1982) to David Desser's essay 'The kung fu craze: Hong Kong cinema's first American reception' (2000), kung fu films are commonly seen to articulate underclass needs and values, and therefore appeal to dispossessed groups such as white working-class youth and the African-American community. Gina Marchetti extends this reading to Jackie Chan's US-released Hong Kong action comedies and first crossover film *Rush Hour* (Brett Ratner, 1998). By unpacking the black connection[11] in four Jackie Chan films, Marchetti argues that Chan represents a dream of physical empowerment to those audiences 'who may be oppressed because of the physical differences of race and gender' (2001: 158). From a different perspective, Yuan Shu (2003) suggests that Chan's success in the US should be understood in terms of the transformation of kung fu cinema from its preoccupation with racial politics, as envisioned by Bruce Lee, to its current embracing of multiculturalism, which aims to accommodate the tastes and needs of the middle class on a global scale.

The third, relatively new, strand in the discussion of transnational Hong Kong action can be termed 'impact studies', and principally surveys the influence of Hong Kong action on and its connection with, action cinemas elsewhere. The edited collection *Hong Kong Connections* (Morris, Leung and Chan 2005) represents such an effort to explore 'the transnational invocation and contextually complex uptake of the Hong Kong action "model"' (Morris 2005: 3) in different national contexts such as Korea, Japan, India and France. As to the role of Hong Kong action in shaping contemporary Hollywood action cinema, Hunt (2003) draws our attention to the contribution of Hong Kong fight choreographers to the success of Hollywood action blockbusters such as *The Matrix* (Andy Wachowski and Lana Wachowski, 1999) and *Charlie's Angels* (McG, 2000), and to the creation of a new 'Cyber-fu' genre that involves heavy use of digital effects, wirework and training non-action stars in martial arts. Elsewhere, Hunt (2008) discusses the role of two types of transnational 'gatekeepers' – represented by Quentin Tarantino and Luc Besson respectively – in the 'Asianisation' of Euro-American cinema through the incorporation of Hong Kong action in either a referential or non-referential way.

The discussions sketched out above provide many valuable insights and perspectives, enabling us to deepen our understanding of the trans-border appeal of Hong Kong action and the role it plays in shaping the global action landscape. However, it should be pointed out that, whether Hong Kong films highlighting action are referred to within the critical discourse as martial arts films, kung fu films, *wuxia* films or action comedies, they are unanimously seen as subgenres of a wider category – action cinema – defined by action films from Hollywood, and studied against a series of discourses conventionally seen in the discussion of Hollywood action cinema. The tendency to indiscriminately label action-oriented Hong Kong films as action cinema has led to many critical clichés, among which the most enduring one might be that Hong Kong action is chopsocky. This disparaging term was originally coined to describe low-tech and low-budget Hong Kong kung fu films exported to the West in the 1960s and 1970s, which are mostly characterised by a disjointed story-line, ridiculous acting, excessive violence and shabby quality. However, this biased, still dominant perception of Hong Kong martial arts/action films as chopsocky in their Western reception, in my view, is also inseparable from the simplistic and problematic categorisation of action-oriented Hong Kong films as action cinema.

As the world's 'most widely distributed popular cultural genre' (Morris 2005: 1), action cinema ironically remains one of the most critically-dismissed genres, despite various critical attempts to treat it seriously (Tasker 1993, 2004; Arroyo 2000). 'Dumb movies for dumb people', a common perception of action films, as revealed by Tasker nearly twenty years ago, still to a large extent predominates the evaluation of this popular genre and its audiences. In contrast to high-culture genres that emphasise psychology, action cinema is firmly defined as a 'physical' genre that foregrounds visual and aural spectacle. Hollywood action films, as Tasker argues, 'have consistently failed to meet the markers of aesthetic and cultural value typically applied within contemporary film culture' as they are 'deemed noisy and brash, judged empty at best and politically reactionary at worst' (2004: 2).

Labelled as action cinema, Hong Kong action-oriented films unsurprisingly bear the stigma of Hollywood action cinema as a low-culture, physical genre, and in fact, have an even poorer reputation in the West. Despite the fact that dubbed kung fu films from Hong Kong 'maintained a powerful presence on U.S. Screens' (Desser 2000: 20) in the 1970s, and that Hong Kong action has been popular in the international video/DVD rental market for decades and has secured a large global fan base, Hong Kong action products are viewed as cheap chopsocky films taking ghetto root in crime, poverty and unrest, or at best, B movies worshipping violence and blood, nowhere near the celebrated Hollywood action genres such as American Westerns. Globally successful 'martial art-house' films are more 'artistically and aesthetically elaborate, with big budgets and grand exterior scenes' (Xu 2006: 90), but they do not seem to have changed the deep-rooted contempt for Chinese/Hong Kong action as mindless entertainment in English-language critical discourse, as evinced by my case study of American critical responses to *Hero* in Chapter 7.

To discuss Hong Kong action-oriented films within the framework of Hollywood action cinema, I would argue, clearly neglects the uniqueness and richness of Hong Kong action traditions. Hong Kong action, deriving from the *wuxia* genre and centring on martial arts performance, has profound connections with Chinese literature, theatre, myth, religion and folklore. Take its literary connection, for example. The *wuxia* genre has existed in Chinese literature for centuries.[12] The enormous popularity of modern and contemporary *wuxia* novels provides a solid foundation and inexhaustible source for the emergence and flourishing of *wuxia* cinema, such as Tsui Hark's groundbreaking *Swordsman* series adapted from Jin Yong's well-known novel *The Smiling, Proud Wanderer*, and Ang Lee's global blockbuster *Crouching Tiger, Hidden Dragon* based on Wang Dulu's novel of the same name written during 1938–42, to name but two. Adaptation is not really an issue in the discussion of Hollywood action cinema, but it would be inadequate to talk about the production and consumption of *wuxia* cinema without referring to its literary origins. Usually adapted from popular *wuxia* novels, and in many cases translated to the screen more than once, the characters in a *wuxia* movie carry abundant inter-textual meanings. Consequently, local audiences (by local, I mean not only Hong Kong audiences but also wider Chinese-speaking audiences) who are familiar with the original novel often have a totally different understanding of a film/character to that of global audiences who lack this pre-knowledge. I briefly touch on the impact of literary connection on the reception of *wuxia* cinema in Chapter 3 where I discuss mainland Chinese fans' reading of *Swordsman II*.

Hong Kong action's close relationship with traditional theatre performance has been elaborated by many critics (Bordwell 2000; Anderson 2001; Yung 2005). Not only were many kung fu stars (Jackie Chan, Sammo Hung) and action choreographers (Yuen Woo-ping, Corey Yuen) trained in Peking Opera before entering the film industry, but many fighting styles seen in both period *wuxia* films and contemporary action comedies evolved from acrobatic stunts on the opera stage. While Hong Kong action, like Hollywood action films, does offer thrilling violence and spectacular bodies, it lays more emphasis on the visual beauty of fighting, no matter whether the combatants are unarmed or using swords or guns. The performativity of Chinese martial arts rather than its function as combat is foregrounded on screen. As mentioned earlier, some critics have tried to theorise the stylised, aestheticised and expressive features of Hong Kong action. However, they mainly aim to address the pleasure of watching Hong Kong action films by drawing a connection between the mental understanding and the physical sensations of viewers, thus basically treating Hong Kong action as a low-culture 'body genre'. As Linda Williams points out, what marks a body genre as low is the perception that 'the body of the spectator is caught up in an almost involuntary mimicry of the emotion or sensation of the body on the screen' (1991: 4). But fighting in the Hong Kong/Chinese action tradition does more than providing visual spectacle and physical sensation. In Chapter 2, I argue that fighting can also help characterisation in a *wuxia* film, by exploring how Jet Li turns fighting into a powerful tool for performing in *Once Upon a Time in China*.

Furthermore, for Chinese filmmakers, action can be used to explore innovative film languages, experiment with new technologies, discuss social issues, and express complicated sentiments. Two pioneers of the Hong Kong New Wave, Tsui Hark and Patrick Tam, chose to start their directorial careers with *wuxia* films – *The Butterfly Murders* (Tsui Hark, 1979) and *The Sword* (Patrick Tam, 1980) – which treat *wuxia* material in an experimental way and became representative of the Hong Kong New Wave; King Hu sought to embody the spirit of Zen in his poetic swordplay films which brought Chinese-language cinema to new technical and artistic heights in the 1960s; John Woo used the bullet to convey his concerns about Hong Kong's future at an unstable historical moment prior to the 1997 handover; Wong Kar-wai continued to discuss his favorite subject – alienated and lonely human beings – in his *wuxia* elegy *Ashes of Time* (Wong Kar-wai, 1994) simply changing the setting from the modern city to the ancient desert; and Ang Lee has described his global success, the *wuxia* epic, *Crouching Tiger, Hidden Dragon*, as a *wuxia* version of *Sense and Sensibility* (Ang Lee, 1995).[13] In Chapter 4, by investigating the popularity of *Fong Sai-yuk* among a group of Mainland military graduates, I further demonstrate, at the level of reception, that action-oriented Chinese/Hong Kong films, far from being a 'body genre', can carry cinematic and cultural significance like any other more 'serious' film genres.

Therefore, in contrast to Hollywood action cinema's low-culture status, and especially in contrast to the Western perception of Hong Kong action as chopsocky, Hong Kong action holds a much more prestigious position in its own film culture, as further evinced by the following facts: (1) action is always the mainstay of the Hong Kong film industry and has played a significant role in the development and internationalisation of Hong Kong cinema; (2) Hong Kong action genres play a remarkable role in producing stars; it is hard to find a major Hong Kong star who has never performed in an action-oriented film; (3) like Hong Kong stars who usually need a couple of action roles to retain their popularity, most established Hong Kong directors make at least one action-oriented film in their career, not to mention latecomers in acting filmmaking such as the renowned mainland Chinese director Zhang Yimou and one of the most successful contemporary foreign directors in Hollywood, Ang Lee. Both directors have declared that every Chinese director has a *wuxia* dream.

By revealing the limitation of 'action cinema' as a designation for Hong Kong films highlighting action, I am not intending to suggest a better name, but rather to draw attention to what has been missed and distorted in the transnationalisation of Hong Kong/Chinese action. The view of Hong Kong action as chopsocky, biased as it is, has to a large extent shaped the crossover image of transnational kung fu stars and reduced their screen presence to that of a fighting machine. While Bordwell affirmatively declares, 'Today Hollywood remains the reference point' (2000: 18), I agree with Adrian Martin that 'Hong Kong cinema can never be reduced to an inspired exaggeration or distortion of Hollywood's codes' (2005: 179). Instead of being viewed as a subgenre of Hollywood action cinema and studied under existing critical models, Hong Kong/Chinese action deserves careful scrutiny within its specific cultural and generic traditions. In this book, I emphasise the importance of researching Hong Kong/Chinese action in its own right in both local and transnational contexts.

Remasculinisation of Chinese action bodies

Where a kung fu star is concerned, the issue of male representation unavoidably emerges. While in Western scholarship, as Willemen (2005) complains, almost all current accounts of action cinema surround the issue of masculinity, this is certainly not the case in the discussion of Hong Kong/Chinese action. As some critics have remarked (Wang 1991; Lu 1997), in Chinese film studies, a 'cultural priority' has been given to femininity. Academic writings overwhelmingly centre on the images and representations of women. By contrast, Chinese male screen images have not received much critical attention, which leads to Chris Berry and Mary Farquhar's (2006) conclusion that there is a failure to treat 'man' in similar depth to 'woman' in China studies. The limited literature that addresses Chinese masculinity has been mainly confined to male-dominated action genres, more specifically, the Hong Kong martial arts/action films of Zhang Che, John Woo, Jackie Chan and Bruce Lee, and the crossover Hollywood action vehicles of Lee and Chan. Intriguingly, despite the diverse male representations in these films, a key theme repeatedly emerging from English-language critical discourse is the remasculinisation of Chinese men.

Hong Kong cinema is widely regarded as offering a macho, tough masculinity through its energetic action genres. This vital masculine tradition is indisputably set forth by director Zhang Che in his new wave *wuxia* films of the late 1960s and the 1970s. Dissatisfied with the female-centred Chinese cinema tradition, Zhang promoted *yanggang* aesthetics, a male-dominated ideology, which marked a break from the Chinese tradition of the 'weak male' and produced a roster of prominent male stars including Wang Yu, Jiang Dawei, Di Long and Fu Sheng. In Zhang Che's cinematic world, *yanggang* means the quality of manhood, embodied in the willingness to sacrifice oneself for friendship or justice, fearlessness in the face of violence and death, and dogged perseverance. Zhang's groundbreaking masterpiece *The Golden Swallow* (Zhange Che, 1968) in Teo's view (1997) presents a new kind of male hero in the character of Silver Roc (Wang Yu) – a violent, lonely, psychologically disturbed young man with 'a martyrdom complex', for whom death/self-destruction seems to be the ultimate way to fulfil his macho self. The character of Silver Roc perfectly exemplifies the notion of *yanggang* and became the prototype for Zhang's later male heroes.

Zhang's preoccupation with male potency and male relationships and his worship of the male body are considered to have been inherited by John Woo in his romantic hero films, which were hugely popular in the late 1980s and early 1990s (Li 1994). Woo himself also acknowledges this influence by pointing out that Hong Kong filmmakers' depictions of masculine characteristics, such as courage and toughness, owe a great debt to Zhang Che's films (quoted in *Cinema Hong Kong* 2003). With his modern version of *wuxia* heroes, Woo is considered to have continued the remasculinisation of Chinese men by advocating Zhang's *yanggang* aesthetics, although male images in the two directors' films exhibit different features. For example, while Zhang's heroes are marked by a martyrdom complex and splendid tragedy, Woo's gangster heroes look more gloomy and are sometimes even anti-heroic. Some critics (Teo 1997) try to relate different types of macho heroes in the films of Zhang and Woo to the different historical contexts in which their films appeared: proud martial arts heroes in the mid-1960s reflect Hong Kong's new economic assertiveness as 'an Asian tiger', and the 'darker' gangster heroes of the late 1980s and the early 1990s are a response to the Hong Kong people's anxiety about 1997.

'Remasculinisation' is also central to the discussion of the screen images of Bruce Lee and Jackie Chan. For example, Marchetti argues that Chan and the Hong Kong action genre generally 'embody a remasculinisation of castrated, marginalised, colonial/postcolonial subjects' (2001: 150). Yet, both stars' roles in remasculinising the Chinese male body have more often been examined within an international context against the discourses of race, class and nationality. For many critics, the significance of Lee's crossover success lies in his articulation for the first time of a tough Chinese masculinity which counters a history of the 'feminisation' of Chinese men on Western screens. As Tasker puts it, 'the hardness of Lee's body and of his star image emerges from a history of softness, a history of images in which both Chinese men and women had been represented as passive and compliant' (1997: 324). For Tasker, the symbolic centrality of a rhetoric of hardness in Lee's films implies a fear of softness, and Lee's image speaks of a struggle to become hard and to negate softness. Similarly, Shu (2003) argues that Lee makes full use of his body to show the fighting skill, agility and superior coordination that a human being can achieve, thereby creating the hard body and tough guy image of the Asian male. Not as much a macho hero as Lee, Chan's crossover image is described as 'courageous but vulnerable, funny but admirable and superman-like but still human' and therefore it 'challenges the Orientalist construction of the Asian male body as being "soft"' (Shu 2003: 57). Moreover, many critics agree that Chan introduces a tough Chinese masculinity probably more through showing the outtakes of stunt mishaps after the film's closing credits to prove that he did all the stunts himself. As Lo remarks, 'Chan becomes a superhero in his outtakes' (2004: 121). It is precisely along the above lines that Lee and Chan are regarded as having remasculinised the Asian/ Chinese male body.

If remasculinisation does to some extent prove an effective way to sum up the originality of the above-mentioned action male heroes, it is at the same time becoming a ready-made way to comment on Chinese male screen images, especially those within a transnational context. In many aspects, remasculinisation has become a defining feature of transnational kung fu stardom. It should be pointed out, however, that the thesis of remasculinisation of Chinese men assumes a pre-existing, problematic Chinese masculinity that needs to be remasculinised, a masculinity often described as 'emasculated', 'feminised' or 'soft'. Indeed, the emasculated/ feminised Chinese man is another oft-repeated critical truism for describing Chinese screen masculinity. Here, I do not intend to debate whether or not Chinese men as represented on screen are emasculated or feminised. Rather, I would like to ask whether a soft, feminised masculinity is always necessarily negative and a manifestation of the loss/lack of masculinity, hence demanding remasculinisation.

Feminised men have had a long presence in Chinese culture. Instead of being despised, the men of the 'effeminate scholar-intellectual type prevalent in Chinese culture' (Lu 2000: 30) are more respected than masculine men, as they are more cultured, refined and subtle. In line with Chinese philosophical ideas such as 'coupling hardness with softness' or 'the balance of *yin* and *yang*', men with some feminine attributes are considered (by both sexes) to be superior to macho men. From *Romance of the Western Chamber* to *Dream of the Red Chamber*, Chinese classical theatre and fiction are populated with many memorable and loveable feminised male characters. Highlighting the exchange of sexual identities in traditional models of Chinese artistic representation, particularly where men display feminine characteristics such as stillness and passivity, Yuejin Wang (1991) claims the feminisation of men to be a form of the collective cultural unconscious. This cultural unconscious is termed 'symbolic femininity' by Wendy Larson in her reading of Fifth-Generation director Chen Kaige's films. According to Larson, in his films Chen splits Chinese male subjectivity into two parts: a symbolically feminised male consciousness and a historically authoritative male self. In contrast to the usual contempt for 'feminised Chinese men' seen in English-language critical discourses, Larson sees femininity embodied in Chen's male characters as a means 'through which male subjectivity can be deepened and made aware of its own lack of belief in or control over . . . history' (1997: 337), thus offering a new possibility for reconstructing male consciousness.

To answer the question I posed earlier, therefore, 'feminised Chinese men' should not be simply related to inadequate or problematic masculinity: they could be read as a cultural product not without merit; or, from an alternative (non male-centred) gender perspective, they could indicate a more complete male subjectivity. The notion of the 'remasculinisation of Chinese men', a predominant theme in English-language academic writing on Chinese male screen images, which presupposes an insufficient Chinese masculinity, thus reveals a Western-centred approach. As Berry and Farquhar rightly point out, when masculinity is discussed in Chinese film studies, 'it is usually within Western paradigms' (2006: 140). However, the Western paradigms of masculinity are often inappropriate to the Chinese case in that 'their application would only prove that Chinese men are "not quite real men" because they fail the (Western) test of masculinity' (Louie 2002: 8–9), as is vividly demonstrated by the critical consensus on the 'remasculinisation of Chinese men'. According to Kimmel and Messner, masculinity is culturally specific in that 'the meaning of masculinity is neither transhistorical nor culturally universal, but rather varies from culture to culture and within any culture over time' (1995: xxi). With a Western-centred approach, however, Chinese masculinity, instead of having its own characteristics, is largely described as a 'modification' or 'aberration' of Western masculinity.

Unsatisfied with the uncritical and inappropriate imposition of a Western model of masculinity on the definition of Chinese male screen images, some critics have begun to adopt a more culturally specific approach, which applies Chinese cultural codes to the theorisation of Chinese male representations. In *Theorising Chinese Masculinity: Society and Gender in China* (2002), Kam Louie suggests the traditional Chinese paradigm of masculinity, namely *wen-wu* (cultural attainment-martial valour), as a key framework for understanding representations of Chinese males in literature and film. Louie emphasises that *wenren* (the scholar) is considered to be no less masculine than *wuren* (the soldier), and an ideal Chinese man is expected to embody a balance of *wen* and *wu*. In one chapter, Louie applies the *wen-wu* paradigm to the analysis of three transnational Chinese male stars, Bruce Lee, Jackie Chan and Chow Yun-fat, by defining their images as 'internationalising *wu* masculinity', a notion revealing that Chinese representations of *wu* masculinity have been modified by Western constructions of masculinity. Like Louie, Berry and Farquhar propose three central Confucian codes – filiality, brotherhood and loyalty – as a way to look at male representations in the films of Jackie Chan, John Woo and Zhang Yimou respectively. They argue that 'the codes persist as mythic symbols of national identity, ideal masculine behavior, and institutional governance that are reconstituted in various ways in films within different national and non-national settings' (2006: 136).

This culturally specific approach engenders a close examination of masculinity within the Chinese cultural context and encourages a definition of Chinese masculinity with unique cultural traits, rather than reading it simply as a 'realignment' of the elements of Western masculinity. Yet, if Western paradigms should not be taken as the 'standard' way to read Chinese male representations, neither should Chinese cultural codes. In an era of globalisation, Chinese male screen images are not only circulated and consumed among Chinese audiences, but also among non-Chinese audiences largely unfamiliar with Chinese cultural codes. Their responses, based on their own cultural backgrounds, are not necessarily misreadings but rather different perceptions of Chinese masculinity. Moreover, given that today the concept of masculinity among many Chinese audiences (the younger generation in particular) is largely influenced by globally-disseminated ideas of masculinity, especially those constructed through Hollywood blockbusters, I am not sure how far a clear-cut cultural perspective among Chinese audiences could be identified. A culturally specific approach can deepen our understanding of how male screen images are constructed in relation to a set of particular cultural codes, or suggest a possible reading among local audiences, but it cannot fully address the wider appeals and multiple meanings of Chinese male representations in an era of film transnationalisation.

Above, I have argued that indiscriminately applying a Western or Hollywood model to the study of transnational kung fu stardom risks ignoring its cultural specificities and often results in critical clichés such as that Hong Kong action is chopsocky and that it concerns the remasculinisation of Chinese men. This is not to say that Western models are invalid for discussing Chinese films or stars, but to resist a critical tendency to read non-Western/non-Hollywood film cultures against a Western/Hollywood standard. Moreover, it would be unfair to blame a West-centric point of view alone for the critical clichés surrounding transnational kung fu stardom, as they can also be attributed to the prevalent text-centred approach to stardom, genre and masculinity in the existing scholarship.

While many works set out to understand the trans-border appeal of kung fu stars and Hong Kong action, very few make a real effort to research how audiences from different locations actually receive them. Instead, critics are keen to speak for an 'imagined' audience positioned by their own reading of film texts. Yingjin Zhang and Mary Farquhar note that audience research remains an underdeveloped area in Chinese film studies. In their edited book *Chinese Film Stars*, the first anthology on the subject, they emphasise the importance of audience to stardom in Chinese film history since the early stages and see the 'imbrication between audience and stardom' (2010: 12) as a significant issue demanding immediate attention. I am entirely in agreement with their assessment. In an area that is predominantly defined by appeal, pleasure and identification, audience reception is as important as the film to our understanding of star image. The audience 'is also part of the making of the image' (Dyer 1986: 5), not simply something manipulated or controlled by marketing strategies of the industry. This especially applies to a transnational star like Jet Li, who appeals to diverse audiences around the world: it is often the position of the audience rather than the film itself that decides Li's meanings for audiences in different cultural and historical contexts. Based on this understanding, this book employs an audience/reception study methodology for the discussion of Li's screen image and transnational stardom. By rejecting the text-centred approach which prevails in star studies and instead emphasising the role of audiences in constructing star image, I hope to avoid indiscriminately applying Western paradigms to the study of a Chinese male star, and to resist some partial and hackneyed analyses present in current critical discourse on transnational kung fu stardom.

Audience/reception studies: a mixed methodology

Discussing key approaches to star studies, Paul McDonald points out that 'the dominance of semiotic and psychoanalytic approaches within contemporary film theory has meant that little work has yet been done on the study of film audiences and their relation to stars' (1995: 92). While some reception/audience-based research on stars has emerged in recent years, to which I refer later, there is still a reluctance to treat audiences seriously in star studies. This reluctance is partly due to the difficulties involved in undertaking an audience/reception study, such as conducting interviews or surveys, or dealing with a huge amount of data. However, I would argue that it might be more to do with a deep-rooted bias which sees audiences as a 'manipulated mass', and a critical tradition of valuing theoretical assumptions over audiences' opinions.

This elitist attitude can be clearly seen in Hollinger's questioning of the use of audience studies in star studies. In Hollinger's view, 'box office statistics, fan magazine polls and letters, fan club news, fan mail, Internet fan sites, and reviewers' opinions have all been used to provide insight into the popularity of certain stars, but they do not always reliably reveal exactly why viewers feel a connection to certain stars' (2004: 43), because the viewers are often 'inarticulate about the reasoning behind their star preferences' (2006: 43). It is astonishing for someone to claim that audiences' accounts are less reliable than critical hypotheses in terms of their own feeling about stars. Moreover, one only needs to visit a couple of Internet fan sites to marvel at how knowledgeable, insightful and articulate today's film fans are.

As a direct result of such critical arrogance, the field of film studies is full of text-constructed 'spectators'. Usually defined within the psychoanalytic-semiotic framework, the spectator of film theory 'remains a somewhat abstract and ultimately passive entity' (Hansen 1991: 4). Spectatorship theory conceptualises audiences as a homogenous mass with unified responses, paying no attention to the audience as a historically constructed and culturally specific subject in relation to a whole range of categories, including class, gender, sexuality, race, ethnicity, nation and age. Opposing hypothetical accounts of what spectators are doing, Janet Staiger (1992; 2000) proposes a historical approach to reception by looking at spectators' responses to films at specific moments in history. She believes that the existence of contextual discourses may explain the evidence of actual comprehension and places particular emphasis on the analysis of published materials such as reviews and articles. This approach indicates a methodological shift, one which Jackie Stacey (1994) describes as being from the 'textually produced spectator' of film studies to the 'spectator as text' within cultural studies.

Star studies has certainly benefited from such a shift. Books like *This Mad Masquerade: Stardom and Masculinity in the Jazz Age* (Studlar 1996), *Masked Men: Masculinity and the Movies in the Fifties* (Cohan 1997), *Gay Fandom and Crossover Stardom: James Dean, Mel Gibson, and Keanu Reeves* (DeAngelis 2001) base their discussion of particular male stars on the examination of a variety of historical materials, such as promotional campaigns, fan and trade magazines and critical commentary. Jackie Stacey (1994) and Rachel Moseley (2002) take a more empirical approach in their studies of the relationship between female audiences and female stars. In *Star Gazing: Hollywood Cinema and Female Spectatorship*, Stacey gathers and analyses correspondence and questionnaires from British women about their memories of Hollywood female stars in the 1940s and 1950s. In her analysis of female spectatorship, Stacey pays special attention to its historical and national specificity, in order to demonstrate the importance of situating spectatorship within specific cultural and historical locations. In *Growing Up With Audrey Hepburn*, Rachel Moseley looks at the accounts given by British women who admired Audrey Hepburn in the 1950s, 1960s and 1990s, in order to uncover the enduring appeal of this actress. Like Stacey's work in many other ways, Moseley's research is distinctive in that it extends the study of the relationship between female star and female audiences to the latter's personal life and everyday practices. Adopting a similar empirical approach to audiences, but with fewer samples, Ian Huffer's articles (2003, 2007) offer an analysis of the relationship between a male star (Sylvester Stallone) and his audiences.

While historical reception studies try to define a historically constructed and culturally specific 'audience', it has been criticised for not representing the views of actual audiences as seen in empirical audience studies. For example, Jeremy G. Butler sees James Damico's reception study of Ingrid Bergman as failing to analyse 'the public's perception' of Bergman: 'He cites general evidence of the furor surrounding her, but the specifics of her affront are presented mostly though the comments of critics and gossip columnists – neither of which is an accurate barometer of public opinion. This essay includes no empirical audience research and no attempt to analyze the discourse of actual viewers' (1991: 241). According to Butler, it is common for historical reception scholars to extrapolate meanings from secondary sources which may or may not accurately represent the perceptions of real audiences.

However, is there a 'real' audience in film studies? If the writings of critics and columnists cannot be equated with the opinions of 'actual viewers', empirical audience research is similarly unable to offer a reliable access to 'real audiences' because respondents' personal investments and researchers' mediations and distortions always exist. Mark Jancovich uses Ien Ang's work on *Dallas* as an example to demonstrate the importance of distinguishing between the activity of consuming films and the activity of talking about them. Jancovich reminds us that when people wrote to Ang about their reaction to the television series, they were fully aware that their opinion would be judged by others, thereby consciously relating their talk to a public discourse, and 'the ideology of mass culture' (2001: 154). Similarly, Judith Mayne (1993) argues that the major problem with an analysis of romantic novels as read by a group of devoted women fans in Janice Radway's *Reading the Romance*, is that, though this claims to be an empirical audience study, the interviewed women are still not in the least 'real readers' because they are mediated by Radway's questions, analysis and narrative.

By quoting Jancovich and Mayne, I intend to argue that there are no 'real audiences' in critical discourse, but only audiences in specific positions. As Robert Allen and Douglas Gomery put it, the notion of a socially and historically specific audience is already an 'abstraction generated by the researcher, since the unstructured group that we refer to as the movie audience is constantly being constituted, dissolved, and reconstituted with each film-going experience' (1985: 156). Therefore, no kind of research data, whether an ethnographic interview or a published review, can be taken as an entirely accurate expression of public opinion. Staiger rightly notes that verbalised manifestations by a subject are not equal to the original experience or its memory, so there is no 'correct' reading of a particular film but 'the range of possible readings and reading processes at historical moments and their relation to groups of historical spectators' (1986: 20).

In this book, I reject the idea of a text-constructed, abstract and passive spectator, but I also reject the notion of a 'real' audience and the idea that empirical audience research offers a more authentic picture of audiences' responses than historical reception studies do. In my view, the audience as a research subject is always critically constructed, and, at the same time, all forms of audience response, whether press reviews, Internet fan discussions or scheduled interviews, are more or less mediated. Nonetheless, all kinds of reception sources can provide an indication of the possible ways in which star image is read and received by particular audience groups, and one should not be prioritised over another. Examining film reviews, or conducting an interview, are equally viable ways to access a historically, culturally constructed audience. Instead of struggling to find a better way to approach the 'real audience', instead of making a strict divide between reception studies and audience studies, I would like to propose a 'mixed methodology', that is, one which combines different methods of handling reception/audience studies.

This book comprises seven case studies in which I examine the responses of selected audience groups to Jet Li films and his star image, and link the readings to their historical situations, cultural specificities and intertextual contexts. While I focus on critical discourse such as press reviews and journal articles in three case studies (Chapters 2, 5, 7), I also devote three chapters (Chapters 3, 6, 8) to the analysis of online fan discourse. The Internet has become an increasingly important location for audience/reception studies because, compared to traditional media, the Internet provides a more convenient, democratic and interactive space for audiences to express their opinions. To some extent, researching online fan discourses bears more similarities to empirical audience studies. If in the past we could approach the silent masses only through interviews, focus groups or questionnaires, today, due to the popularity of the Internet, we see 'average' audiences finding a new channel to freely express and share their opinions. In some senses, fans who publish their postings and get involved in online discussions are probably less mediated than audience members in an empirical audience study.

Besides investigating critical discourse and fan discussion, in one chapter I have also engaged in ethnographic audience studies by interviewing a group of military graduates about their memories of Li's *Fong Sai-yuk* (Chapter 4). I have limited the application of empirical audience studies to one chapter, to highlight the fact that it is no more than a small experiment, and reflect my intention of combining two critical methods of audience research into one project. In so doing, I want to demonstrate that what matters is not only how scholars collect reception material, but also how they use it to engage with their research topic, in this case, Jet Li. This attempt to utilise a 'mixed methodology' will hopefully offer a fuller picture of how Li's star image and cinematic masculinity are constructed and transformed in the process of audience consumption across time and space. In general, at the level of reception, this book understands 'Jet Li' as discursively produced through critical discourse, fan discussion and personal memory.

We should realise, however, that no approach to film audiences is perfect and unproblematic. Commenting on the intertextual approach to star studies, McDonald writes, 'in constructing a context out of texts, historical analysis is faced with a basic problem. How do we tell which texts are significant and which are not, and how many texts do we need to reconstruct a context convincingly?' (1995: 85). McDonald's questions can well be applied to the audience/reception studies conducted in this book. How do I decide which audiences/responses are significant? And how many audiences/responses do I need to consider in order to reconstruct a convincing picture of reception? I explain in each case study why I have chosen to examine a specific audience group or reception site, but two general features have been foregrounded throughout the book, in order to address the limitations of the audience/reception studies method.

The first is 'comparative reading'. When exploring the reception of *All about Eve* (Joseph L. Mankiewicz, 1950), Martin Shingler suggests that 'a historiographical approach to film reception that is dependent upon reviews and journalistic features in mainstream publications is limited to revealing the construction of dominant or "preferred" meanings' (2001: 59). In response to this accusation, in most of the case studies, I examine the reading of a select group of audiences in contrast to another popular or sometimes dominant reading. The main categories compared in the book include critical review/fan reading, Chinese critics/Western critics, and Chinese-language reception/English-language reception. Furthermore, while kung fu stardom and Hong Kong action have been mostly discussed in either an international context or a Hong Kong context, their uptake in the Mainland has received little critical attention. This book seeks to address this scarcity by investigating three groups of audiences from mainland China. By highlighting the comparative dimension, however, I do not intend to reinforce some existing binaries such as Chinese audiences/Western audiences. First, both 'Chinese' and 'Western' are terms which are too large to describe complex forms of spectatorship. Second, audience perception is shaped by many elements; whether you are Chinese or a Westerner is not necessarily a determining factor. Yet cultural background does sometimes play a crucial role in the reading and interpretation of star image and male representation, as demonstrated by some of my case studies.

The other criterion in my choice-making is 'changing meanings', which has been highlighted in response to the criticism of Barbara Klinger and others[14] of reception studies' lack of attention to how meaning changes over time. As Klinger notes, historical reception studies have shown a tendency to concentrate on single practices during the original moments of reception, but have not 'systematically explored the fuller range of effects that historical context might have on cinematic identity' (1994: xvii). Klinger thus emphasises the need to examine the issue of meaning in a 'trans-historical, trans-contextual manner'. Li's border-crossing career trajectory in the past three decades allows an examination of the changing meanings of Li as received and constructed in different cultural locations and at different historical moments. Six case studies of audience responses to Jet Li's on-screen image focus on two significant periods in Li's career: the Hong Kong *wuxia* film period in the early 1990s and the Hollywood and transnational film period from 1998 to the present. Accordingly, the audiences I choose to research come mainly from these two periods: for example, Hong Kong critics of the early 1990s, and mainland Chinese critics and American critics at the beginning of the twenty-first century.

This brings us to another methodological difficulty of audience/reception studies; namely, how many audiences/responses are sufficient to represent the reception picture of a wider audience? Theoretically speaking, any amount of responses will not be enough since there are, so to speak, a thousand Hamlets in a thousand people's eyes. While all studies of audiences are partial and provisional, in my view, it does not really matter how many audiences/responses are examined as long as they are able to represent the opinion of a specifically defined audience group. For example, eight critical reviews from prestigious Hong Kong film magazine *City Entertainment* can indicate Hong Kong critics' opinion of

Li's performance in *Once Upon a Time in China* (Chapter 2) just as fifty-six articles from nine Mainland film journals on *Hero* only give a glimpse of mainland critical views of the film (Chapter 7). Similarly, the accounts from fifteen military graduates of their memory of Li's *Fong Sai-yuk* (Chapter 4) are no less representative than hundreds of user comments from *The Internet Movie Database* on Li's characters' relationships with women in his English-language films (Chapter 6).

Chapter summary

This book comprises eight chapters and is divided into two parts. The first part of the book examines Jet Li as a Chinese *wuxia* hero as constructed in Chinese audiences' responses to his Hong Kong *wuxia* films. Chapter 2 functions as an introduction to the first part of the book. It defines the new *wuxia* cinema of the early 1990s in Hong Kong, from which Li grew into a superstar, by elaborating its three notable traits – technology-based visual spectacle, parodic and comic text and obsession with gender-bending – and how they pose a telling threat to the traditional representation of male heroes as well as kung fu stars. Chapter 2 looks at Hong Kong critical reviews in *City Entertainment* of Li's *Once Upon a Time in China*. It argues that for Hong Kong critics, fighting and acting are two interdependent rather than discrete elements within Li's performance, and that cinematic technology helps Li project the image of an elegant and prestigious master. Chapter 3 examines mainland Chinese fans' readings of *Swordsman II*. Within fans' heterosexualised reading of this homosexual story, Li escapes from homosexual anxiety and gender confusion, and maintains his incorruptible heterosexual patriarchal image. In Chapter 4, an analysis of the memories of a group of Mainland military graduates of *Fong Sai-yuk* reveals that Li's comic 'mother's boy' image functions merely as a masquerade for a repressed and unchangeable 'father's son', a central form of male representation in Chinese cinema.

The second part of the book examines Jet Li as a transnational kung fu/action star for global audiences. Chapter 5 investigates Western press reviews of Li's English-language films. In Western critical discourse, Li's image is that of a charismatic villain, dispassionate killer and childlike Chinese man, and Li survives in Hollywood at the price of his heroism being toned down or even denied. Chapter 6 examines user comments from *The Internet Movie Database* on the relationships of Li's characters with the female leads in his English-language films. Li's Western roles, on the one hand, perpetuate the 'asexual Chinese male' myth, while, on the other hand, he has started to introduce a soft, Eastern-flavoured sexuality into the West. Chapter 7 compares Chinese and American critical responses to *Hero*. Li functions respectively as a 'national hero' and a 'symbol of spectacle' in Chinese and American critical discourses, and this neatly sums up his national and transnational identity. Li's appeal as a transnational Chinese film star is built upon a constant negotiation between changing national and transnational identities.

The final chapter discusses the way in which Jet Li fans on *The Official Jet Li Website* make sense of Li's off-screen personalities. In fan discourse, Li stands as an 'ordinary hero', a 'sex icon' and a 'moral model'. It is precisely through the correspondence and conflict between Li's on-screen and off-screen images, that, in the eyes of a new generation of North-American Jet Li fans, contradictory terms such as 'superhero/normal guy', 'shy man/sex idol', and 'fighter/preacher of non-violence' are perfectly reconciled in Li. In conclusion, my research on the transcultural reception of Li demonstrates that Li's star image has been constantly constructed, negotiated and modified by audiences from different cultural locations and at different historical moments. Li's border-crossing career typifies the process of a non-Hollywood star becoming a transnational star.

Notes

1. For example, *Sessue Hayakawa: Silent Cinema and Transnational Stardom* (Daisuke Miyao 2007); 'Transnational Stardom: The Case of Maggie Cheung Man-yuk' (Tony Williams 2003); 'Asian's Beloved Sassy Girl: Jun Ji-Hyun's Star Image and Her Transnational Stardom' (JaeYoon Park 2009). In her recent article on Chow Yun-fat's transnational stardom, Feng Lin (2011) makes an interesting distinction between international, global and transnational stardom at the level of marketing and distribution.
2. There are some exceptions. For example, Hong Kong star Maggie Cheung never made a film in Hollywood but became a transnational star by working in the French film industry.
3. A more recent example is Christian Bale who is cast in Zhang Yimou's latest film *Jin ling shi san chai* (*The Flowers of War*) (2011).
4. I explain this term in more detail in Chapter 1.
5. In Leon Hunt's definition, 'traditionally the more accurate Mandarin name for Chinese martial arts, *wushu* became the name of the specific art practiced in the People's Republic...*wushu* is designed for performance and mixes traditional martial arts with gymnastics and techniques from *jingju* [Beijing Opera]' (2003: 31).
6. A 1996 Hong Kong film, *Comrade, Almost a Love Story*, vividly depicts the contemptuous attitude towards Mainlanders in Hong Kong society. See also Eric Kit-wai Ma's work on Hong Kong identity (2002).

7. See more discussion on this topic in 'Border crossing: Mainland China's presence in Hong Kong cinema' (Esther Ching-mei Yau 1994).
8. 17 out of the 18 films Li made in Hong Kong in the 1990s earned over HK$10 million at the box office. In 1993, his salary was over HK$16 million, which was second only to Jackie Chan, and surpassed other local superstars such as Stephen Chow, Andy Lau and Chow Yun-fat.
9. The most substantial account of Li appears in Leon Hunt's *Kung Fu Cult Masters* (2003).
10. There have been numerous articles on these two films and an edited book on *Hero* (G. Rawnsley and M. Rawnsley 2010).
11. The relationship between kung fu films and black culture has been examined in a number of articles. See also Ma (2000), Kim (2004) and Cha-jua (2008).
12. The earliest record about *xia* can be traced back to 'You *xia* Lie Zhuang', a section of *Shi Ji* (Records of the Grand Historian), the first university history of China, written by Sima Qian (c. 145–86 BC). See the work of Chen Pingyuan (1992) and Stephen Teo (2005) for a discussion on *wuxia* literature.
13. Ang Lee directed *Sense and Sensibility* in English, which is adapted from Jane Austen's novel of the same title.
14. See also *The Place of the Audience: Cultural Geographies of Film Consumption* (Mark Jancovich and Lucy Faire with Sarah Stubbings 2003).

Part I
Jet Li as Chinese *wuxia* hero

1

Jet Li and the new *wuxia* cinema in the 1990s

In the first part of this book, I examine Jet Li's star image as it developed in his Hong Kong films in the early 1990s, and to do this I investigate how three important *wuxia* films, which he made during this period – *Once Upon a Time in China* (1991), *Swordsman II* (1992) and *Fong Sai-yuk* (1993) – have been received by three different audience groups from Hong Kong and mainland China respectively. The current chapter aims to define the new *wuxia* cinema as a film cycle in the early 1990s and thereby to sketch the background from which Jet Li emerged as a superstar. As pointed out in the Introduction to this book, the discussion of transnational kung fu stardom has revolved around the issue of transnational action. Kung fu films and kung fu/action comedies that won the global fame for Bruce Lee and Jackie Chan respectively have been studied in great detail. New *wuxia* films, by contrast, have not gained similar international visibility, probably due to their perceived 'untranslatableness' (Law et al. 1997). Their appeal in the global market, according to Teo, is 'limited to a cult minority audience' (2005: 199). Nevertheless, while enjoying remarkable commercial success in Greater China and pan-Asian popularity, new *wuxia* cinema has also produced numerous *wuxia* classics. For many Chinese-speaking audiences, the global success of *Crouching Tiger, Hidden Dragon* (2000) and *Hero* (2002) is incomprehensible, as in their view, such martial art-house films cannot compete with many of the new *wuxia* masterpieces. In many ways, new *wuxia* films have been under-discussed and underestimated, but in order to trace Li's transnational career, and to re-evaluate Li's status as a kung fu star as significant as Lee and Chan, new *wuxia* films provide a good starting point.

First, however, it is important to explain what *wuxia* cinema is. Ang Lee neatly defines *wuxia* as 'a kind of unique Chinese fantasy' (quoted in Zhang 2005: 189). As already pointed out in the Introduction, *wuxia* is one of the most typical forms of Chinese culture and has existed in folklore, literature and drama in China for centuries. The term *wuxia* consists of two Chinese characters, *wu* meaning the Chinese martial arts and *xia* referring to the chivalrous spirit (*xiayi*) which is manifested through actions such as protecting the weak, fighting injustice, and sacrificing oneself for the sake of loyalty and friendship, and so on. '*Xia*' can also refer to a particular Chinese type of hero (*xiake*) who has excellent martial arts skills and incarnates the spirit of *xiayi*. As a modern artistic form of *wuxia* culture, *wuxia* film is one of the most popular and enduring Chinese film genres, almost as old as Chinese cinema itself. It incorporates a hero canon as well as carefully choreographed fighting scenes, usually set in a legendary past. In Zhang Che's words, *wuxia* pictures 'use the form of martial arts (*wu*) to express the content of chivalry (*xia*)' (1999: 18). As Teo points out, Hong Kong/Chinese filmmakers regard *wuxia* cinema as a '"national form" possessing historical and cultural characteristics and attributes of "Chineseness"' (2005: 198).

In the West, Chinese martial arts films are widely known as kung fu films. However, in the Chinese context, *wuxia* film is a more familiar name for martial arts narratives, and kung fu films are mainly seen as a subgenre of *wuxia* films, different from the other subgenre which is swordplay films. While kung fu films became popular with the films of Bruce Lee and tend to show more realistic, face-to-face combat, swordplay films emphasise the supernatural, stylised display of heroism. It is noteworthy, though, that there are different interpretations of these terms. For example, Teo (2009) considers both kung fu films and *wuxia* films as subgenres of Chinese martial arts cinema. For Teo and some other, mostly Western, critics, *wuxia* is synonymous with swordplay films. Commenting on the diverse opinions about the categorisation of kung fu films and *wuxia* films, Leon Hunt concludes that 'the relationship between the terms "kung fu" and "*wuxia*" is both complex and context-specific' (2006: 2). In this book, I adopt the most common Chinese perception and treat kung fu films as a subgenre of *wuxia* films. When the star is referred to, however, I use 'kung fu star' or 'martial arts star' instead of '*wuxia* star', because the first two are more generally accepted, especially in a transnational context.

As a vigorous and successful film genre, *wuxia* film has been developing for more than eight decades, during which time it has consistently been revived after a temporary fading away. The 1970s saw a fad for kung fu films, but this was followed by a period of dormancy for all *wuxia* films in the 1980s. The commercial success of *Swordsman* (Ching Siu-tung, King Hu, Raymond Lee and Tsui Hark, 1990) started to revitalise the declining *wuxia* genre and ushered in a period during which *wuxia* films would rule the box office in Hong Kong for a few years. Some statistics may give us an idea of the popularity of *wuxia* films at the time: five of the top ten box office hits in 1992 were *wuxia* films; and of the thirty-five films for which box office takings exceeded HK$10 million in 1993, 18 were *wuxia* films (Jin 1995). The amazing speed with which spin-offs were produced offers further evidence of this *wuxia* upsurge. For example, only three months after the release of the very successful *The Bride with White Hair* (Ronny Yu, 1993), its sequel came out with the same leading actors. These *wuxia* films were also very popular with audiences in Taiwan, Korea, Japan and other Asian countries. According to local critic Sek Kei (1997), overseas demand for *wuxia* films raised the prices of rights to Hong Kong films in the early 1990s and led to Taiwanese investment in Hong Kong cinema. These period *wuxia* films, produced in bulk in the early 1990s, have been dubbed the 'new *wuxia* cinema' by some critics (Jin 1995; Jia 1999), and mark the third golden age in the history of *wuxia* cinema.[1]

While there have been some academic studies of individual new *wuxia* films (for example, *Once Upon a Time in China*) and leading directors (mostly Tsui Hark), the new *wuxia* cinema as a film cycle has not been properly defined and the major stars coming out of this cycle, Jet Li in particular, have received little critical attention. However, when the new *wuxia* cinema is under discussion, few people fail to mention Jet Li. It is this very film cycle that made Li a martial arts superstar in Asia, and it was Li who ensured the popularity of the new *wuxia* films. From 1991 to 1994, Li made eleven *wuxia* films, ten of which took more than HK$10 million at the box office,[2] and rapidly became a superstar. Films starring Li became guaranteed hits, not only in Hong Kong, but also in Taiwan, mainland China, South-East and East Asia (not to mention a significant cult following amongst martial arts fans worldwide).

Working with a host of famous filmmakers, including Tsui Hark, Corey Yuen, Yuen Woo-ping, Ching Siu-tung and Wong Jing, Li incarnates a range of familiar *wuxia* heroes of diverse styles: the legendary Cantonese folk heroes Wong Fei-hung, Fong Sai-yuk and Hung Hei-kuan; the tough historical figure Chen Zhen,[3] the leader of the *Wudang* (one of the two biggest martial arts schools) Taoist Zhang Sanfeng; two most charismatic *wuxia* heroes from the popular *wuxia* novels of Jin Yong, Ling Hucong and Zhang Wuji. As Hunt writes, '[I]n the early 1990s, he seemed determined to play every classic martial arts hero, like a one-man kung fu star system' (2003: 141). A careful examination of the new *wuxia* cinema will help to shed light on the significance of Jet Li to this film cycle, and more importantly, to understand how Li's star image has been constructed in relation to it.

When it comes to the new *wuxia* films, critics habitually try to make direct or indirect connections between the film texts and the historical context of their production (Sek 1997; Teo 1997; Stokes and Hoover 1999; Bhaskar Sarkar 2001), namely, the unquiet period after the 1989 Tiananmen Square protests and before the 1997 handover of Hong Kong, thereby allegorically interpreting the new *wuxia* films as a cinematic engagement with the fears and anxieties of the Hong Kong people at the time. While I do not intend to deny the possible impact of particular social and psychological contexts on new *wuxia* cinema, I think that this somewhat clichéd reading not only disguises the rich themes and forms that new *wuxia* cinema has created, but also precludes the abundant reading possibilities provided for its audiences by new *wuxia* texts. Instead, I would like to draw attention to the ways in which new *wuxia* films redefine the *wuxia* genre and reconstruct *wuxia* masculinity. In the rest of this chapter, I examine three salient traits of new *wuxia* films, which distinguish them from previous *wuxia* films, that is, their parodic and hysterical textual nature, the technology-based, exaggerated visual spectacle they provide, and their fascination with gender-bending and cross-dressing. I argue that it is exactly these traits that pose a significant challenge to traditional representations of *wuxia* heroes and also to kung fu stardom.

When *wuxia* meets *mo-lei-tau*: the parodied hero

Bhaskar Sarkar suggests we read the new *wuxia* films as hysterical texts. For Sarkar, history and reality have been allegorically played out in a magic, fantastic *wuxia* world with hysterical abandon. He observes, 'Hysteria often executes a parodic function against repressive social structures ... Unable to imagine the new structures adequately, the films articulate the anxieties by parodic repetitions of symbolic structures (myth)' (2001: 171). Indeed, parody may be the most popular strategy employed by new *wuxia* films. The objects of parody, or in Sarkar's words, the repressive or symbolic structures, could be anything: chauvinistic nationalists, a hypocritical *xiake*, outdated Chinese traditional mores, pretentious Western science and rationality, even new *wuxia* films themselves. The means of parody are various: modern ideas and expressions are uttered from the mouths of ancient swordsmen to produce a comic and absurd effect (*Fong Sai-yuk*); classic scenes or characters from other new *wuxia* films are ironically transplanted into a new film in order to create a blatant pastiche in which the original, serious meaning becomes a source of slapstick (*Royal Tramp II* [Ching Siu-tung and Wong Jing, 1993]); crucial moments or serious issues are exaggeratedly or grotesquely presented (*Once Upon a Time in China* [1991]; *New Dragon Gate Inn* [Raymond Lee, 1992]), and so on. Parody widely applied in the new *wuxia* cinema is seen as an efficient way to offer 'unruly allegories' (ibid. 171), while at the same time, it should be noted that it is also subject to the dictates of the market.

When discussing the parodic and hysterical style of the new *wuxia* cinema, it would be remiss not to mention Stephen Chow. Chow's influential comedies not only continuously attracted huge box office receipts in the early 1990s, but also gave birth to a new film genre, the so-called '*mo-lei-tau*' (nonsense comedies), which are well-known for their nonsensical parodies and frantic gags. Through excessive farce, pastiche and self-mockery, *mo-lei-tau* comedies ruthlessly deconstruct everything related to orthodoxy or authority. As Yingjin Zhang puts it, 'the meaning of Chiau's [Chow] nonsense or irrationality derives from its outrageous deconstruction of reason and nonsense and its staging of a carnival subversion of normality and decency' (2004: 263). Despite not being a martial arts star, Chow contributed to the popularity of new *wuxia* films by starring in numerous *wuxia* comedies such as *Justice, My Foot* (Johnnie To, 1992), *Royal Tramp* (Ching Siu-tung and Wong Jing, 1992), *Royal Tramp II*, *King of Beggars* (Gordon Chan, 1992), and *Flirting Scholar* (Lik-chi Lee, 1993). Amazingly, it was his *Justice, My Foot* and the *Royal Tramp* series that earned the highest profits of all the new *wuxia* films. Chow's remarkable presence in the new *wuxia* cycle presents two great challenges for the *wuxia* genre and its stars. First, the wacky, clown-like hero, which characterises Chow's screen image and is brought into his portrayal of *wuxia* heroes, ridicules and deconstructs the traditional *wuxia* hero image in a drastic and unrestrained way. Second, as an actor without any martial arts skills who is still able to make the most profitable *wuxia* films, Chow undoubtedly questions the status of those martial artists-turned-actors such as Jet Li and Donnie Yen.

In fact, there is a constant complaint that the conventional representation of heroes has been deconstructed in the overwhelming atmosphere of 'parodying everything' which permeates the new *wuxia* cinema. In his article about the transformations of Wong Fei-hung's hero image, Ng Ho (1997) suggests that in Hong Kong cinema Wong has experienced three phases. The first one is the traditional hero in classical times, who is the defender of Confucian morality, as portrayed by Kwan Tak-hing in the 1950s and 1960s. The second is the anti-hero of modern times, who challenges the orthodox social system, represented by Jackie Chan's comic Wong. The third is the mock hero in postmodern times, who feels impotent in the face of a changing world and doubts everything, including his own existence, as manifested in the *Once Upon a Time in China* series starring Jet Li in the early 1990s. Ng concludes that Li's Wong is such a confused hero that he marks the finale of the heroic legend.

Ng's view of Li's Wong as a mock hero is debatable. As I demonstrate in Chapter 2, many Hong Kong critics consider that in *Once Upon a Time in China* Li succeeds in portraying a prestigious kung fu master. Nonetheless, I agree with Ng that the heroes in the new *wuxia* world seem to have ambivalent and unstable value systems and standards of behaviour, while in a traditional *wuxia* world, whether the heroes keep a straight or comic face, at least they have steadfast beliefs and will finally show audiences what is right through defeating evil or through self-sacrifice. Take Li's new *wuxia* heroes as examples: they are usually caught in the conflict between lofty causes and personal emotion (Ling Hucong in *Swordsman II*), or Chinese traditional mores and modern Western values (Wong Fei-hung in the *Once Upon a Time in China* films); they experience a period of losing themselves (Zhang Sanfeng in *Tai Chi Master* [Yuen Woo-ping, 1993]) and choose to retreat from *jianghu*[4] after fulfilling their tasks (Fong Sai-yuk in *Fong Sai-yuk*, Chen Zhen in *Fist of Legend* [Gordon Chan, 1994]). Confusion and abdication characterise many of Li's new *wuxia* heroes and betray an uncompromising heroism in crisis.

Compared to Tsui Hark and Ching Siu-tung, directors like Wong Jing and Jeffrey Lau show even less interest in the heroic narratives seen in previous *wuxia* films and are prepared to overthrow the generic construction of *wuxia* heroes in a highly playful way. In their films, inept and burlesque swordsmen often replace omnipotent, reputable *xiake* as the ultimate winners. Funnily enough, Jet Li plays Wong Fei-hung again in *Last Hero in China* (1993) directed by Wong Jing, but in a distorted and farcical way so that his character is nowhere near to a revered master. Some Hong Kong critics have discerned a scepticism about the ideals of traditional chivalry and secularisation of the *wuxia* hero image found in martial arts films produced after 1968 (Lin 1981). The new *wuxia* goes further to subvert old-style *wuxia* narratives, primarily through a banalised or caricatured representation of *wuxia* heroes and a nihilistic attitude that sees *xiayi* (chivalry) as meaningless. Probably in this sense, Stokes and Hoover entitle their chapter about *wuxia* films in the early 1990s 'Last Hero(es) in Hong Kong' (1999: 89).

However, while the critics are keen to discuss 'the death of the *wuxia* hero' in either a positive or negative tone, we cannot ignore the fact that new *wuxia* films have contributed to the genre a range of classic hero images, such as those portrayed by Li. Moreover, the unparalleled popularity enjoyed by the new *wuxia* cycle in Hong Kong may be partly because it satisfied the common desire for a hero among local audiences, especially in turbulent times. Indeed, while taking a postmodern approach to the portrayal of a *wuxia* hero, many new *wuxia* films also suspend the parodic stance from time to time in favour of nostalgia for traditional values such as chivalry and patriotism, which in Sarkar's view, is a manifestation of a 'schizophrenic incoherence' (2001: 172). Alternatively, I prefer to read it as a unique way of portraying *wuxia* heroes and would argue that it is as significant to explore how the new *wuxia* cinema reconstructs the *xiake* image in a more complex, creative way, as to discuss how it deconstructs the traditional representation of *wuxia* heroes.

When *wuxia* meets special effects: the technologised hero

Another noticeable feature of the new *wuxia* cinema is its exuberant and exaggerated visual style. Sarkar defines the 'expressionist stylistics' characteristic of the new *wuxia* cinema as something which 'conveys a sense of breathless pace and dizzying energy: the camera movements and editing have become faster, the angles are more askew, the special effects more spectacular' (2001: 170). Likewise, Stokes and Hoover notice that in the films of Tsui Hark and Ching Siu-tung, 'the wire stunts come fast and furious' (1999: 104). Indeed, the new *wuxia* cinema of the early 1990s distinguishes itself from previous *wuxia* films through its flamboyant visual spectacle, built on the mastery of special effects, montage editing and an abundance of wirework. *Wuxia* films had never before been so dependent on filmic techniques.

As a homegrown expertise, wirework has been applied for a long time in the filming of fighting in *wuxia* cinema, but not until the early 1990s was it widely used to make on-screen heroes look real, and to achieve an aesthetic, romantic martial arts style. Many talented action chorographers, such as Yuen Woo-ping, Ching Siu-tung, Sammo Hung and Corey Yuen have, with the help of wirework, created numerous highly imaginative fight scenes and evoke a magical, fantastic *wuxia* world that can 'coexist with real, historical characters and situations' (Sarkar 2001: 165). At the same time, the move to high-tech special effects had come to dominate the rapid development and transformation of *wuxia* film in the early 1990s, as a result of the resolutely experimental intention of the new *wuxia* filmmakers, in particular Tsui Hark. Since his debut with *The Butterfly Murders* (1979), Tsui has never given up the endeavuor to renew traditional Chinese martial arts through modern technology. Unsatisfied with displaying martial arts only through fists and kicks, Tsui seeks to convey the mysterious and fantastic *wuxia* world by trying all kinds of special effects in a freewheeling and unrestricted way. Special effects are applied in fight scenes to create a supernatural *wuxia* world where the swordsman and swordswoman can do everything that the ordinary mortal cannot: flying through the air, plunging into the earth, stirring up the waters, producing magical contrivances capable of killing an adversary in one second, and so on.

While the new *wuxia* cinema ushers in a visual revolution for the genre, it also carries it to an extreme, to 'the point of loss of control and total overload' (Li 1993: 51). Teo describes Tsui's work as 'a wondrous farrago of special effects achieving a seemingly endless succession of stunning, comic-strip imagery, at times even overwhelming the narrative which disintegrates into a montage of "attractions"' (1997: 166). Technical intervention in the *wuxia* genre not only faces the charge of overemphasising form at the expense of content, but more strikingly, puts male heroes (both on screen and off screen) into crisis. Esther Yau observes a 'technologised masculinity' in the James Bond films, which 'involves hard and swift bodies that operate and manipulate a wide variety of information, weaponry and machinery, as well as bodies that presumably have an unprecedented geographical or territorial mobility' (1997: 107). She argues that technology has become the protagonist and the Bond males are responding to a techno-fetish. According to Yau, director Zhang Che updated the *wuxia* genre in the 1970s by combining pre-modern, native legends and modern cinematic mise-en-scène realised at varying speeds so that the *wuxia* cinema could join in the international competition for supreme techno-masculinity.

The new *wuxia* cinema undoubtedly further reinforces the idea of 'technologised masculinity', given its wholehearted embrace of cinematic technology. Like Yau's criticism of the James Bond films, some scholars talk about the triumph of special effects over the male hero in Tsui's early 1990s *wuxia* work. For instance, Ackbar Abbas (1997) argues that the real heroes here are not kung fu stars, but special effects. Based on his observation of the gradual disappearance of muscular bodies in Hong Kong popular culture from the realistic kung fu films inaugurated by Bruce Lee to Tsui Hark's new *wuxia* films starring Jet Li, Kwai-cheung Lo concludes that 'no body' exists in 'excessive technical prowess, over-rapid editing, breakneck-speed narration and video-game-like cinematography' (2004: 122), and the muscle men are simply support props for the intensive effects work. For Abbas and Lo, it is modern technology rather than traditional heroism that is worshipped in *wuxia* films of the early 1990s.

From the above discussions, then, it would seem that *wuxia* heroes have been disempowered by giving away their strength to special effects and other cinematic techniques. However, it should be noticed that such a view exists mostly in English-language critical discourse. There are different points of view about the technologised male body within different reception contexts. Take as an example two new *wuxia* films starring Jet Li, one performing best and the other worst in his box office record, *Swordsman II* and *Fist of Legend*. While *Swordsman II* is seen by many Western critics and fans as Li's most heavily wire-injected, and hence unrealistic work, mainland Chinese fans laud it as a *wuxia* masterpiece in which Li brings to life a *wuxia* hero who best embodies the unrestrained *wuxia* spirit (Chapter 3). Meanwhile, *Fist of Legend*, undoubtedly a cult film in the West which 'has frequently performed the role of "authenticating" Jet Li, of offering documentary proof of his abilities' (Hunt 2003: 27), met with unexpected failure at the box office in Hong Kong. These polarised opinions attest to the importance of discussing screen masculinity in culturally and socially specific contexts.

Another challenge which technology brings to kung fu stardom is that, with the help of cinematic technology, anyone can look like a super martial artist on screen, no matter whether he or she is the king of comedy (Stephen Chow), the prince of art cinema (Leslie Cheung), or the queen of romantic drama (Brigitte Lin). This therefore raises an important question: are actors with martial arts skills still necessary for the genre? Since there is a common perception that martial artists-turned-actors usually have limited acting skills, why not simply use good actors to portray *wuxia* heroes while letting special effects and wirework take care of their physical shortcomings? Or, to ask this question in a different way: when technology makes real martial artists unreal and makes unreal martial artists real, how should/did a 'real' kung fu star like Jet Li respond to the challenge of technology and maintain his status in the genre?

When *wuxia* meets Asia the Invincible: the castrated hero

Some critics detect a fascination with cross-dressing and gender-bending in the new *wuxia* films (Teo, 1997; Sek, 1997; Sarkar, 2001). Cross-dressing is a common trick in the *wuxia* narrative, enabling swordswomen to disguise their real identity. But in the new *wuxia* films, cross-dressing has been an indispensable element: swordswomen in male attire can be found in almost every new *wuxia* film; even male heroes occasionally dress up as women (for example, Jet Li in *Fong Sai-yuk*), which is quite venturesome for a male-dominated, sometimes misogynistic genre. The gender categories are further blurred by all the kinds of gender-bending characters frequently seen in new *wuxia* films: the self-castrated transsexual (*Swordsman II*; *The East is Red* [Ching Siu-tung and Raymond Lee, 1993]; *Holy Weapon* [Wong Jing, 1993]), the bisexual swordsman/woman (*Ashes of Time* [1994]), or the androgynous clan leader (*The Bride with White Hair*).

This gender-bending trend was undoubtedly initiated by the character Asia the Invincible in *Swordsman II* and *The East is Red*, an ambitious South China tribal chief who castrates himself to learn the supernatural martial arts recorded in a sacred scroll but unexpectedly falls in love with his adversary, the male hero Ling Hucong (Jet Li). As one of the most memorable characters in the *wuxia* genre, Asia the Invincible was so influential at the time that the theme of sexual ambiguity quickly became a fashion, not only in *wuxia* films but across the whole of Hong Kong cinema in the early 1990s. At the same time, it rejuvenated the career of the actress playing the part, Brigitte Lin, and made her another big star of the new *wuxia* cycle, alongside Jet Li. Interestingly, most of Lin's new *wuxia* roles involve either cross-dressing or gender-bending. She even plays a male hero in some films (*The Three Swordsmen* [Taylor Wong, 1994]), hence further intensifying the crisis of kung fu stars: not only a non-martial artist, but even an actress can play a male *wuxia* hero!

In the new *wuxia* texts, gender transformation through cross-dressing and gender-bending is so easy and spontaneous that gender becomes merely a mask as well as an effective narrative strategy. As a consequence, homosexuality and heterosexuality are no longer clear-cut. That a heterosexual woman/man falls in love with another woman/man due to sexual misrecognition becomes a popular narrative, which leads to a funny or tragic love story. No other *wuxia* films, or even Chinese films, have ever created so many radical gender fantasies as the new *wuxia* cinema of the 1990s. Transgressive gender discourse, together with frantic parody and excessive visual spectacle, make the new *wuxia* an 'ecstatic cinema', a term David Bordwell (1997) suggests to define Hong Kong action films as a whole.

There are two main attitudes towards the prevalence of gender-bending narrative within the new *wuxia* cinema. Some read it positively as a response to the sentiments of feminism and gay liberation. For example, Teo opines that gender-bending is a 'surprising manifestation of the search for sexual identity' (1997: 250) and reflects the changing sexual mores and attitudes towards women and homosexuals in Hong Kong society. Similarly, Stokes and Hoover (1999) argue that the 'she-demons' and 'power-hungry castrators' appearing in many new *wuxia* films testify to the improved social position of Hong Kong women since the 1980s, as well as the male anxiety caused by women's empowerment. By contrast, some critics see the gender-bending and homosexual implications in these *wuxia* fantasies as elements of sheer entertainment, which help to create parodic texts and stir sensuous excitement. Sek Kei (1997) points out that the 'homosexual' characters mostly become 'straight' in the end and revert to heterosexuality. He thereby claims that gender-bending is only a fad, a fashion, without any serious intention to explore homosexuality in depth. It may be true that none of the new *wuxia* films could be called a 'feminist film' or a 'gay/lesbian film'; it may also be true that the new *wuxia* filmmakers' discussion of gender remains largely intuitive rather than conscious. Yet, the rich gender texts offered by the new *wuxia* films undeniably present a series of challenges to *wuxia* masculinity.

One such challenge is the emphasis on women's roles. Women have never appeared in such striking roles before in a genre which traditionally excludes women, though the *xianü* (female *wuxia* hero) has been portrayed in *wuxia* films throughout the history of the genre. On the one hand, the new *wuxia* cinema offers a range of independent, strong-minded female hero images which declare that heroism is not inherently masculine (Qiu Moyan in *New Dragon Gate Inn* [Raymond Lee, 1992]; Wing Chun in *Wing Chun* [Yuen Woo-ping, 1994]). On the other hand, the roles of the obedient, submissive female and the aggressive, dominant male are often turned upside down in the new *wuxia* texts (Jin Xiangyu and Zhou Huaian in *New Dragon Gate Inn*, Lian Nishang and Zhuo Yihang in *The Bride with White Hair*). Moreover, some new *wuxia* films exclusively portray swordswomen as the central characters, with swordsmen taking on insignificant supporting roles (*Holy Weapon*).

The challenge presented by female *wuxia* heroes is also embodied by their intervention in the male heroes' emotional world. In previous *wuxia* films such as Zhang Che's *yanggang wuxia* films, women are usually sidelined into being the love interests of male heroes. Traditional male *wuxia* heroes are tough in the sense that neither the enemy nor women can shake them. The male heroes in the new *wuxia* films, however, seem to be much more vulnerable, especially when involved in a romance. No matter how superb their martial arts are, they have to live in pain and loneliness when they lose their love (Ou Yangfeng in *Ashes of Time*, Zhuo Yihang in *The Bride with White Hair*). Even in those films where the male hero is finally united with his love, his heroic masculinity is not impeccable. In the *Once Upon a Time in China* films, Aunt Thirteen, a woman educated in Britain and dressed in Western clothes, is presented as the symbol of Western culture and a threat to the celibate male *wuxia* hero Wong Fei-hung. In spite of being an unbeatable kung fu master, Wong is embarrassed in front of Aunt Thirteen and refuses to admit his real affection. Lie Fu (1997) suggests that Wong's discomfort and repression, in contrast to Aunt Thirteen's uninhibited passion, interestingly exhibits the male hero's disquiet and mistrustful attitude towards increasingly powerful women and the unknown modern culture of the West. If female heroes and romance have to some extent redefined the male hero image in the new *wuxia* cinema, the gender-bending narrative permeating new *wuxia* films poses an even greater threat for the heterosexual male hero, an issue which deserves further exploration.

As the leading man of the new *wuxia* cinema, Li best exemplifies and sometimes intensifies and complicates the contradictions, crises and transformations surrounding male heroes and kung fu stars brought about by the new *wuxia* cinema's unrestrained indulgence in parody, special effects and gender-bending. Since the release of the *Once Upon a Time in China* films and *Swordsman II*, Li has been seen as the most wired-up kung fu star, one who embraces high-tech unreservedly;[5] but ironically he was also a national martial arts champion and gained his initial fame from his 'authentic' martial arts performance in *Shaolin Temple* (1982). A frequently heard complaint is that the Hong Kong cinema's 'Jet Li' has substituted cinematic artifice for his genuine skills. This paradox on the one hand seems to support or even aggravate the contention that technology damages the authenticity of kung fu stars and on the other suggests that there must be something more than 'authenticity' behind a real martial artist's choice to incorporate cinematic techniques into his performance.

The conflict between parodic interpretation and traditional representation of the *wuxia* hero is made especially salient by Li's complex identities. While *mo-lei-tau*-style parody is labelled 'made in Hong Kong' and reflects the 'Hong Kong audiences' craving for less "spiritual burdens"' (Sek 1997: 122), Li is 'very Chinese' in the eyes of local audiences and critics, due to his Mainland background. And the new *wuxia* cinema, which Li leads, has been seen as a part of the 'China Fashion' in early 1990s Hong Kong cinema, which conveyed a nostalgia for a China from the past. How, then, do Li's heroes negotiate nostalgia and parody, traditional mores and modern values, China and the West, in such a way as to become extremely popular in the larger context of the early 1990s? Finally, the gender-bending theme mounts a more striking challenge to Li's heroism, given the apparent sexual innocence originating in his previous, widely-circulated image as the 'little monk' (built upon his three *Shaolin Temple* films) and his most adventurous romance with transsexual Asia the Invincible as the male hero Ling Hucong in *Swordsman II*.

In the following three chapters, I address these three issues by looking at three Jet Li films: *Once Upon a Time in China*, in which Li establishes his techno-mediated fighting style; *Swordsman II*, in which he meets his gender-bending lover; and *Fong Sai-yuk*, in which he gives his most comic performance. Apart from their all relating to the above three issues, these films share other similarities. First, they were all major successes at the box office. Secondly, these three films are significant in terms of either the genre or Li's career. *Once Upon a Time in China* and *Swordsman II* respectively revived the kung fu subgenre and the swordplay subgenre in the early 1990s, while *Fong Sai-yuk* was the first film made by Li's own production company. Furthermore, these three films made over three consecutive years offer three different types of *wuxia* hero, thus indicating the changing meanings of Li's star image.

Instead of pursuing a conventional text-centred approach, I intend to concentrate instead on the various meanings constructed for Jet Li by audiences from culturally and historically specific locations. Sarkar suggests that the pan-Asian commercial success of the 1990s' Hong Kong *wuxia* films bears witness to their ability to 'tap into certain common concerns' (2001: 174) arising from similarly destabilising changes. Yet, at the same time, he also reminds us that '[h]ow the particular texts are received and decoded, what place they occupy in popular discourse and what kinds of intensity and pleasure they generate in different milieux remain a rich area of study' (ibid. 174). It is noticeable that new *wuxia* films have been discussed mainly within the Hong Kong context, while there is little research to show how they were received by Mainland audiences, although the new *wuxia* cinema might have been celebrated more by Mainland fans who had little access to Hong Kong *wuxia* films of the 1960s and 1970s, and for whom new *wuxia* films constituted their first *wuxia* memory. To address this critical imbalance, two out of the three case studies in Part One will examine the reception of Jet Li films among selected audience groups from mainland China. But we will start with the Hong Kong critical response to Li's first Hong Kong work, *Once Upon a Time in China*, which proved crucial for him to establish his trans-border stardom after the ephemeral popularity he enjoyed as a result of *Shaolin Temple*, almost ten years previously.

Notes

1. The first boom in *wuxia* cinema was in the silent film era in Shanghai during the 1920s and the second was in Hong Kong from the late 1960s to the 1970s, represented by Zhang Che and King Hu's new style *wuxia pian*, and the kung fu films of Bruce Lee and Jackie Chan.
2. These ten films are *Once Upon a Time in China*, *Once Upon a Time in China II*, *Swordsman II*, *Once Upon a Time in China III*, *Fong Sai-yuk*, *Fong Sai-yuk II*, *Last Hero in China*, *Tai Chi Master*, *Kung Fu Cult Master*, *The New Legend of Shaolin*.
3. Bruce Lee also plays Chen Zhen in *Fists of Fury* (Lo Wei, 1972).
4. *Jianghu*, a mythic underworld, is a key concept central to Chinese *wuxia*

imagination. It is a 'reckless and anarchic world where everyone wants to perform and excel' (Chan 2001: 491), but it has its own set of laws and codes of ethics such as loyalty, righteousness and honour. *Jianghu* is a place where *xiake* can embody the *xiayi* spirit.
5. The ubiquitous wirework seen in the new *wuxia* films, which allows fighters to defy gravity, has led some fans to re-dub the genre 'wire-fu'.

2

Kung fu master: martial arts and acting in *Once Upon a Time in China* (1991)

Tony Williams (2000) suggests that the *Once Upon a Time in China* series represents one of the major achievements of 1990s Hong Kong cinema; and Bey Logan (1995) notes that *Once Upon a Time in China* (hereinafter *OUATIC*)) was one of the first *wuxia* films to receive serious critical attention. Indeed, in academic writing *OUATIC* has been discussed as an influential work in terms of its significance as: (1) a typical '97 Syndrome' Hong Kong film; (2) a re-invigorating force for the kung fu subgenre in the 1990s; (3) a breakthrough Tsui Hark film. Surprisingly, however, it is hardly ever presented as a Jet Li film, though it is acknowledged that the film resurrected Li's fame, fading at that point since his *Shaolin Temple* days, and made him a new kung fu superstar, following the footsteps of Bruce Lee and Jackie Chan. Few film scholars have shown an interest in exploring how Li's performance and star appeal contribute to the film's enormous popularity. I have chosen *OUATIC* as my first case study, because of this long-term underestimation of Li's significance in discussions of the film, and also because of two important, interrelated debates sparked by the film which have continued to surround Li since then: first, can a kung fu star act? Second, does cinematic technology damage the authenticity of kung fu stars?

'Only special people can do this': the authenticity of kung fu stars

It has been a commonplace within Western critical discourse to state that action stars cannot act. Similarly, 'good martial artists with limited acting ability' seems to represent the wider view of Chinese kung fu stars, especially in English-language scholarly writing. On the one hand, such an opinion reveals a deep-rooted bias, that is, the supposition that martial arts/action stars are people who know less about acting than they do about fighting. On the other hand, it reflects a dominant idea about film performance – that facial expression/psychology is favoured over body movement/physicality. Given the assumption that a kung fu star cannot act subtly and has to rely mostly on his physical capability, the substantial application of technology in the new *wuxia* films inevitably raises doubts about the *raison d'être* of kung fu stars, as has been pointed out in the previous chapter. These doubts can only grow in the age of digital reproduction, when more and more CGI (computer-generated imagery) is used in the creation of fight scenes.

As a steadfast advocate and example of displaying genuine martial skills in the cinema, Jackie Chan once expressed his discontent with the new *wuxia* films pioneered by Tsui Hark in the early 1990s:

> I don't like the *wuxia pian* (film), the flying, the exaggerated kung fu skills. It's not real. You can make anyone fly like Superman or Batman, but only we special people can do my style of fighting. (Quoted in Reid 1994: 21)

In Chan's view, it takes a star with physical skills to guarantee the 'uniqueness' and 'authenticity' of the *wuxia* film. 'Authenticity' is another crucial issue for kung fu stars. According to Leon Hunt, 'authenticity' is a term 'that sometimes refers to the martial arts themselves, to the "invisibility" of cinematic representation (wide framing, unobtrusive editing) or to the body itself as guarantee of the real (athletic virtuosity, physical risk)' (2003: 19). Hunt sees the kung fu film as a genre with a particular investment in the real, that is, the presence of special people (either martial artists or trained actors) doing what normal actors cannot do. He suggests that the 'new wave' martial arts films exemplified by the *OUATIC* series embody a new collision of technology and the kung fu star's body, more specifically, a tension between the visual excess facilitated by the increasing application of special effects and the emphasis on realism. Hunt confesses that he would like to see more authenticity for Li by ensuring that he himself performs each move and concludes that 'martial arts films simply do not need their stars to be trained martial artists anymore' (2003: 46).

Amongst Hunt's and other (mainly English-language) critical discourses surrounding *wuxia* films, 'authenticity' always provokes an intense debate, which sometimes reveals a sentimental nostalgia for a former golden period (especially the time when Bruce Lee made his name). While different views of authenticity emerge in different critical contexts, the popular view runs as follows: there are no longer authentic kung fu stars, since all the marvels of fighting can be simulated by special effects or wirework. The emphasis on authenticity conveys a strong message – that 'only special people can do real fighting', and at the same time it implies a similarly strong claim that 'special people can only do fighting', which easily leads to the belief I mentioned earlier, that is, that kung fu stars cannot act.

Li unquestionably falls into the category of the 'special people' whom Chan and Hunt refer to. He learned martial arts from the age of seven; he was five times a national martial arts champion; he made his name from his martial arts virtuosity, as showcased in his early films (*Shaolin Temple* [1982]; *Shaolin Temple II: Kids from Shaolin* [Zhang Xinyan, 1984]). Audiences have good reason to believe that Li can display genuine martial arts skills as well as any other kung fu star can. However, surprisingly, Li is criticised (notably in English-language writings) for subordinating his real skills to cinematic technology in *OUATIC*. Ackbar Abbas argues, 'Tsui Hark's star Jet Li knows his kung fu, but there are no more authentic stars/heroes of the order of Bruce Lee, as the real is more and more being "coproduced" through special effects' (1997: 31). The rumour that, after breaking his ankle, Li used stunt doubles during some fight sequences has aggravated the charge of 'inauthenticity'.

Despite such criticism, *OUATIC* was a big hit at the local box office. It was not only placed in the Box Office Top 10 in Hong Kong in 1991, but was also lauded by Hong Kong film critics as one of the ten best Chinese-language movies of the year. As a groundbreaking *wuxia* film, *OUATIC* revived the declining genre and initiated a new *wuxia* trend in the early 1990s. Why was the film such a huge success when Li was criticised for not giving an authentic exhibition of martial arts? If the 'authenticity' of martial arts is mostly a Western concern, how do local critics respond to Li's kung fu body as mediated by cinematic technology? Is it true that a martial arts star cannot act? How does Li negotiate his dual identities as a martial artist and an actor? What kind of star image does Li construct in this film?

In the discussion which follows, I attempt to address these questions by examining Hong Kong critical responses to the film, as evidenced in *City Entertainment*. Established in 1979, *City Entertainment* was the most authoritative film journal in Hong Kong and is highly regarded. During its more than thirty-year existence,[1] the journal witnessed the development, prosperity and decline of Hong Kong cinema. For example, *City Entertainment* first used the term 'Hong Kong New Wave' to define the emergence of the new wave directors in the late 1970s;[2] and in 1982 it set up the annual Hong Kong Film Awards, which have become the most prestigious film awards in Chinese-language cinema. The other important Hong Kong film awards – the Golden Bauhinia Awards (awarded by the Hong Kong Film Critics Association [HKFCA]) are also closely related to *City Entertainment*, not only because the journal's former chief editor,

Chen Baisheng, was also the key figure in HKFCA, but because many members of HKFCA were writing for the journal. After the release of *OUATIC*, several reviews of the film were published in three consecutive issues of *City Entertainment*, in August and September 1991. Given the journal's influential status within the Hong Kong film industry, these reviews can provide a glimpse of Hong Kong's critical opinion of the film at the time. Before taking a closer look at the articles, it is necessary to give a brief introduction to the film.

From kid to master

Wong Fei-hung is one of the most revered folk heroes in Chinese culture. Born in 1847, in the province of Guangdong in the south of China, Wong is celebrated as a dazzling martial artist and a proficient healer. According to Hector Rodriguez, Wong is simultaneously 'a paternalistic protector of the underdog against corrupt landlords and criminals, and a conservative champion of Confucian morality and a progressive fighter against feudal superstitions' (1997: 2). After his death in 1924, several newspapers published a series of novels fictionalising Wong's exploits; not much is known about his real life. The first Wong Fei-hung movie, *The Story of Wong Fei-hung* (Hu Peng, 1949), was released in 1949, and Wong became a major figure in Cantonese cinema between 1949 and 1970. During this period, more than seventy feature movies about this legendary martial artist were made, most of them starring the prolific actor, Kwan Tak-hing. Kwan portrayed a peace-loving, omnipotent and traditional Confucian hero so successfully that Hong Kong audiences saw him as synonymous with Wong Fei-hung.

Both Wong Fei-hung and Wong Fei-hung films have become legendary in the popular culture of Hong Kong. Not only does Wong Fei-hung symbolise the quintessential *wuxia* hero, but the films made about him 'served as a training ground for many of the leaders of kung fu filmmaking in the decades to follow' (Bordwell 2000: 204). After Kwan Tak-hing's classic portrayals, many subsequent endeavours to remake Wong Fei-hung adventures were largely unsuccessful, because there was simply no substitute for the venerated Kwan. One exception was Jackie Chan's reinvention of Wong in *Drunken Master* (Yuen Woo-ping, 1978), which tactfully changed the serious patriarchal hero to a mischievous adolescent and established Chan as a kung fu comedy superstar.[3] Wade Major therefore claims that 'any actor seeking the part would face comparisons not only to the real Wong, but also a pair of Hong Kong film legends' (2000: 153).

When director Tsui Hark came to rework the Wong Fei-hung legend in 1991, he approached the subject in a totally different way. While the earlier Wong Fei-hung films were confined to domestic dramas and stories which revolved around local communities, Tsui deliberately placed the hero within a wider historical context, foregrounding 'the Chinese coming to terms with foreign things' (Wu 1991: 35). The film is set at the end of the nineteenth century, when the Western powers were carving up China and forcing the weak Manchu government to sign a series of unequal treaties. Featured as a national hero, Wong has to defeat various enemies, including deceptive Americans who recruit Chinese labour with the promise of the 'mountain of gold' in the US, wicked local gangsters who help Americans kidnap Chinese women, corrupt and incompetent Chinese officials who always compromise with the foreigners and the stubborn northern master, Yim (Yee Kwan-yan), who desperately tries to defeat Wong in order to become the most superior kung fu master. In addition to fighting his foes, Wong is also intellectually confronted by the challenge of Western technology and culture. Interestingly, this challenge is often presented by his romantic interest, Aunt Thirteen (Rosamund Kwan), a woman educated in England, with a Western mindset.

Tsui's bold decision to reinvent Wong using Jet Li was regarded with suspicion at first. It was nearly ten years since *Shaolin Temple* had made the nineteen-year-old Li a household name within the Chinese world. In that film, Li plays the young monk Jue Yuan, who struggles to avenge his father's death. Li's deft physical skills and unaffected performance contributed to the film's unexpected popularity, and made the 'Shaolin kid' his trademark role. Hong Kong audiences were so familiar with Li's boyish, vigorous kung fu teenager image that few could imagine him as a prestigious national hero. In addition, some purists complained that Jet Li's northern martial arts style hardly prepared him to portray a Cantonese kung fu hero (Bordwell 2000). Li also admitted that he was under great pressure when playing a master because audiences had got used to his 'kung fu kid' image (quoted in Yang 1991). However, the success of the film to a great extent banished those doubts.

After the release of *OUATIC* in Hong Kong in 1991, several film critics at *City Entertainment* used the same words to describe their feeling about the film: a 'pleasant surprise'. Kang Xueying writes, 'It is a bit strange to cast Li with boyish features as a revered master, but unexpectedly he makes it' (1991: 67). She says that before watching this film, she thought that Li would transform Wong's image from a serious master to a mischievous teenager, but in fact Li's performance is no less dignified than Kwan Tak-hing's. Kang sees Li's brilliant martial arts skills as a guarantee of the film's success. Zhang Zhicheng also notes that 'Li's previous image of a vigorous kid has been totally got rid of' (1991: 62). Zhang mentions the rumour that Li used stunt doubles in some fight sequences, but he does not think that it matters. 'With his dignified and graceful physical expression, Li still convincingly impersonates a serious, prestigious martial arts master' (ibid.). In another article, Yang Xiaowen suggests that 'the previous kid has grown up. Li's wonderful martial arts performance accurately delivers a renowned master's steadiness and demeanour' (1991: 23).

From the above comments, it is not difficult to detect a common opinion – that Li's martial arts performance was crucial to his success in bringing a prestigious *wuxia* master to life. None of the *City Entertainment* critics seemed to be concerned that film technology might compromise Li's martial capabilities or make them unreal, as suggested by some English-language reviews discussed earlier. Instead, they speak highly of the combination of film techniques and Li's martial arts skills. Kang writes, 'It is exhilarating when Tsui's visual style meets Li's solid martial skills' (1991: 67). Zhang points out that 'this film again attests to the fact that fight scenes with only fists are limited, but with the help of film techniques, a fight scene full of imagination can be created' (1991: 63). Clearly, the *City Entertainment* reviewers tend to ignore the 'unreal' aspect of Li's physical performance. For them, the important thing is not how much wirework Li applies in his fighting or whether or not he uses stunt doubles, but whether or not he successfully exhibits his martial arts skills to convey Wong's dignity and adeptness as a prestigious master. In other words, it is the performativity of the martial arts sequences rather than their authenticity that is accentuated by Hong Kong critics as the key appeal of Li's reinvention of Wong Fei-hung.

These comments, on the one hand, suggest the presence of a holistic attitude towards martial arts performance amongst Hong Kong critics, rather than the rigid distinction between 'fighting' and 'acting' so often seen in English-language critical discourse, and, on the other hand, indicate a performative tendency among kung fu stars in the early 1990s. By this time, due to the introduction of Western cinematic technology and a gradually maturing system of martial arts choreography, stars with little or no prior martial arts experience, such as Brigitte Lin and Leslie Cheung, could look like expert martial artists on screen. It was obviously difficult to become a new generation kung fu star by relying solely on martial arts ability. How did Li, with his boyish face and previous 'kung fu kid' image, convincingly impersonate a revered kung fu master in *OUATIC*? To answer this question, attention may be drawn to two *City Entertainment* interviews with Li, in 1991 and 1993, in which Li makes clear his opinions on the martial arts in the film.

'Performing' martial arts

On his official website, Li admits that in the movies he made in the 1980s, he knew nothing about how martial arts would work on screen; he simply took all the things he had learned in the previous ten years of martial arts training and threw them together.[4] This may partly explain why Li did not develop into a kung fu star before the 1990s, despite his influential debut. By the beginning of the 1990s, Li had obviously gained a new understanding of cinematic martial arts when he came to play Wong Fei-hung. In the 1991 *City Entertainment* interview, Li articulates his enthusiasm for spreading Chinese martial arts through *wuxia* films, but he insists that the key thing for a *wuxia* film is to create some new fighting methods, rather than display authentic martial arts. 'We often try to go beyond our limit to do some impossible, original kung fu until the atmosphere or effect has been created' (quoted in Yang 1991: 24). When asked how, with his northern background, he managed to adjust to the southern martial arts, Li answered, 'It is hard to define my fighting style in the film as northern or southern. In fact I do not think audiences really care about it. They just want to see you fighting like a master' (ibid.). In the 1993 magazine interview, regarding the relationship between cinema and martial arts, Li declares: 'Certainly I use martial arts as a means to enhance the character. No matter how chaotic the situation is, Wong Fei-hung remains unperturbed. It is better to integrate his martial arts with his personality, using the former to cater to or enrich the latter' (quoted in Deng 1993: 40). In Li's view, 'martial arts are always limited. Each *wuxia* film only requires a little bit of breakthrough in its action scenes. It is more important to have a good script and an attractive character' (ibid.).

Li's words convey two major points. First, it was the originality and expressivity of the martial arts and not their authenticity that were pursued in *OUATIC*. Second, when audiences were constantly evolving and growing familiar with various martial arts styles, and when the rapid development of cinematic technology made 'unreal' fighting seem 'real', Li realised that acting was becoming increasingly essential to a kung fu star. In other words, instead of displaying martial arts impassively and mechanically, kung fu stars have to act/perform as well as fight. Based on this understanding, Li changed the straightforward martial arts skills which he had shown in his 1980s films to a new fighting style which is graceful and dignified, as the *City Entertainment* critics commented, and which could better deliver Wong's master image. Li did this by on the one hand infusing theatrical elements into his displays of martial arts, and on the other by allowing his skills to be negotiated by cinematic technology.

Unlike his previous *wuxia* movies, in which Li maintained continuous body motion most of the time to showcase his martial skills, *OUATIC* incorporates extensive 'pauses' and 'poses' in order to foreground Wong's repose and dignity. Each time that Li/Wong begins or finishes a bout of combat with his adversary, or lands from mid-air, either a 'pause' will be highlighted or a 'pose' will be presented, such as a half-squat with legs crossed and arms outstretched, one of Li/Wong's trademark poses. Both 'pause' and 'pose', as director Tsui Hark acknowledges, are borrowed from Chinese opera traditions:

> [On the stage] you see somersaults and flips and fights and it's very visual and then at a high point before the climax it stops for tension or suspense and then it goes on and they do a fantastic demonstration and the people say: 'Good!' and then they applaud. When we structure something by building up and then holding it back for suspense, that's the influence of Peking opera ... Now we try to make things less than Peking opera and more cinematic. (Quoted in Hwang 1998: 18)

Here, Tsui is talking about the way in which the film uses the combination of pause and movement, a typical rhythm in Peking opera, to create atmosphere in the fight sequences. The rhythm of pause/burst/pause, as David Bordwell (1997, 2000) observes, is deeply characteristic of the fight scenes in Hong Kong cinema. It not only contributes to the clarity and dynamics of Hong Kong action, but is also used to arouse and channel emotion in the fight scenes. Indeed, in *OUATIC*, the alternation of fight and stasis reconciles Li/Wong's intensity with his calm, his fury with his poise, his violence with his peace, thereby perfectly conveying the dignity of a revered master.

While Li's glamorous poses betray his Mainland *wushu* background (which attaches importance to the expressivity of martial arts), they also show the influence of another Chinese opera tradition – '*liang xiang*', a term, as Hunt writes, suggesting 'an opening of the body to let light shine', a 'key presencing moment' in Peking opera (2003: 44). Whenever Li/Wong poses, a close-up is used to emphasise his soul-piercing eyes and foreground his luminous presence. In *OUATIC*, 'pose' has been expertly fused into Li/Wong's fighting style and has become an important way of portraying the character. This can be clearly observed each time that Wong fights with Master Yim. While Yim desperately initiates one attack after another, emitting furious noises, Wong is always waiting for him in a still pose with a half-smile on his face. Wong's calm and Yim's hysteria form such a strong contrast that audiences probably do not need to wait until the last minute to know who will be the winner. The different fighting styles convey the different personalities of two martial arts masters.

Figure 2 Jet Li as Wong Fei-hung in *Once Upon a Time in China II* (Tsui Hark, 1992). (Source: Kobal Collection.)

The deployment of these poses helps Li to create a graceful and serene fighting style, thus vibrantly demonstrating what made Wong a respected kung fu master, namely, his commitment to peace – using his skills as the last recourse, instead of attacking or showing off.

'Pause' and 'pose' not only give the fight sequences a vigorous rhythm and tension, but also add aesthetic beauty and elegance to Li's martial arts performance. More importantly, by incorporating theatrical elements into the displays of his martial arts, Li fully expresses Wong's dominance in each combat and his self-possession and self-confidence as a superior kung fu master. This is probably what Hunt has in mind when he ponders that 'there is more to kung fu stardom than authentic ability', and suggests that 'Chinese performance traditions have made their own special contribution to film stardom' (2003: 43).

As mentioned before, Li is often criticised for substituting wirework and special effects for physical skills. For some (Abbas 1997), the aura of kung fu stars has been erased by technology. However, *City Entertainment* critics represent another (probably no less popular) perspective, namely that cinematic technology enhances Li's martial arts performance rather than damaging his physical 'authenticity'. In their reviews, Li/Wong's fighting style is described as 'graceful', 'dignified' and 'peaceful', and this has been to some extent attributed to the influence of cinematic techniques. It is not difficult to find evidence in the film to support this opinion. For example, one of Wong's trademark kung fu techniques, the 'Shadowless

Kick', cannot be created without the help of cinematic techniques, as it requires Li to land seven kicks in mid-air. Tsui claims that, although it looks a little exaggerated, 'you have the feeling of being very romantic and very visual' (quoted in Hwang 1998: 18). Indeed, the 'Shadowless Kick' powerfully foregrounds Wong's dignity as an invincible kung fu master. With this technique, Wong can always defeat the strongest opponent at the last minute.

Another good example is the extensive application of slow motion in Li/Wong's kicks, punches, rotations and landings. Slow motion, as Bordwell observes, is a staple of the *wuxia* film; it can be highly expressive and 'imbue the performer with strength and adroitness' (2000: 234). In *OUAIC*, slow motion is masterfully employed to showcase the beauty of Li's/Wong's physical performance and highlight his heroic presence. One of the most memorable scenes depicts Li/Wong jumping from a teahouse in order to chase a local gangster. His jump is paced with the gradual unfolding of an umbrella. His beautiful landing is aided by wirework and presented in slow motion, leaving audiences both on and off the screen impressed by Li/Wong's outstanding physical skills and unmatchable magnificence.

For Hong Kong critics, cinematic technology in *OUATIC* helped create some of the most dynamic, imaginative fight sequences ever made. One of the sequences of this kind which is often mentioned is the final duel between Wong and Master Yim in a warehouse. As numerous ladders are thrown about and deployed as weapons, the two men scamper to the top of long bamboo ladders, dodging each other's blows as they jump and leap from one ladder to the next. This fight sequence is said to have been filmed over two weeks (Bordwell 2000: 123), involving a good deal of wirework and special effects. Enhanced by cinematic technology, this sequence showcases Li/Wong's graceful martial arts style at its best. Highly original and expressive, it has become one of the most memorable fight sequences in *wuxia* film history and offers a good example of how to balance 'real' physical skills with 'unreal' cinematic techniques.

We may conclude that, through the intentions of director Tsui Hark and star Jet Li, and more importantly, from the perspective of Hong Kong critics: (1) technology is used in the film as a supplement to the kung fu star's body and to help Li perform martial arts gracefully and serenely; (2) fighting and acting are two interdependent rather than discrete elements within Li's portrayal of Wong Fei-hung. By contrast, as noted above, the criticism that technology impairs Li's martial arts performance comes mainly from English-language critical discourse. What leads to this discrepancy in the transcultural reception of *OUATIC*? Among a number of possible reasons, the genre heritage stands out. As Tom Ryall suggests, 'The "rules" of a genre – the body of conventions – specify the ways in which the individual work is to be read and understood, forming the implicit context in which that work acquires significance and meaning' (1998: 328).

Indeed, genre constitutes an effective and pertinent context for the reading of this film. The Chinese martial arts world of Western audiences may be mostly made up of Bruce Lee and Jackie Chan's realistic displays of their physical skills, but among Chinese audiences *wuxia* cinema has a much longer history and much more diverse dimensions. If for Western audiences Chinese martial arts films tend to form a subgenre of action films which seek to stage 'real-life' fights (Reid 1993–4), for Chinese audiences, martial arts play out a kind of cultural fantasy which is largely based on imagination. A brief overview of the history of kung fu stars may give a clearer idea of the way in which martial arts and acting, the authenticity and performativity of the kung fu body interact and interrelate in the traditions of *wuxia* cinema.

Martial arts versus acting: a brief history of kung fu stars

Mostly set in ancient dynasties, the early *wuxia* films emerging in the 1920s and 1930s in Shanghai embraced a mythical, superhuman *wuxia* tradition and often featured 'flying swords', 'palm power' and 'weightless flight'. The heroes with their supernatural skills could fly or leap with the aid of a range of cinematic tricks such as hidden trampolines, double exposures and, most famously, wirework. Hence, from an early period, cinematic techniques have been applied to *wuxia* films to help create spectacular feats and fantastic effects. Moreover, martial arts in *wuxia* films have never consisted purely of fighting, given the fact that many action sequences were inherited and developed from the stylised combat which occurs in Peking opera, and that early *wuxia* films, often inspired by or adapted from *wuxia* literature, were eager to reproduce those magical martial arts depicted on paper, rather than adhere to 'real' fighting techniques. High expressivity and high levels of imagination have characterised Chinese cinematic martial arts from the very beginning.

Generally speaking, in the 1920s and 1930s, it was the story, rather than the martial arts or the performer, that was central to the *wuxia* genre. Martial arts at the time might be seen more as the product of the cultural (and cinematic) imagination than a form of film performance. It is noticeable, however, that the early *wuxia* films required their actors to have some capacity to display martial arts skills on screen and consequently the *wuxia* performers of the day usually came from an opera background (Jia 2005).

This tradition was carried on in the following decades and produced a number of talented kung fu stars. More importantly, it indicates that, for kung fu stars, martial arts and acting are not necessarily two separate, conflicting elements, even though, as demonstrated throughout the history of *wuxia* film it is not always easy to combine them harmoniously.

With the genre's relocation to Hong Kong in the late 1940s, the martial arts themselves started to be highlighted, as well as the kung fu star's performing body, and they gradually became the main attraction of the genre. Cantonese *wuxia* films in the 1950s and 1960s, represented by the long-running Wong Fei-hung series, usually opted for a more realistic exhibition of martial arts, distinguishing themselves from previous swordplay films, which were filled with displays of superhuman feats. The Wong Fei-hung films are commonly regarded as recording precious martial arts traditions (Rodriguez 1997), thereby exemplifying what Hunt calls 'archival authenticity' (2003: 29). However, although the Wong Fei-hung films are memorable for their depiction of 'authentic Chinese martial arts for the first time' (Sek 1980: 28), according to Loon Sheng (a Hong Kong martial arts choreographer), they were not much concerned with martial arts or their aesthetics: 'What was important at that time was the Wong Fei-hung character, his personality, the way he behaved and the Confucian morality' (quoted in Morrissette, 31 August 2002). Kwan Tak-hing, the actor who plays Wong, cannot be regarded as an authentic martial artist because he was mainly trained in Peking opera and had limited knowledge of martial arts. Kwan brought Wong to life mostly by his unique interpretation of the historical figure, for example his fierce eyes and distinct utterances, 'which emit the dignity of the character' (quoted in Lau 1999: 38), as Lau Kar-leung observes.

From the mid-1960s, Shaw Brothers' Mandarin *wuxia* films began to dominate the local box office. Martial arts, in the hands of the two prestigious *wuxia* directors, King Hu and Zhang Che, started to transcend the limitations of opera-derived combat and developed a new visual emphasis. King Hu, who is celebrated for his stylised and montage-based *wuxia* movies, frankly claimed that he regarded combat scenes as ballets, not as plausible fights (quoted in Bordwell 2000). His heroes and heroines display fantastic skills, such as effortlessly flying and leaping on top of branches or roofs, thereby creating poetic airborne fight scenes. Zhang Che, who was keen to showcase the male body and promote a tough Chinese masculinity in his *yanggang wuxia* films, insisted that 'it is not enough to have action in a scene – the action must be powerful and contain aesthetic beauty' (1999: 20). Elsewhere, Zhang (quoted in *Yang ± Yin* 1997) declares that realism did not come into the films made by Hu and himself, as they used *wuxia* to explore their fantasies. Despite paying more attention to the aesthetics of the fighting, Hu and Zhang used only trained martial artists as choreographers, stuntmen and supporting players, while leading players such as Wang Yu, David Chiang and Zheng Peipei did not come from a strict martial arts background.[5] It is therefore safe to conclude that martial arts stars before the 1970s mainly built their screen images upon their acting rather than on their displays of martial arts skills.

A new trend within *wuxia* films, which emphasised the authentic martial abilities of kung fu stars, was launched by Bruce Lee at the beginning of the 1970s. Applying special effects at a minimal level and insisting on longer takes and full-body framing to guarantee the authenticity of his skills, Lee expressed a tough, competitive male persona through his superb martial arts and endowed *wuxia* films with an unprecedented level of realism. As Lau Tai-muk remarks, 'the worship of body and the praise of good physique culminated in the peculiar temperament of Bruce Lee' (1999: 32). By highlighting physical skills, Lee brought Chinese *wuxia* film and the masculine kung fu body to global attention and initiated the first 'kung fu craze' on Western screens in the early 1970s. Through Lee, whose body is often seen as a symbol of nationalism and masculinity, martial arts has become 'a fetishized object that represents the identity of the modern Chinese to the West' (1993: 93), as Kwai-cheung Lo puts it. At the same time, by largely relying on martial arts to express his emotions, such as anger or determination, Lee began to use martial arts as a powerful form of cinematic performance.

Influenced by Lee's huge success, *wuxia* films featuring realistic martial arts became popular during the 1970s. Apart from Zhang Che, who shifted his focus to *wuxia* films set in the later years of the Qing Dynasty, in which martial arts from the southern school such as *Hung Gar* and *Wing Chun* were frequently deployed, Lau Kar-leung, the first martial arts choreographer to become a *wuxia* director, may be the most important figure in terms of the showcasing of authentic martial arts in *wuxia* films. Accordingly, kung fu stars with martial abilities headed the genre in the 1970s and 1980s. On the one hand, traditional kung fu stars such as Di Long and David Chiang acquired some martial arts skills from the training school at the Shaw Brothers studio, as martial arts choreographers continued to train stars to perform their moves. On the other hand, some performers who were previously trained in the opera school and had skills of their own, such as Sammo Hung and Yuen Biao, grew up to be a new generation of kung fu stars.

Jackie Chan, another martial arts superstar, also came out of this tradition. Following Lee, Chan in his films further accentuates the significance and irreplaceability of authentic martial arts by doing all the stunts himself. Chan created a humorous variant of the martial arts which was distinct from Lee's earnest style of kung fu, encompassing comical acrobatics derived from his training in the opera school and developing his trademark kung fu comedy. The transnational popularity of Jackie Chan films further foregrounds the spectacular manifestation of martial arts as the main appeal of the genre. However, an overemphasis on 'authentic' physical capabilities can easily result in the criticism of 'the neglect of acting'. This partly explains why, except for the stars mentioned above, most kung fu performers in the 1970s and 1980s turned into fighting machines and were unable to keep their names in the pantheon of kung fu stars. Moreover, we should note that even those actors who prefer a more realistic display of martial arts also use some cinematic techniques to achieve effects or amplify expressivity.

To summarise, in the history of kung fu stars, sometimes acting is given more attention and sometimes it is martial arts capability which prevails, but both are indispensable elements for a kung fu star's performance. This may partly explain why Hong Kong critics, and Chinese audiences in general, seem to have less investment in such issues as the authenticity of kung fu stars. For them, whether cinematic techniques help create imaginative, atmospheric fight sequences, or whether martial arts performance contributes to the portrayal of the character, is much more important than the degree to which martial arts on screen are authentic. In the eyes of Hong Kong critics, Li undoubtedly succeeded wonderfully in *OUATIC* by perfectly combining two traditions of kung fu stars, one emphasising acting and performance, the other focusing on martial arts and the body.

'Impersonation in fighting': elegant kung fu star

In considering Li's star image built around *OUATIC*, the views of another *City Entertainment* reviewer, Luo Weiming, are instructive. He writes:

> What overcomes audiences is [the film's] dizzying fight scenes and Jet Li's poised martial arts. It is a rare, wonderful performance after the *wuxia* film genre had been out of fashion for so many years. Wong/Li embodies generous elegance both in his martial arts and non-martial arts performance. Compared with tough Bruce Lee, funny Jackie Chan, and impetuous Lau Kar-hui [another Wong Fei-hung player], Jet Li is a scholarly and calm hero rarely seen in the *wuxia* film. Li will definitely become a new idol in Hong Kong. (1991: 38)

Here, Luo on the one hand confirms that Li successfully balances martial arts and acting and on the other describes a new category of masculine *wuxia* hero, embodied by Li in his fresh interpretation of Wong Fei-hung: one that is 'elegant', 'scholarly' and 'calm', qualities which clearly distinguish Li from previous kung fu stars.

A comparison between Jet Li and Bruce Lee may help to identify the meaning of Li's new kung fu star image. Both Lee and Li are superb martial artists, and both of them are famous for portraying national heroes. While Lee's hero is a pure nationalist who prepares to fight against any enemy of China, Li plays a revisionist Wong Fei-hung who would like to learn the advantages of the West. While Lee's character is adored for his physical superiority, Li's Wong is celebrated for his ardent defence of Chinese culture. Lee's masculinity is hard, unbending and rough, as embodied in his aggressive, fiery fighting style; by contrast, Li's male hero looks soft, flexible and reflective, and this is manifested in his graceful and serene manner of fighting. While Lee established his star persona through his intention to showcase martial arts authentically, Li built his screen image by emphasising a more aesthetic display of martial arts.

The appearance and popularity of Li's elegant kung fu star image reflect some of the social and psychological changes in Hong Kong at the time. Referring to the emergence of muscular male action stars in the Hollywood cinema of the 1980s and 1990s, Paul McDonald suggests that 'these new hard-body stars show by their obvious physicality how bodies act as key signifiers of cultural beliefs' (1998: 181). As such, the significance of kung fu star bodies can be read in terms of the ways in which they embody cultural identity. In the 1970s, the Hong Kong people, faced by rigorous colonial domination and a chaotic 'fatherland' (during the Cultural Revolution), pressed for a tough and uncompromising hero image in the Bruce Lee mould to arouse national self-confidence and identify with an imaginary, powerful China. By the early 1990s, with a highly developed economy and impending handover to the Mainland, the Hong Kong people began to reflect on the impact of Western culture in a new way, and began to examine their own identity on a more complex level. A gentle, flexible and adaptable *wuxia* hero such as Li was therefore closer to the sentiment of the day.

The transition of kung fu stars from Bruce Lee to Jet Li also results from different approaches to martial arts performance. As Barry King (1991) and McDonald (1998), among many other critics, articulate, there are two main modes of acting, namely 'impersonation' and 'personification'. 'Impersonation' is produced by the actor who transforms his or her body and voice in ways that signify the differences between the characters he or she plays. 'Personification', on the other hand, foregrounds the continuity of the star's image over and above different characters. While an actor who *impersonates* plausibly integrates herself/himself into the narrative circumstances, an actor who *personifies* always plays herself/himself. This distinction in terms of acting can be borrowed to categorise two different approaches to martial arts performance, namely, personification and impersonation in fighting. A martial arts actor who maintains his particular fighting style in playing each character can be regarded as practising 'personification in fighting'. By contrast, 'impersonation in fighting' means that a martial arts actor transforms his fighting style to adjust to different characters. If Bruce Lee and Jackie Chan are good examples of the former, Li's performance in *OUATIC* perfectly illustrates the latter.

As mentioned earlier, Lee tended to deny the performativity of his on-screen martial arts and highlight his authenticity and superiority as a martial arts master. He invented his own style of martial arts, which he called 'Jeet Kune Do', and performed it in each of his films. Similarly, Chan rejects an exaggerated expression of martial arts and insists on the body itself as a guarantee of the real. Chan's little tricks in his comedic martial arts, as Yuen Woo-ping describes them – 'somersaults, creeping down and up, nimble hands and body' (quoted in *The Making of Martial Arts Films* 1999: 64) – can be found in nearly every Jackie Chan film. For Lee and Chan, authenticating their martial arts performance has became a useful means to fuse their film roles with their off-screen identities, thus constructing their star personae. By practising their unique martial arts in each film, Lee and Chan make all the characters they play look like 'angry Bruce Lee' or 'funny Jackie Chan'. In this sense, they could be seen as always playing (including 'fighting as') themselves, thereby embodying 'personification in fighting'.

In his re-interpretation of Wong Fei-hung, Jet Li brings a different approach, that of impersonation, to his performance. Despite coming from a northern martial arts background, Li confidently portrays a southern martial artist; though a martial arts national champion, Li allows cinematic techniques to mediate his fighting in order to perform some 'unreal' martial arts actions. For Li, martial arts function as a mask enabling him to impersonate a character, instead of playing himself. While in all their movies, Lee and Chan use their trademark martial arts to express their invariable selves, Li employs different fighting styles to depict different *wuxia* heroes. For example, unlike the graceful, peaceful presentation of martial arts which appropriately conveys Wong's dignity and elegance in *OUATIC*, Li displays more fantastic, romantic martial skills in his portrayal of the drunken, free-spirited Ling Hucong in *Swordsman II* (1992), and later, adopts an adroit, amusing way of fighting to depict mischievous Fong Sai-yuk in *Fong Sai-yuk* (1993) and *Fong Sai-yuk II* (1993). As

Major rightly notes, 'unlike Jackie Chan, whose most popular characters are nearly all variations on himself, Li had built a career playing individuals whose personalities often contrasted sharply with his own, characters frequently at odds with their own nature' (2000: 174). Indeed, it was the adoption of 'impersonation in fighting', or, in other words, the emphasis on the performativity of martial arts and acting, that would make Li a more flexible kung fu star than Lee and Chan in the years to come.

Conclusion

While the success of *OUATIC* is usually credited to director Tsui Hark, in particular in English-language scholarly accounts, Hong Kong critical responses suggest that it also benefited enormously from Li's subtle martial arts performance. In the view of Hong Kong critics at *City Entertainment*, instead of substituting cinematic artifice for his real skills, Li combines the two; instead of losing his aura, he acquires a more charismatic, elegant presence with the help of cinematic technology. As discussed in this chapter, through incorporating theatricality and technology into his martial arts performance in *OUATIC*, Li foregrounds martial arts as a forceful means of portraying a character. By smoothly combining two traditions of kung fu stars (emphasising martial arts/the body and acting/performance respectively) and bringing in 'impersonation in fighting', Li takes fighting beyond the physical dimension so that it acquires a new cinematic and cultural significance. As Yan Mingyu puts it, Li's body is not simply a flesh and blood somatic construction made to perform heroic deeds and for purely visual consumption; instead, it is 'an oxymoronic cultural construct as part of the historical heritage, intertextual embodiment and commercial market' (quoted in Cheung and Ku 2004). Li's performance in *OUATIC* tellingly proves that the kung fu star can act, and that martial arts and acting are not always two split and conflicting elements in a kung fu star's performance.

Li's excellent performance in *OUATIC* resulted in two breakthroughs. One concerns Wong Fei-hung. This film completed the change of this legendary character from a conservative, patriarchal Confucian martial hero to a reflective, complex modern kung fu master, therefore continuing the most enduring legend in Hong Kong film history. The other concerns Li himself. This film helped Li to fulfil numerous transformations both on and off screen: from a boyish kung fu kid to a prestigious master; from a Mainland martial arts performer who knew little about film to a transborder kung fu star who began to build his star persona on his interpretations of different *wuxia* heroes. As Major (2000) comments, when Li appeared as Wong in *OUATIC*, it was as if audiences were rediscovering two heroes from the past spiritually joined together in one movie. However, Li's newly-built star image as a scholarly *wuxia* hero would once again be overthrown when he played the lover of a transsexual male villain in *Swordsman II* the following year.

Notes

1. It was temporarily closed down in January 2007 and re-emerged as an online magazine in December 2007.
2. The Hong Kong New Wave in the late 1970s and early 1980s is one of the most famous film trends in Hong Kong cinema.
3. Chan later returned to the role in Lau Kar-leung's *Drunken Master II* (1994).
4. Quoted from Jet Li, '*Shaolin Temple*', *The Official Jet Li Website*, http://www.jetli.com/jet/index.php?l=en&s=work&ss=essays&p=1
5. For Zhang, this practice changed as his choreographer Lau Kar-leung exerted greater creative control over his films.

3

Gay lover? Gender trouble and male identification in *Swordsman II* (1992)

After two successful Wong Fei-hung films, Li made his most adventurous film, *Swordsman II*, in 1992. Two paradoxes in this film are worth noting. First, it is viewed as one of the earliest Hong Kong films to touch on a homosexual theme, but it stars 'the chastest, most sexually reticent, of all martial arts stars' (Hunt 2003: 134): Jet Li. Second, despite its perceived transgressive subject, it became a hit at the Hong Kong box office. In fact, it has proved the highest-grossing Jet Li film in Hong Kong to date.[1] Before exploring these contradictory facts, I will first briefly review an intriguing debate surrounding male representations in *wuxia* films, that is, a homosexual interpretation of male relationship in *wuxia* narratives and the resistance to such an interpretation among *wuxia* filmmakers.

Male bonding versus gay ideology

Action genres are mainly male-dominated and strictly heterosexual-oriented. However, *wuxia* cinema is characterised by a more complicated representation of gender and sexuality. In addition to the remarkable existence of the *wuxia* heroine (*xianü*) who excels in martial arts skills and often exists in her own right rather than as the love interest of the male hero, and to the gender-bending characters prevalent in the new *wuxia* films of the early 1990s, who sometimes blur the boundary between heterosexuality and homosexuality (both of which are discussed in Chapter 1), the fact that the relationship between men in *wuxia* films is often subject to homoerotic readings provides further evidence of the complexity of this representation. Unlike a typical Hollywood action narrative in which the hero will have a love interest, *wuxia* films usually foreground male friendship, or brotherhood, and downgrade romance. For example, in kung fu films by Bruce Lee, Jackie Chan and Sammo Hung, as Cheng Yu notes, 'normal heterosexual relationships are secondary to brotherly love' (1984: 25). In his *yanggang wuxia* films, Zhang Che more undisguisedly worships male bonding by 'going to great lengths to make his movies more violent and more homogeneous (literally so, by using completely male casts) without diversion into romantic sub-plots' (Teo 1997: 100). Such a tradition of celebrating male bonding has led many critics to discern a homosexual undertone in *wuxia* films.

Tian Yan (1984) argues that Zhang Che films covertly but leniently represent a repressed gay ideology through the depiction of male bonding and symbolic scenes, which feature the heroes, always with a weapon protruding from their stomachs, spilling blood as if ejaculating. Jillian Sandell suggests that John Woo's 'modern version *wuxia*' – romantic hero films – express a masculinity 'which celebrates both strength and intimacy, and where male bonding can suggest an erotic charge without the associated anxiety such relationships often trigger within the Hollywood action genres' (1997: 23–4). While a homosexual reading of the *wuxia* male representation proves quite popular in English-language critical discourse, it has been criticised by local filmmakers as a Westernised perspective, which fails to acknowledge male bonding as a 'cultural fantasy' of Chinese men.

In an interview conducted by Stanley Kwan in his highly personal documentary *Yang ± Yin: Gender in Chinese Cinema* (1997), Zhang Che overtly rejects a homosexual interpretation of the male bonding portrayed in his films and explains that his worship of male friendship is based on his understanding of Chinese tradition. He claims that, according to this tradition, the Chinese hero 'has no truck with women. He is much more concerned with his male friends'. Zhang regards the blood-brothers Liu, Guan and Zhang in the classic novel *The Three Kingdoms* as 'Chinese men's highest ideal'. He emphasises that 'no Chinese reader thinks of homosexuals when he reads a book like *The Three Kingdoms*. Nobody thinks the heroes of *The Water Margin*[2] are gay.' In this same documentary, John Woo similarly denies any conscious homoeroticism in his films and clarifies his intention to portray male friendship in a romantic and emotional rather than a sexual way.

If the refusal of a homoerotic reading of male bonding in *wuxia* films is justifiable, especially within a Chinese cultural context, it is intriguing to see the director of a film which does involve a homosexual subtext makes a similar denial. *Swordsman II* is a bizarre film mixing gender-bending, male bonding and a gay story. Although it was shown at the San Francisco International Gay Film Festival where it won the Audience Award, and although its role in initiating the representation of gender trouble in Hong Kong cinema of the 1990s is widely acknowledged, few critics relate it to gay films. At most, in Leung's definition, it is seen as a 'queerscape' film, a kind of film that expresses 'desire, eroticism, and sexuality that momentarily disrupt what heterocentric ideology assumes to be an immutable, coherent relation between biological sex, gender and sexual desire' (2004: 462).

Notably, director Tsui Hark is reluctant to admit the film's homosexual implications. In *Yang ± Yin,* Kwan criticises Tsui's films for always ending by reaffirming heterosexual norms, though most of them touch on the theme of gender confusion. He asks Tsui what draws him to the sexual conundrum in *Swordsman II* and Tsui responds in a very ambiguous way. He admits that the film is about transsexuality, but says that he did not think much about gender confusion when filming it. Tsui then goes on to claim that 'some gay films are touching not because they are gay, but because of their humanity'. Yet, at the same time, he controversially asserts that an 'unreal' love (involving some gender blurring) is more romantic than a 'real' one (a heterosexual love story). Tsui's words evidently reveal his motivation: he wants to incorporate the sexual conundrum into the film in order to make it both entertaining and profitable, but he does not want to push it into unequivocally homosexual terrain.

By investigating the resistance of a few famous Hong Kong directors to a homosexual reading of their *wuxia*/action films, my intention is to provide a critical and industrial context from which *Swordsman II* was produced and received. My interest lies not in deciding whether *Swordsman II* should be categorised as a gay film, but in finding out how Jet Li is posited and read in this transitional, pre-gay film (if it is not fully recognised as a gay film), and whether or not his image as a *wuxia* hero has been endangered by this bold attempt to involve him in a transsexual love story.

Swordsman II: a transsexual love story

Swordsman II is a sequel to another successful film, *Swordsman* (1990), and is one of the few sequels that is universally regarded as equal in quality to the original. Although the first film's credits are shared by four directors and the second one is directed by Ching Siu-tung, the fact that Tsui Hark was the producer and screenwriter has meant that both films are labelled as Tsui Hark films.[3] The *Swordsman* series films are adapted from Jin Yong's well-known *wuxia* novel *The Smiling, Proud Wanderer*, which tells the story of power struggles in the *wuxia* world. According to Tsui, of all the Jin Yong novels, *The Smiling, Proud Wanderer* is best suited for screen adaptation, because 'it is a brilliant political allegory with contemporary relevance, loaded with subtle parallels to relations between Hong Kong and China and pointed allusions to real-life figures' (quoted in Ho and Ho 2002: 182). However, in *Swordsman II*, due to the introduction of a love story between the male hero Ling Hucong (Jet Li) and the transsexual villain Asia the Invincible (Brigitte Lin) (Asia hereinafter), the gender metaphor is as poignant as the film's political allegory.

Following the first film's storyline, Ling and his fellow disciple Kiddo (Michelle Reis), disheartened by their master's betrayal, decided to retire from *jianghu* along with their Wudang Mountain brothers. But Ying (Rosamund Kwan), his former lover, delays his retirement and involves him in an internal power struggle between Ying's father Wu and Asia, who seizes Wu's leadership position in the Sun Moon sect and imprisons him. For the purpose of gaining supernatural power to fulfil his ambition of dominating China, Asia learns mysterious martial arts from a sacred scroll at the price of castrating himself, which results in a gradual loss of his male physical features. But after he meets Ling and is attracted to him, he begins a deliberate transformation of himself into a woman, through cross-dressing and makeup. Unaware of this, and falling in love with the transsexual Asia, Ling has to face a final duel with him. Asia's martial ability is far beyond Ling's, but he does not want to use his full power to fight Ling, which leads to his defeat. When Asia is falling from Black Wood Cliff, he refuses to answer Ling's question – whether or not he is the one who has spent one night with Ling – and leaves Ling in confusion and regret for ever.

The biggest difference between the screen version and the original novel is that in the novel, Asia's lover is Yang Lianting, another male villain, while in the film the romance is between Asia and the male hero Ling. It is this very difference that rewrites Ling, Asia and the whole story. Whereas the demon in the novel is humanised and romanticised, the hero on screen is entangled in perplexing gender confusion and a morality crisis. This transgressive love story unexpectedly opens up a wider, richer space for the discussion of gender issues in the film. Two opposite standpoints are apparent in the critical discourse on *Swordsman II*. While some critics acclaim its positive feminist view and a flexible sense of gender identity, others insist that it is only a confirmation of, and sign of allegiance to, patriarchy and heterosexuality. For example, Stephen Teo (1997) suggests that the character of Asia offers a new type of gender-bending hero/heroine who bends not only genders, but character types (villainess and romantic protagonist), therefore presenting a telling attack on the stereotype of the male hero. From another angle, Rolanda Chu points out that the concept of idealised love set out at the end of *Swordsman II* is not defined clearly as 'staid, coherent and heterosexual' (1994: 33).

By contrast, some critics read this film as a sheer patricentric construction. Through an interesting comparison between the consciousness and situation of the male lead, Ling, in the film and Chinese men in real life, Kuang Youhua (1992) warns that the misogyny and homophobia hidden in the film text aim to repress both women and men who do not want to obey gender rules. She writes that for Asia's mistress, Cici, spending the night with Ling as a stand-in is a patriarchal strategy to redeem the male hero's morality and defend heterosexual authority. Similarly, Lang Tian (1992) argues that what seems to be a plea on behalf of disempowered women and gays cannot conceal the intrinsic gender violence of this film. Asia's sacrifice for Ling speaks to the unchangeable fate of women/homosexuals, that is, submission to patriarchal domination.

It therefore seems that the film's ambiguous gender narrative offers many possible readings. However, it is important to point out three less-addressed areas in the critical discourse on *Swordsman II*. First, when critics try to explore this film's gender significance, they focus mostly on the text, paying little attention to the audience, even though it was highly unusual for a film with a homosexual subtext to become so popular in the still conservative Hong Kong society of the early 1990s. In fact, there exists a common tendency in the discussion of homosexual representation in Hong Kong cinema, namely, to emphasise the ambiguity of the film text as the sole source of pleasure to its audience while downplaying other factors, such as the gendered, social and cultural position of the audience, the specific reading strategies adopted by different audiences and the meanings associated with a star persona. This textual-centred approach is unable to answer such important questions as: why were Hong Kong audiences fascinated by *Swordsman II*? Was it because of its subversion or its reaffirmation of heterosexual gender norms?

Second, almost all the existing critical articles on this film are written by Western or Hong Kong critics/academics. Mainland scholars show little interest in *Swordsman II*, probably because it was not officially released in Mainland cinemas, but more possibly because for a long time orthodox Mainland scholars have dismissed *wuxia* films in general as a commercial film genre without merit, to say nothing of a sexually adventurous *wuxia* film. It is noteworthy, though, that in contrast to Mainland scholars' disregard, mainland Chinese fans have canonised this film as an unsurpassable *wuxia* classic. In the ten or more years since it was first imported from Hong Kong, this film has been repeatedly consumed and circulated among Mainland fans. Numerous reviews of it can easily be found on the Internet. In some sense, *Swordsman II* has become the embodiment of the *wuxia* dream for a generation of mainland Chinese fans (roughly speaking,

Figure 3 Jet Li as Ling Hucong in *Swordsman II* (Ching Siu-tung, 1992). (Source: Kobal Collection.)

those born between 1965 and 1980). Emerging from a different cultural and social context, Mainland fan discourse can provide a comparative dimension to Western/Hong Kong critical readings of the film.

Third, though *Swordsman II* has stimulated much academic interest, the discussion mostly focuses on the transsexual Asia/Lin and the tension and anxiety she/he symbolises, while little attention has been paid to the male hero Ling as played by Jet Li. Indeed, this film strikes rather a discordant note in Li's career, not only because it is a rare attempt to cast Li as the 'reluctant' *wuxia* hero Ling Hucong, who has a happy-go-lucky philosophy and indulges in wine and women, instead of devoting himself to noble causes, but also because as a leading actor in the Hong Kong film industry in the early 1990s, Li had to share attention with, and was even overshadowed by the actress Brigitte Lin. In critical discourse, Lin is undoubtedly the focus of attention and the centre of the film while Li is mainly viewed as a foil, or even a 'fool' (Stoke and Hoover 1999: 105). Consequently, *Swordsman II* is simply regarded as an exceptional Jet Li film, without further discussion. However, if, as Teo (1997) puts it, the film is an unambiguous attack on the stereotype of the male hero, this attack should not only be presented by the transsexual Asia, but also by Ling, who, as an accepted *wuxia* male hero, unexpectedly falls in love with a villain, and, more defiantly, a half-male half-female villain. What equally deserves attention is that the film does not seem to have done any harm to Li's heterosexual hero image, as suggested by its commercial success in Hong Kong and its long-standing popularity among mainland Chinese fans.

Why is a transgressive film contradictory to common mores so popular among mainland Chinese fans? How do fans read and understand the imperfect hero Ling and his gender-bending lover Asia? Do they read it as a gay love story? Does fan adoration of this film manifest a more open and tolerant attitude to minority sexual identity? How do fans reconcile the film's homoerotic implications with Li's heterosexual star image? Does Jet Li really become second to Brigitte Lin in this film? In the rest of the chapter, I explore these questions by examining fan discourse on *Swordsman II* at *Dingding Studio: Kung Fu Star*,[4] a *wuxia* film fan site based in mainland China.

Fans' reading: a heterosexual love story

The *Dingding Studio* fan site was established in 2002 by Dingding, a twenty-eight-year-old male *wuxia* fan. He confessesed that his motivation to create this site came entirely from his passion for *wuxia* movies.[5] In the 'About Us' section of the site, he declares his ambition to make *Dingding Studio* the biggest Chinese kung fu film database and BBS (Bulletin Board System). Indeed, among numerous *wuxia* film fan sites in mainland China, *Dingding Studio*, stands out for its abundance of information and well-populated forum. It provides comprehensive introductions to the major kung fu film talents, including stars, directors and fight choreographers.[6] As a fan comments, it supplies 'some interesting materials you cannot find in other websites'.[7] In its forum, the most lively section of the website, all kinds of topics are freely set out and discussed under eighteen sub-forums such as Shaw Brothers Films, Kicker Masters, Donnie Yen Forum, or Yuen Woo-ping's Action World. From its emergence in 2002 to the date when I made my calculations in 2006, this film forum had 7,522 members and innumerable visitors. Some 30,022 postings under 4,569 topics had been published. My examination of fan discourse on *Swordsman II* mainly focuses on the 'Tsui Hark Chivalry Forum' and the 'Jet Li Chinese Forum'. According to a report in *Dazhong dianying* (Popular Cinema), one of the most prestigious Mainland film journals, the 'Jet Li Chinese Forum' at *Dingding Studio* is 'currently the most popular Jet Li BBS among Mainland fans' (2005: 31). As their personal information shows, the members of *Dingding Studio* are mostly between twenty and thirty-five years old. While male fans still make up the majority of them, female fans are by no means scarce. For instance, the hosts of 'Jet Li Chinese Forum', Jianbao and Xiaoyu, are both young women.

Swordsman II is one of the most frequently-mentioned titles in both the 'Tsui Hark Chivalry Forum' and the 'Jet Li Chinese Forum'. The fans express their unreserved fondness for it, as seen in such threads/articles as 'Meet *Swordsman II*', '*Swordsman II* is My Most Favourite', and '*Swordsman II:* Unfading Legend'. While the fans frequently mention their experience watching this film – 'Last night I watched *Swordsman II* for the eighteenth time, I still couldn't help crying' (Cao Yun, 30 June 2003); 'I was deeply moved when I first saw it. I have had a totally new understanding and perspective on *wuxia* film since then' (Abby, 30 April 2004) – they are also keen on discovering its inexhaustible meanings (for example, 'Asia the Invincible and Asha: Anima or Animus?'). Two differences between fan discussion and critical discourse are worth noting.

First, unlike a 'non Jet-specific' film in critical reviews, in various polls held on the site *Swordsman II* is commonly viewed as one of the best Jet Li films. The original novel has been adapted as a film and television drama many times over, but the version embodying Li's Ling is agreed to be the most successful. For example, JetLiang writes, 'Li's portrayal of Ling is peerless. Ling's adventurous spirit, heroism and affection are best embodied by Li' (22 November 2002). Second, although critics are keen to discuss gender issues in the film, surprisingly they hardly ever address the love between the two protagonists. In contrast, the fans express their unreserved sympathy and admiration for the tragic love story between Ling and Asia. Lousany (5 May 2003) says that it is a beautiful love story which delivers the message: political ambition can never ultimately overcome human nature. Sui Feng writes, 'Starting from mutual understanding and admiration for each other, Ling and Asia gradually truly fall in love. It is so touching!' (14 February 2004) However, do these compliments indicate an acceptance of the homoerotic feeling between the two leads?

When closely examining the fans' discussion, it becomes apparent that Asia is actually read as a charismatic woman, rather than an abnormal transsexual man, or as Chu describes her, a 'monstrous feminine' (1994: 35). Much evidence supports this observation. For instance, two similar polls were held, asking 'Who is the most beautiful heroine in Jet Li movies?' under the title 'Hero and beauty'[8] and the other 'Who is the Number 1 beauty in Tsui Hark films?'[9] In the first vote, many fans declared that it is undoubtedly Brigitte Lin/Asia (*Swordsman II* is the only film to have teamed Li and Lin together). In the latter, Lin scores 17 out of 30 votes. Although Lin appears in more than one Tsui Hark film, her Asia is the most memorable character she plays. Some fans openly call her 'Asia *sister*'! (My italics. Doudou, 13 December 2003); 'I like Asia, like Brigitte Lin' (Alr, 8 February 2003). Whenever Asia is referred to in fan discussion, the pronoun 'she' rather than 'he' is used. The fans marvel at Asia's beauty and charisma as a captivating woman, while his or her cruelty and perversity as a transsexual male leader seem to be largely forgotten. Chaoyear describes Asia as like 'a princess from a fairy tale' (6 March 2003). Similarly, Fengyu sings her praises, 'Many audiences' first impression of Asia is that of a "goddess", an incarnation of beauty and power' (6 April 2004).

Given the agreement that Asia is a female, it becomes easy to understand why the fans can enjoy Li/Ling's heartbroken romance without feeling at all uncomfortable with the fact that their hero has fallen in love with a castrated man. Simultaneously, it is no surprise that the fans at *Dingding Studio* hardly address the homosexual undercurrent throughout the film. They try to define the romance between Ling and Asia in various ways, but avoid reading it as a homosexual story. For example, JetLiang (22 November 2002) sees it as an intriguing love story between a good guy and a bad girl. Another fan (Anon., 5 March 2003) reads it as a heterosexual love containing some characteristics of male bonding, such as mutual appreciation and trust. Clearly, among the fans, the Ling-Asia romance is accepted as a love story between a man and a woman, not between two men or a man and a transsexual man. This is not only because, in the eyes of the fans, Asia is supposed to be a woman, but also because they see Ling as unequivocally heterosexual. As Tiantian says in his defence, 'It is absurd to call Ling a gay as from the outset he has never seen Asia as a man!' (8 July 2003) Romantic adventure and gender trouble in *Swordsman II* appear to be completely smoothed over in the fans' readings in this instance.

Nevertheless, this is not to say that the fans at *Dingding Studio* are unaware of the homosexual implications of this film. Let us have a look at the following two posts. '*Swordsman II* tells a love story between two men. It was difficult for audiences to accept this kind of story in 1992, before the appearance of *Lan Yu*'[10] (Li Xiangrui, 27 February 2003); 'Asia's self-castration is used to allude to the darkness of political conflict and the extermination of humanity in the original novel. However Tsui Hark skillfully relates sexual disorientation to homoerotic sensibility, the latter becoming very popular later. He is seeing into the future, but this subject matter could not be accepted at that time' (Lou Sang, 23 February 2003). The fans' awareness of homoerotic undertones in the film can also be detected from their attitude to the film's finale. Unlike the usual expectation for a heterosexual love story, that is, that the hero and his lover can be together at the end of the film, *Dingding Studio* fans speak highly of *Swordsman II*'s tragic ending. Seriously hurt by Ling both physically and emotionally, Asia chooses to give up both his ambition and his life by refusing Ling's rescue. Asia's final farewell to Ling is regarded as the most touching and impressive scene in the film. One fan acclaims that 'it pushes the whole movie to the climax, making the romance sublime and ideal. It's irreplaceable!' (Song, 11 November 2003). Most fans agree that Asia's death is the best ending to this love story. As Sui Feng comments, 'Indeed, it is sad. But if not there, then where could this love story go?' (17 December 2003). As far as I am aware, only Tutor11 expresses a wish that Li could be united with Asia at the end. But he immediately admits his desire is irrational and inadmissible and concludes, 'An aberrant love story ends in a rational way. No other better resolution!' (14 February 2003).

Cross-dressing and male identification

Unlike Western/Hong Kong critics, mainland Chinese fans at *Dingding Studio* seem not to be at all disturbed by the gender-blurring narrative and homosexual implications in *Swordsman II*. But from the quotations taken from the fan discourse above, this is clearly not because Western/Hong Kong critics are more sophisticated and Mainland fans more naive in recognising the gender confusion in this film. The fact is that Mainland fans have the same, if not more knowledge about this film's homosexual subtext, because Asia's sexual transformation and homosexual inclinations are made very clear in the original novel. In the novel, Asia and his similarly evil male lover are easily disparaged as emblems of wickedness and perversion. What makes the fans change their initial view of Asia as an abnormal villain to an appreciation of him as a sympathetic, romantic heroine? How can the fans ignore the film's overt homoerotic message and read it as a heterosexual love story? How do the fans succeed in making sure that Li, an accepted *wuxia* hero, who always stands for morality and heterosexuality, is exempt from the gender trouble? I tackle these questions by revealing how cross-dressing, a striking feature of this film, functions in mainland Chinese fan readings.

In her analysis of gender misrecognition in *Swordsman II*, Chu (1994) references Annette Kuhn's discussion of the relationship between spectator and cross-dressing narrative, and claims that the casting of the famous actress Brigitte Lin as Asia encourages the viewer to perceive the male Asia as a woman. Chu's argument is certainly justifiable, but I would like to add that the male hero Li/Ling's role is as important as Lin's, if not more so, in facilitating this misrecognition, as found in the fan discussion at *Dingding Studio*. Like Chu, I also use Kuhn's work as a starting-point. In her chapter 'Sexual Disguise and Cinema', Kuhn (1985) argues that cross-dressing can be used as a means to denaturalise fixed and unproblematic sexual differences but its potential to subvert or confirm the dominant gender order depends on genre, spectator-text relations and internal textual organisation. Kuhn divides narrative films involving sexual disguise into two main genres, thriller and comedy. In comedy, Kuhn argues, spectators have an all-embracing narrative point of view, termed the 'view behind', and they are never in doubt as to which of the characters is 'really' male and which 'really' female, as some characters are in the film. So from a secure vantage point, spectators can laugh at the travesty, 'the comedy of errors attending the ignorance and confusion of the fiction's characters' (1985: 62–3). In this sense, Kuhn concludes, comedy with cross-dressing narration does not denaturalise sexual difference. However, when watching a cross-dressing thriller, spectators have the 'view with'; they are placed in the same uncertainty as the other characters about the gender of particular characters, and therefore feel anxiety and curiosity to know the truth, which integrates them into the world of the characters. Kuhn claims that this latter point of view may temporarily shake the spectator's conviction that gender distinctions are absolute.

Cross-dressing in the *wuxia* genre can also be used to create comic or thrilling effects, but this is more to do with the tradition of *xianü*, as mentioned in Chapter 1, and less commonly to do with male castration, as seen in *Swordsman II*. Cross-dressing functions in mainland Chinese fan readings of *Swordsman II* in a way which combines the two points of view which Kuhn has theorised from the spectator-text relations in classic Hollywood narrative films. The difference is that, while the 'view behind' arouses anxiety, it is the 'view with' which mitigates this anxiety. Undoubtedly, the fans hold the 'view behind' when they are watching the film. They know everything that the male hero Ling does not know: Asia is a castrated man and it is Asia's mistress, Cici, who as a stand-in spends one night with him. With this 'view behind', the fans have to face the fact that, albeit unwittingly, Ling does fall in love with a man. But from the fan discussion above, we can see that the fans are willingly indulging themselves in Ling's tear-sodden romance, while turning their backs on its homosexual feelings and gender confusion. This surely indicates that, in the viewing process, the fans have unconsciously (or consciously?) given up their 'view behind' and changed so as to 'view with' the male hero Ling. When Ling first meets Asia in the lake, he mistakes him for a woman due to his red cloak and good looks. Asia is shocked to hear Ling address him as 'lady' but he quickly chooses to keep silent in order to maintain

Ling's misrecognition (at this point, Asia has castrated himself but still has a male voice which later gradually transforms into a female voice). Throughout the film, Ling sees Asia as a charming, beautiful woman to whom he is easily attracted. Although knowing that Asia's appearance is deceptive, the fans prefer to suspend their knowledge and identify with Ling's perception of Asia as a glamorous woman, which guarantees them a safer position from which to enjoy the transgressive romance, and downplays any homoerotic suggestion.

Kuhn observes that even though their stories problematise gender identity and sexual difference, classic Hollywood narrative films involving cross-dressing aspire to resolve the questions that they raise, at least in their endings. This gives the films a considerable suggestion of closure and limits the denaturalising potential of the cross-dressing narrative. *Swordsman II* may be one of the few films in which such a re-transformation does not happen, because Asia refuses to reveal his true sexual identity and leaves Ling in unresolved doubt. However, the satisfaction of the fans with this ending, as I discussed above, does not suggest that they welcome the subversion of normative heterosexuality. The fans' attitude shows that they change back to the 'view behind', thereby fully conceding that Asia's death is the best way to maintain heterosexual rule, as well as the sexual innocence of the male hero Ling/Li.

By skilfully shifting between 'view behind' and 'view with', and above all by identifying with the male hero's point of view, the *Dingding Studio* fans successfully manage to heterosexualise a homosexual story. In this regard, while on the surface Lin's Asia catches the eyes of the fans, in their interpretation his or her meaning actually depends on Li's Ling. It is Ling's perspective that makes the fans change their initial verdict on Asia, from a transsexual careerist to a romantic heroine: through Ling's eyes, the fans begin to appreciate Asia's beauty and overlook his or her perversions, and when Ling falls in love with Asia, the fans gradually see Asia as a human being instead of a monster. Asia largely exists as a spectacle, gazed at by both the male lead and the fans. If, as Jin Yong (quoted in Ho and Ho 2002) says, Asia is beautified and romanticised in this film, it is not only because of Lin/Asia's charisma, but, perhaps to a greater extent, because of the male hero Li/Ling's adoration for him/her. Without Ling's love, for the fans at *Dingding Studio* Asia would have remained a symbol of evil and abnormality, as depicted in the original novel. As one fan mockingly says, 'Every normal reader of the original novel will feel disgusted with Asia, a transsexual monster who always calls his/her male lover, Yang, in a half-male, half-female voice' (Xiao Yu, 4 February 2004). The fans' identification with Li/Ling's male, heterosexual viewpoint therefore legitimates not only Asia, but also this love story. By adopting this 'view behind'/'view with' reading strategy, the fans effectively disavow the homosexual undertones and gender confusion which critics find fascinating in the film. The fans' reading even ultimately denies that *Swordsman II* is a cross-dressing film. If Asia is believed to be a woman, who is cross-dressing?[11]

Above, I argue that while the cross-dressing narrative in *Swordsman II* allows for ambiguous play with sex/gender, it is the viewer's perspective that generates different readings and meanings. From a feminist perspective, or the perspective of gay politics, Hong Kong/Western critics take issue over whether the film subverts or upholds gender normativity. From a male-centred perspective, mainland Chinese fans at *Dingding Studio* downplay its troubling gender message and define it as a heterosexual love story. This male-centred perspective, apart from being deep-rooted in a society characterised by strong homophobia, should be understood in relation to industry strategy as well as to Jet Li's star image.

A number of academic accounts have attempted to address the explosion of the homosexual narrative in 1990s' Hong Kong cinema and attributed it to two events – the decriminalisation of homosexuality in Hong Kong in 1991 and the 1997 handover (Grossman 2000; Leung 2004). While the former supposedly indicates a new openness to gay and lesbian themes among Hong Kong audiences, the latter is seen as a catalyst for such films. Meanwhile, some critics also point out that the decriminalisation of homosexuality did not alter the stigma attached to homosexuals, and the public's acceptance of homosexuality was still quite limited (Leung 2004; Lilley 1998). Therefore, while many Hong Kong directors in the 1990s were keen to sell a film on the basis of its gender fantasies, they tended to handle homosexual material in a heterosexual and more acceptable way, which is less offensive to mainstream audiences. This strategy produced two visible traits characteristic of Hong Kong films in the 1990s involving a homosexual narrative (for example, *Swordsman II*; *He's a Woman, She's a Man* [Peter Chan, 1994]; *Hu-Du-Men* [Shu Kei, 1996]; *Intimates* [Jacob Cheung, 1997]): an ambiguous portrayal of same-sex desire and commercial success. To some extent, this could be seen as an example of what Harry Benshoff (1997) calls homosexploitation, namely, using gender blurring or a homosexual subtext to provoke curiosity and anxiety, but finally comforting the spectator and reinforcing cultural assumptions about gender roles, sexuality and heroism.

As the initiator of this homosexploitation trend, *Swordsman II*'s submission to heterosexual norms may be less betrayed by its ending – the death of Asia – than by its tricky casting: letting an actress play the male villain, Asia, who cross-dresses as a female in the diegesis. The casting of the renowned 'screen goddess' Brigitte Lin as Asia indeed makes it hard for audiences not to see Asia as a beautiful woman. Not only are Mainland fans enthralled by Lin's charisma, but the comment of the veteran Hong Kong critic Law Kar on Lin's gender-blurring image evinces a similar confusion: 'I have never taken her as anything but female. I like her charm, not because she plays men or seems androgynous. She always looks great' (quoted in *Yang ± Yin* 1997).

The homophobic undertone in this casting choice is sharply laid bare by Leslie Cheung, the only major Hong Kong star who has publicly admitted his gay identity:

> In terms of Chinese morality, it's much easier for a woman to play a man than vice versa. When a woman plays a man, everyone is indulgent. If she seems 60% masculine, she'll be appreciated. But if a man plays a woman and seems 80% feminine, people will still be hostile. That is typical of Chinese morality. If you ask if Lin is believable as a man, I think not, too bad. She is not convincing as a man. But she is pretty...it should be more fair. If they can accept a woman playing men, then a man playing women should be okay too. (Ibid.)

Indeed, it is 'a man playing a woman' that the Hong Kong film industry strains every nerve to avoid. From the perspective of gay and lesbian politics, Asia certainly should be played by a male actor.[12] But if he or she had been, it is uncertain whether mainland Chinese fans would have extolled Li/Ling's transgressive romance as heartily as they do now and whether the film could have become such a big hit in Hong Kong in the early 1990s. An interesting dispute at the *Dingding Studio* fan forum indicates the unfeasibility of this casting. When Qian Xue (25 October 2003) ventured a hypothesis – that it would probably have been equally terrific if Leslie Cheung had been cast as Asia – he was immediately strongly attacked by other fans: 'We admit Cheung's excellent acting ability and his effeminacy, but could you bear it if Li fell in love with Cheung?' (Yin Huise, 25 October 2003); 'No Chinese audience could stand seeing Li and Cheung flirt on screen! The film would be banned in China' (Foshan, 11 April 2004).

Jet Li's star image also plays an important role in the fans' heterosexualised reading of the film. Li is without doubt heterosexual, both in his movies and in real life. In terms of his on-screen romantic relationships, Li perfectly represents the sexual image of traditional Chinese male heroes – conservative, reserved, serious and simultaneously shy, embarrassed in front of women – as can be seen from his well-known, chaste romance with Aunt Thirteen in the Wong Fei-hung film series. It is probably in this sense that Hunt refers to Li as the chastest, most sexually reticent martial arts star ever. It seems that even the slightest charge of sexual abnormality must not stain Li's screen image. Regarding his personal love life, *Dingding Studio* fans show huge interest in Li's two marriages, first to Mainland martial arts actress Huang Qiuyan and then to famous Hong Kong beauty Li Zhi. In the fans' discussion, Li is a sensitive man, heart-stirringly romantic and a perfect husband who devotedly loves his wife. It is quite difficult for fans to relate Li to any homosexual tendency.

In addition, Li's attitude to the film deserves special attention. According to the public accounts Li has given regarding his films, it is easy to get the impression that *Swordsman II* is the film he dislikes most. Though Li has expressed his discomfort with it on different occasions, let me quote from an article published on his official website[13] and re-posted at *Dingding Studio*, in which he talks about the filming of *Swordsman II*. Li recalls that he had a hard time getting into the role of Ling Hucong, as he could not identify with much of his behaviour. 'The part of the plot that I couldn't get straight involved Ling's multiple love relationship . . . involving five different women'. Notably, Li here defines all his love interests in the film as women. Throughout the article, Li tries his best to distance himself from the role by saying, 'I wasn't able to give that role the same energy that I invested in my portrayals of Wong Fei-hung or Fong Sai-yuk. In those films, I became the character. In this film, I was just acting a role'; or 'after *Swordsman II*, I set up my own production company. I wanted to make sure that I wouldn't have to take any other roles that would feel too forced'. Li mentions that the film was considered a great success and made a good deal of money, but he has never been able to understand the character and this disturbs him. His article ends by saying 'As for his (Ling's) romantic temperament, I don't think I will ever understand that as long as I live'. Li's account, on the one hand, reveals his own understanding of Ling's romance as heterosexual and, on the other, can be taken as an intentional strategy to defend his sexual innocence and to dispel any possible doubts about his sexual preferences which this role may have aroused in audiences, thereby maintaining his image as a heterosexual hero.

Conclusion

In the view of many Western/Hong Kong critics, *Swordsman II*'s best moments belong to Brigitte Lin as Asia, while Li/Ling, 'despite his lead billing, often seems to be on hand largely for weapons expertise' (Major 2000: 159). Yet my examination of mainland Chinese fans' reception of the film demonstrates that the significance of Li as Ling has been substantially underestimated within existing critical discourse. Mainland fans also show great admiration for Lin/Asia, but Li/Ling is not at all overshadowed by Lin/Asia's glamour. In the eyes of the fans, Li/Ling is still unshakeably the 'real' hero in the film. Li/Ling stands as an omnipresent 'father', controlling both Asia's fate on screen and the fans' reading off screen. By identifying with Li/Ling's perspective, the fans, on the one hand, see the formidable androgynous Asia as a charming, lovelorn woman, thereby effectively dissolving his or her threat to the male hero Li/Ling, and, on the other, they heterosexualise a homosexual story, thus perfectly defending Li/Ling's moral integrity and maintaining the patriarchal gender construction.

In the reading of mainland Chinese fans, Li/Ling functions as a barrier to counteract any homosexual suggestion. Li/Ling's heterosexual feelings for Asia save the fans from having to deal with Asia's homosexual feelings for Ling and help evade the issue altogether. Furthermore, Li/Ling stands for normality and authority, while Asia is constructed and consumed as exotic, perverse and spectacular. According to Benshoff (1997), the monster queer may be a sexy, alluring, politically progressive figure, but in any traditional model of monsters and normality, he or she is still a social threat which must be eradicated. Indeed, in *Swordsman II*, Li's sexuality and his hero image meet unprecedented challenges – as Dai Jinghua suggests, 'Dongfangbubai [Asia], as an image of misidentified gender and gender ambiguity, works as an obstacle to the male protagonist's firm grasp on his own identity' (2005: 91–2) – but they are still far from being subverted.

To a large extent, mainland Chinese fans' reception of the gender issue in *Swordsman II* is closed and conservative, in that it excludes the possibility of mobilising or reconstructing rigid, sometimes repressive, gender categories: a possibility offered by the film's cross-dressing and gender-bending narrative. Yet, from another angle, the fans' reading nicely supports Judith Butler's (1990) idea of gender as performance. The notion of a natural and true gender identity in this film is indeed unsubstantiated, as both gender and sexuality are constantly being constructed and modified in the text, as well as by its reception. It seems that audiences may play a larger role than filmmakers and performers in this construction. In the fans' heterosexual reading, Li/Ling stands as a heterosexual male hero, but this heterosexuality is by no means seamless, if we consider the following facts: (1) Before Asia falls off the cliff, Ling's anxious plea – 'Tell me that you are Cici' – betrays his secret desire to be with Asia even after knowing that he is actually a castrated man; (2) though trying to deny the homosexual undertone, Mainland fans' glorification of the Ling-Asia romance still unconsciously reveals a pleasure that comes from what Kuhn describes as 'a vision of fluidity of gender options', 'a glimpse of a world outside the order normally seen or thought about' and 'a utopian prospect of release from the ties of sexual difference that bind us into meaning, discourse, culture' (1985: 50).

Despite his openly-stated dislike of the film, Li's Ling has become a classic hero image of the new *wuxia* cinema of the early 1990s. The film marks another milestone in Li's career, not only because of its huge success at the Hong Kong box office, but also because Ling is probably one of the most complicated characters Li has ever portrayed. One fan at *Dingding Studio* (Mo Yan, 3 March 2003) even goes so far as to claim that Ling stands for Li's highest achievement as an actor. This complexity and achievement can partly be attributed to the film's ambiguous gender representation. Interestingly, in Li's subsequent work, the Fong Sai-yuk films, for which Li was also the producer, he not only has two wives, which is certainly runs counter to his usual chaste hero image, but in one scene himself cross-dresses as a woman! It may be that playing Ling Hucong unexpectedly offered a means to question or even deconstruct the unshakeable, static patriarchal image Li had built up in his Wong Fei-hung films, thus endowing Li with a new flexibility towards his sexual image on screen. Nevertheless, after *Swordsman II*, gender and sexuality would not be a visible issue in the discussion of Jet Li films until he transferred to the West. Then his sexuality would once again become an intriguing topic of discussion among audiences in a different cultural context.

Notes

1. According to the figures from the Hong Kong Film Archive, during the first five-week run in Hong Kong, it took HK $34,462,000 and actually outperformed all the *OUATIC* series, both *Fong Sai Yuk* films and other popular Jet Li movies. This record was not even broken by his two more recent blockbusters *Hero* (HK$ 26,648,345) and *Fearless* (HK$30,201,600), although the latter grossed most at the Hong Kong box office in 2006.
2. Both *The Three Kingdoms* and *The Water Margin* are classical novels in which male bonding/brotherhood is portrayed and highlighted.
3. Tsui Hark films are usually characterised by dynamic camera movements, unlimited imagination, intense emotional expression and profound political allegory.
4. After I conducted my research on the site in 2004, the website has changed its outlook and its name to *Kung Fu Film Dynasty* but it uses the same address www.kfstar.com.
5. Dingding, e-mail message to the author, 14 September 2004.

6. It is divided into a range of film worlds of stars, directors and choreographers, such as the Jet Li Film World, Sammo Hung Film World, Tsui Hark Film World, Zhang Che Film World.
7. Quoted from www.kfstar.com. Unless stated otherwise, all quotations are from this address, accessed in November and December 2004.
8. This poll took place in October 2002.
9. This poll took place between December 25, 2002 and November 5, 2004.
10. A famous gay film about the story of a gay couple based in Beijing, directed by Stanley Kwan in 1998.
11. In *Swordsman II*, there is another cross-dressing character, Kiddo, but she is relatively insignificant in terms of the diegesis of the film.
12. At the San Francisco International Gay Film Festival, the character of Asia was reportedly adored by gays and lesbians from all over the world, but a common opinion was that the character should have been portrayed by a male actor.
13. Quoted from Jet Li, '*Swordsman II*', *The Official Jet Li Website*, http://www.jetli.com/jet/index.php?l=en&s=work&ss=essays&p=11

4

Mother's boy: adolescent hero and male masquerade in *Fong Sai-yuk* (1993)

Jet Li's most productive year appears to have been 1993; six films starring him were released and all of them performed well at the box office.[1] Of these films, *Fong Sai-yuk* is undoubtedly the most important, not only because it was the first film produced by Li's own company, Eastern Productions, with Li as the producer, but also because of its widespread popularity at the time and in later years. Based on the adventures of a real-life Southern hero, *Fong Sai-yuk* and its sequel were Li's most successful films in the early 1990s, alongside the Wong Fei-hung series and *Swordsman II* (1992). In this chapter, I want to move my discussion from Li's negotiation between martial arts and acting in *Once Upon a Time in China* (1991) (Chapter 2) and his entrapment in gender trouble in *Swordsman II* (Chapter 3) to his reinvention as a comic 'mother's boy' in *Fong Sai-yuk*, which distances him from the patriarchal image he built up in the former two films: in *OUATIC*, he portrays a prestigious 'father' figure of the *wuxia* world, master Wong Fei-hung; in *Swordsman II*, his Ling Hucong represents a symbolic 'father' for both his female admirers and his transsexual lover.

Becoming a father: kung fu comedy and adolescent hero

Despite the significant existence of *xianü*, *wuxia* cinema is predominantly a male genre and focuses on the portrayal of male relationships. Apart from male bonding, another male relationship highlighted in many *wuxia* films is the father-son relationship or its variant – the master-disciple relationship. In fact, the complicated relationship between father and son has always been a prominent theme in Chinese-language cinema; as Stanley Kwan inspiringly demonstrates in *Yang ± Yin: Gender in Chinese Cinema* (1997), 'fathers are everywhere'. The well-known Chinese directors interviewed by Kwan, such as Hou Hsiao-hsien, Ang Lee, Edward Yang and Chen Kaige, all admit the deep influence of their fathers on their lives and their filmmaking. Indeed, as the central structure of Chinese society and the core discourse of Confucian culture, the father-son relationship has played a crucial role in moulding Chinese male identity, both on screen and in social life. Within the Chinese context, facing a powerful and ubiquitous 'father', the son has to be obedient, deferential and disciplined, as this is the only way to fit himself into social morality and political reality. Yet, fatherhood and sonhood are inseparable and interchangeable. To a large extent, for a Chinese male, 'becoming a man' means 'becoming a father' – a dominant fiction which functions to perpetuate patriarchy.

The complex love and hatred between father and son becomes a rich topic which Chinese filmmakers find they can endlessly explore. For example, the father-son relationship is conventionally used as the metaphor for a clash between tradition and modernity, old and new, authority and anti-authority, as exemplified by a number of excellent films by directors from all three Chinas, among them Allen Fong's *Father and Son* (1981), Ang Lee's 'Father Knows Best' trilogy (*Pushing Hands* [1992]; *The Wedding Banquet* [1993]; *Eat Drink Man Woman* [1994]) and Zhang Yang's *Shower* (1999), though as Stephen Teo observes, 'the paradox in all father and son relationships and their history of conflict is lodged in this final acceptance of the father by the son' (1997: 65). The repressive nature of the father-son relationship can be found most evidently in socialist films, where the Chinese Communist Party (CCP) and 'the Party's son' form a symbolic father-son relationship. 'The Party's son' is usually denied all forms of male power except those conforming to the Party, which, according to Esther Yau (1989), evinces a 'rhetoric of castration'. Typically represented as a 'father's son', Chinese male screen images have to a large extent been defined by either patriarchal domination or political authority.

Wuxia heroes are not usually bound to family. They are homeless and wandering around *jianghu*. Yet, while *wuxia* heroes do not usually have a blood father, they are mostly accompanied by a *shifu* (master), who represents an omnipresent 'father' figure in the *wuxia* world. In some cases, *wuxia* heroes have neither father nor master, but the central goal of their lives is to avenge the death of their father or master, and this forms a classic theme of the genre. It is worth noting, however, that the father-son relationship in a typical *wuxia* narrative is rather different from that in other kinds of Chinese film, in that it is less of a conflict. *Wuxia* heroes seem to pay more respect to and show more identification with their father or symbolic father – the master. In other words, while in many other Chinese films, the patriarchal figure is continually questioned, challenged and restored, in many *wuxia* films he somehow remains as a romanticised or idealised object.

It was not until the emergence of the kung fu comedy trend in the late 1970s, initiated by *Snake in the Eagle's Shadow* (Yuen Woo-ping, 1978) and *Drunken Master* (1978), both starring Jackie Chan, that the inviolable father-son/master-disciple relationship in *wuxia* films started to be secularised, even parodied. As Leon Hunt notices, most kung fu comedies are 'about Master/Pupil relationships, but with an irreverent or cynical flavour' (2003: 103). In kung fu comedies, while the image of father/master is no longer defined by impeccable heroism and unquestionable authority, the son/disciple is usually 'a bright but hopelessly lazy kid, who lacks both the staying power needed for martial arts training and respect for his *shifu*' (Ng 1980: 43). However, although many kung fu comedies try to elaborate transgressions and rebellion against the father/master's authority, in the end they prove to be merely the adventures of the young hero and part of the process of becoming a father. It is probably in this sense that Chris Berry and Mary Farquhar suggest reading the features of Jackie Chan's masculinity as typical of adolescence, 'a time of identity formation and risk-taking in the transition from childhood to adulthood' (2006: 150), the period before becoming a man, in particular a 'father'. In their eyes, all the troubles, risks and traumas presented in such an exaggeratedly comic way speak of Chan's having to negotiate between 'his adolescent search for a separate male identity while simultaneously constrained by a family that demands submission to the father' (ibid. 145).

Kung fu comedy faded after 1982 when its leading figures, Jackie Chan and Sammo Hung, transferred to the domain of action filmmaking in contemporary settings, but comic heroes (with a different look) would come back to the *wuxia* genre in the early 1990s, as discussed in Chapter 1. The Fong Sai-yuk films, as Hunt (2003) points out, highlight a dominant strategy used in reinventing martial arts in the early 1990s: pastiche and parody. The comic elements seen in the Wong Fei-hung films have become ubiquitous in *Fong Sai-yuk* and its sequel. Like earlier kung fu comedies, *Fong Sai-yuk* tries to parody the classic father-son relationship, but at the same time, it unconventionally foregrounds the relationship between mother and son. Kung fu comedies notoriously exclude women; both heroes and villains are 'men without women' (Ng 1980). By contrast, *Fong Sai-yuk* offers some eye-catching female roles: Li/Fong's romantic interest Tingting aside, the heroic mothers of both characters have superior martial arts skills and always protect their husbands and children when they are in danger.

The mother figure in Chinese cinema often appears marginalised and dispensable. In most cases, the mother functions as a mouthpiece of the father and an agent or a catalyst between father and son, because the latter two always have difficulty in understanding and communicating with one another. Instead of achieving any independent personality, the mother is largely meant to 'serve and bolster the patriarchal system' (Teo 1997: 62). Compared with the conflicting and complicated father-son relationship, the mother-son relationship is simply defined as unreserved love and giving, without any need for further discussion. Therefore, the most innovative part of *Fong Sai-yuk* may not be its comic tone, but its reconstruction of the Confucian family structure through a comic presentation, that is, using 'weak father, strong mother and mother's boy' to replace 'strong father, weak mother and father's son'.

Fong Sai-yuk: a fresh hero or a reluctant hero?

As one of the earliest films made jointly by the three Chinas – it was financed by a Taiwanese film production company, made by a Hong Kong crew with a mixed cast from Hong Kong, Taiwan and mainland China and filmed in the Mainland – *Fong Sai-yuk* was a huge success in all three places.[2] It ranked fifth at the box office in Hong Kong in 1993 (HK$30,666,842),[3] and fourth in Taiwan (NT$65,000,000) (quoted in *China Film Year Book 1994*, 1994: 401). Its sequel *Fong Sai-yuk II* (1993), which came out four months later, proved similarly successful, ranking tenth in Hong Kong and ninth in Taiwan. In mainland China, in 1993, when most domestically produced films did badly at the box office, according to Wang Zhiqiang's (1994) report, the most profitable films were all co-productions, such as *Once Upon a Time in China III* (1993) and *Fong Sai-yuk*. Unlike many mass-produced kung fu films which would quickly be forgotten by audiences, *Fong Sai-yuk*'s status as a kung fu classic has been secured by its being repeatedly shown on television over a long period, both in mainland China and overseas.[4]

Apart from its box office triumph throughout the Chinese-speaking world, the film is significant for Li's career because it offers another trademark screen image of him – the mischievous and carefree Fong Sai-yuk, revitalising a legendary hero whose stories had been presented on the screen more than thirty times before (for example, *Fong Sai-yuk and Miu Chui-fa* [Feng Zhigang, 1948]; *Two Heroes* [Zhang Che, 1974]). Wade Major sees *Fong Sai-yuk* and its sequel as Li's conscious effort to 'forge a new persona closer to his own personality, while simultaneously distancing himself from Wong Fei-hong' (2000: 159). Major's perception is probably based on Li's own statements on different occasions that he liked and identified with the character (Deng 1993). Whether or not these

Figure 4 Jet Li as Fong Sai-yuk and Josephine Siao as Fong's mother, Miao Cuihua, in *Fong Sai-yuk* (Corey Yuen, 1993). (Source: Kobal Collection.)

claims are true, Fong Sai-yuk is undoubtedly one of the most celebrated *wuxia* heroes Li has portrayed.

The film depicts, probably for the first time in the genre, a delightful mother's son.[5] Fong (Jet Li) prefers to practise martial arts with his mother, Miao Cuihua (Josephine Siao), than to learn ancient poems under his father's supervision. He enjoys doing slightly unconventional things with Miao and then, with her, has to take the father's punishment. Whenever he is in danger, he calls on his mother for help. He gets along very well with his mother, and they are like two good friends. Beyond simply loving each other, the relationship between Fong and Miao is also defined by mutual understanding, appreciation and cooperation. In the film, the father figure is astonishingly diminished and caricatured while the mother seems to be the son's ideal. Despite its popularity and originality, however, the film has received much less critical attention than the *Once Upon a Time in China* series. Moreover, the limited existing critical discourse does not speak highly of its fresh characterisation.

Hunt comments that 'rather than chastening and galvanising the hero into "becoming a man" by severing maternal ties, the narrative allows Fong to do the exact opposite' (2003: 148). Hunt concludes that Fong Sai-yuk may be an 'immature' mother's boy, but at least he survives. Two reviews published in *City Entertainment* are rather negative regarding Li's new image. A Lisi complains, 'Fong Sai-yuk does not grow up to adulthood even after personal tragedy' (1993: 104), and suspects that excessive love from his family, especially his mother, undermines his appeal, as well as his potential to become a hero. Similarly, another Hong Kong critic,

Yang Xiaowen, criticises Li/Fong for 'lacking the serious thoughts about the country and people seen in Tsui Hark's *Once Upon a Time in China* films' and consequently 'lacking depth' (1993: 106). It appears that for Hunt, A and Yang, a mother's boy will never grow up to be a man/hero, but must remain an immature, frivolous teenager whose status as a *wuxia* hero is largely in doubt.

While box office statistics show that the film was warmly welcomed by Chinese audiences in different places, the critical opinion on Li/Fong as a reluctant hero offers few clues as to why it was and still is popular, what exactly are the 'new' traits which Li's comic 'mother's boy' offers in this film, and how Li's adolescent hero image is related to his previous star persona. In the rest of this chapter, I deal with these questions by analysing the accounts of audience members, more specifically, a group of mainland Chinese military graduates who watched *Fong Sai-yuk* in 1994 when they were still at university, whom I interviewed about their memories of the film.

Tracing personal memory: a case study

First of all, I should explain why I chose this specific audience group to conduct my empirical research. There were two major reasons. The first one concerns my own personal memory. Fifteen years ago, I was pursuing my bachelor's degree in a military university in China. My university aims to train future military officers who are competent in different languages. We were educated in a similar way to students in other, non-military, universities, but under a rigidly militarised administration. The compulsory viewing of films, a very military-based activity, bears witness to the nature of this administration and stands out as a unique experience for military students. I remember that every Tuesday evening, all the students would bring small chairs and queue to enter an open square to watch a film. The films, chosen by the Army Propaganda Department, were usually used as ideological conditioning tools, and were mostly politically safe but aesthetically shabby. When asked about their experience of watching compulsory films, most interviewees described it as 'intolerably boring' though some of them admitted they were sometimes amused by the sloppy plots and far-fetched performances. But exceptions always exist and one of those was *Fong Sai-yuk*. As I remember, throughout the screening, laughter could be heard all over the square. The excitement lasted for a long time afterwards, while the students enthusiastically quoted passages of dialogue from the film. *Fong Sai-yuk* therefore was a rare, pleasant mandatory viewing, both for me and, I believe, for many military students of the day.

Motivated by this memory, I decided to interview some of my previous classmates about their opinions of the film. Compared to Hong Kong critics writing for *City Entertainment* in Chapter 2 and mainland Chinese fans on the *Dingding Studio* site in Chapter 3, this audience has a different relationship with me as the researcher. However, I must declare, in spite of having more background knowledge about this audience group and a different means of gaining their response, I treat their accounts equally as evidence of the reception of a Jet Li film and analyse them in the same way as I handled the reception material in the previous two chapters.

Second, while I am aware that military graduates are only a special group within a wider audience, and I would not wish to present them as representative of larger-scale audiences in any way, I do find that a military university is highly appropriate for representing a coercive China, an image which has been built up in film studies since the Tiananmen Square incident in 1989. As mentioned in Chapter 1, the new *wuxia* films of the early 1990s, including *Fong Sai-yuk*, are categorised as 'June 4 Syndrome' films or '97 Syndrome' films, and their popularity is often read as a sign of the anxieties haunting Hong Kong people at the time in the face of an arbitrary future ruler. I have long wondered why these films were equally popular in other places outside Hong Kong; was it due to similar reasons or to different but rarely addressed ones? Military universities in mainland China at that time are notorious for their heavy-handed control of students, and I see my university as one of the places where patriarchal oppression could be felt to the utmost. The military graduates whom I interviewed thus bear at least one similarity to the Hong Kong audiences of the early 1990s, that is, they were all faced with an oppressive father/ruler, either in reality or in imagination. Researching their responses to *Fong Sai-yuk* can, I hope, offer a comparative picture of the way in which the film and Jet Li struck audiences in different places. Moreover, I want to challenge the monolithic, exclusive definition of the audiences for Hong Kong cinema which has been constructed in most critical writings relating to the Hong Kong films of the late 1980s and early 1990s, that is, as local people who were living in the shadow of the 1997 handover.

I interviewed fifteen of my previous classmates from this military university, nine females and six males.[6] This is a small sample of an audience, however, as I stated in the Introduction, it is difficult to decide what number is large enough for an audience study. Fifteen people's accounts might not provide an exhaustive reception picture, but it can certainly give a glimpse of how the film was received by military students in the early 1990s. Due to the distance involved (I was in the UK during the period of this research, but even had I managed to go back to China it would not have been possible to meet most of them, as they were living in different cities), I conducted most of my interviews in September and October 2005, and four of them in May 2007, through various means: one face-to-face, two by telephone, four online in instant conversations via MSN Messenger, and eight through email communication. I asked some scheduled questions (which are presented below) and then discussed with my interviewees the answers they had already given. As regards the email interviews, after sending out the first email with questions, I usually followed up with one more email in which I asked further questions based on their first responses. I describe the methods used to collect the information as 'interviews', in that the process was two-way and dialogic, though not always in the form of oral communication.

Yet, I am fully aware of the difficulties associated with tracing people's memories. The request for a person's impressions of a film from so long ago might be risky for two reasons. First, the interviewee's memory might be too vague to offer any valuable information, hence resulting in invalid data. This problem fortunately did not arise in my interviews, thanks to the fact that the film had made a great impression upon the interviewees. But I should make it clear that the memories which I analyse here are solicited memories and not self-generated ones. Second, no memory can be held to be a 'straightforward representation of past events' (Stacey 1994: 63). Memories of the cinema are always negotiated by many factors, such as changing discursive contexts, the changing identity of the cinema audience, or the star's subsequent career. To a large extent, memory is an inaccurate reflection of the past. No doubt for this reason, Jackie Stacey suggests that 'a critical analysis of the forms and mechanisms of memory is pertinent to all ethnographic studies of media audiences' (ibid.).

The above-mentioned factors certainly affected my interviewees' memories of *Fong Sai-yuk*. For example, asked if he liked this film, Chen J. said, 'I liked it before, as *wuxia* films were my favourite when I was younger. But it doesn't appeal to me now'. Chen's words suggest that the status of the interviewees, in relation to the ways their lives have changed and the possibility that their feelings have changed, actively structures the memories produced for this research. Generally speaking, I take the accounts offered by my interviewees as their responses to the film, but retold in retrospect and modified by their current perspectives. They are not accurate original responses, but I hope nevertheless that they may indicate the way in which the film was consumed by Mainland military university students at the time.

Mother's boy: the new look of the *wuxia* hero

My opening question to the respondents was: 'Do you still remember *Fong Sai-yuk*, which was screened in the university in 1994?' Regarding a film they watched 11 (or 13) years ago, apart from Chen Q. who confused its sequel *Fong Sai-yuk II* with the original, the interviewees gave an affirmative answer. Wang Y. told me that even today she and her boyfriend often quoted funny dialogue from the film to each other. In response to my next question – 'What was your impression of this film?', the interviewees frequently used the words '*haokan*' (literally 'nice-looking', meaning 'good'), '*gaoxiao*' (comic or humorous) or '*qingsong*' (light-hearted) to describe the film. All the interviewees readily acknowledged that they liked this film. For example, Ren X. confessed, '*Wuda*[7] films are not my type. I can never even finish a *wuxia* novel as I simply dislike violence. I don't like period films either. But *Fong Sai-yuk* was an exception. I really enjoyed watching it'. The consensus of the interviewees confirmed not only what the box office statistics have told us – that the film was popular at the time, but also what they did not tell us – that the film has a special place in the memories of many people who have watched it.

Regarding the question 'Which character impressed you most in the film?', the interviewees voted as follows: Miao (Sun, Liu, Li L., Wang P., Cao, Jia, Wen, Wang Y.); Fong (Xie, Li M., Cheng J.); both Miao and Fong (Ren, Chen Q.); Tiger Lei (the father of Fong's lover) (Ye, Cao). The mother figure seems to have made the strongest impression on the interviewees. She is seen as 'the soul of the film' (Jia), and defined as a 'new woman' who can protect her husband and others (Wen). Liu K. commented, 'Miao Cuihua is an extraordinary character, who combines wisdom, bravery, humour and goodness'. Ren held a slightly different view: 'This mother is not perfect. She often makes trouble and produces some comic situations. It is rare to have a mother image who is a parody and at the same time likeable'. By contrast, Fong's father seems a rather forgettable figure. Asked about their opinion of him, most interviewees responded that they could not really remember his image. Jia told me that she did not like this character and called him 'an odd man'. Wang P. described the gender dislocation embodied by Fong's parents, that is, the traditional model of 'male knight-errant versus smart and pretty female' was reinvented as 'female knight-errant versus knowledgeable but weak male'. Interestingly, the other father in the film, the clownish Tiger Lei, a semi-villain, was remembered very clearly by the students. Many interviewees mentioned his famous line '*yi de fu ren*' ('cultivate the people through morality'), which became very popular among students after watching this film.

Since a majority of the interviewees regarded Miao as the most impressive character in the film, I wondered if, in their view, Li/Fong's masculine heroism had been overshadowed by his strong, glamorous mother. To this, only four of the interviewees answered 'Yes',[8] while eleven claimed that Fong's status as a hero had been underpinned instead of being undermined by his mother. Many interviewees agreed that in this film an exuberant mother image serves as a foil, a backup, in order to foreground a perfect male hero. Sun M. asked, 'Can you imagine a capable mother having an incapable son?' The film was read as a growing-up story and Miao was regarded as playing a key role in the formation of Fong's personality. So, for Ye, 'The more remarkable Miao is, the more heroic Fong will be'. The male hero and his mother, in most interviewees' eyes, complemented rather than conflicted with each other. In fact, one of the richest discourses coming out of my interviews was the interviewees' comments on mother-son bonding as portrayed in this film.

Unlike the critical opinions interpreting Fong's close relationship with his mother as a handicap to becoming a man/hero, and far from the popular perception in Western discourse that a son's emotional dependence on his mother should be diagnosed as an 'Oedipus complex' which a man must get rid of on his way to adulthood, almost all the interviewees expressed their appreciation of mother-son bonding highlighted in the film, and suggested that being a 'mother's boy' makes Li/Fong a more convincing and accessible hero. 'Fong's close relationship with his mother reveals the human nature of a male hero, which had not had enough attention paid to it in previous Chinese films' (Ren); 'As a teenager, Fong's dependence on his mother is understandable and natural. What makes the film successful is precisely its refusal to offer an omnipotent, larger-than-life hero' (Li M., Jia). While the interviewees agreed that the portrayal of Fong's affection for his mother humanises the once tough, self-sufficient *wuxia* hero, they frequently made the comparison between the serious father-son relationship and the intimate mother-son relationship. Wang P. remarked, 'Contrary to the inherently antagonistic father-son relationship, mother and son are supposed to be close and interdependent'. Li L. suggested, 'While a father always cares about finding ways to establish his authority, which is often repressive, in front of his son, a mother is like a friend, who gives her son more encouragement and less pressure'.

Fong's attachment to Miao, then, not only makes him a more realistic and sympathetic *wuxia* hero for the interviewees, but foregrounds a 'family love' which is not typical of a *wuxia* hero, thereby offering a new, family-based hero image. Chen Q. said, '*Wuxia* films used to portray a hero who devotes himself to loyalty or brotherhood. This film impressed me because of its focus on filiality. Fong always puts family love in first place. He might not be a *da* [big] hero but I can really identify with him in this respect'. Jia also claimed, 'it is nice to see the film paying attention to Fong's relationship with his mother, instead of his lover'. With the character of Fong, Li seems to distance himself from his 'master' image as Wong Fei-hung in the *Once Upon a Time in China* series and from his 'lover' image as Ling Hucong in *Swordsman II*, and reinvents himself as a 'son', according to the military graduates.

I asked all the respondents 'What do you think is the difference between Li's Fong and his previous hero images, such as Wong Fei-hung? Which one do you like more?' In terms of the difference between Fong and Wong, a common opinion was that they represented *shaoxia* (the adolescent hero) and *daxia* (the adult hero) respectively. While Fong was described as carefree, funny, with faults and likeable, by comparison, Wong was steady, responsible, mature and prestigious. Six people liked Fong more (Li L., Ye, Chen Q., Ren, Wen, Jia), three preferred Wong (Wang P., Wang Y., Sun), four liked both equally (Li M., Liu, Zan, Chen J.) and two did not choose between them (Cao, Xie). The interviewees who liked Fong more gave various reasons: 'Wong is undoubtedly more perfect, but Fong is a people's hero. I feel closer to him' (Li L.); 'Compared with the mature Wong, the younger Fong is more lovable and less boring' (Wen); 'I prefer Li to be a son, rather than a master' (Ye). It might be safe to conclude that to these military graduates the 'mother's boy' image does not endanger Li/Fong's masculine heroism, but instead makes him a family-based, more approachable adolescent hero.

Given the interviewees' identification with the breakthrough mother image and fresh mother-son construction, I asked another question, 'Is this film still patricentric or trying to challenge patricentrism?' Of the twelve people who answered this question, Li L. and Chen Q. who thought that the film to some extent challenged male domination by highlighting a female hero, but the rest of them read it as an absolutely male-centered film. The sense that the patriarchal theme is maintained was explained by the interviewees from two main standpoints. First, the father's authority is not questioned in any way. Sun pointed out that, no matter how anti-traditional and excellent in martial arts Miao may be, she is always obedient to her husband. Wen insisted on the supremacy of Fong's father in the film. 'Although more attention has been paid to the mother-son bonding, the father's authority is still untouchable. Miao and Fong are more like sister and younger brother, partners in mischief-making, under the supervision of the father'. Second, though Josephine Siao as Miao was considered to have stolen a fair number of scenes, the interviewees still view Li/Fong as the real centre of the movie. Miao was regarded as either somebody who is responsible for producing comic effect (Zan), or a perfect foil who serves to make the male hero Fong stand out (Xie, Li M., Chen Q., Wang P.). Jia detected the 'exploitation of women' in the film, and suggested that Miao simply functions to help deliver Fong's humour and integrity. She commented, 'Female characters are still secondary in the film'.

When I asked their opinion of Li's comic image in the film, all the interviewees acknowledged that Li's performance as the lively and mischievous Fong was good. However, most of them did not see Li/Fong as a comic figure in the same way as a Stephen Chow or Jackie Chan character would be. They preferred to use 'humorous' instead of 'parodic/ farcical' to describe Li/Fong. Chen J. compared Chan and Li: 'You can spot Chan's comedic tricks even in his fighting, but Li's fighting style here is still sincere'. Wang Y. made reference to Chow by insisting that 'Li cannot intentionally self-parody, as Chow does. He looks better with some serious or positive elements in his image'. The interviewees tended to view Li/Fong's image as semi-comic and semi-serious, which makes him multi-dimensional and lovable, but at the same time keeps his hero status unshakable. Wang Y. and Ren told me that all the comic scenes they can remember in this film are related to Siao/Miao, while Li still remained in their memory as a gallant, chivalrous *wuxia* hero, as he had always been, only with mischievous teenager traits added. While Jia and Xie saw Li's comic performance as 'under control' so that it would not damage his heroism, Chen Q. claimed that Li/Fong was characterised by both comedy and tragedy. Zan's comment probably represents a common perception: 'Fong is playful in everyday life, but once he faces a showdown with the villain, he becomes as serious as Wong, or any other of Li's heroes. So the comedic elements are just cosmetic, it is his serious hero image that embodies value and ideology'.

Intertext and context: why do we like it?

According to the interviews, as I have presented them so far, the reasons why this film appealed to the interviewees include its funny dialogues, spectacular fighting, a successful portrayal of mother-son bonding, excellent performances, and above all its parodic or comic features. However, the film alone cannot fully explain why it is so memorable for a specific group of people unless it is placed within a wider context. As Mike Budd puts it, 'Readings are determined not only by the structuration of the text but also by the intertextual, subjective, and social situation into which that text is inserted' (1990: 52). An attempt to understand or analyse audiences' responses to a film should be accompanied by a process of unscrambling the context in which particular audiences are located, as my study of the military students' reception of *Fong Sai-yuk* demonstrates.

When the interviewees talked about why they liked this film, they often used the epithet 'new' to back up their reasons, no matter whether they were describing the film's comic style or its light-hearted construction of the hero. This reveals that intertextual discourse plays an important role in their reading of the film. In other words, the experience of viewing films of this kind helped shape their responses to *Fong Sai-yuk*, as the following accounts show. 'I like this film because of its novelty. The *wuxia* films we watched before were very serious but this one is funny' (Wen); 'The traditional *wuxia* hero is serious and idealised. By contrast, Li's comic version of Fong Sai-yuk is more realistic and attractive' (Li M.). As we know, kung fu comedy was not newly created in the 1990s. It came into fashion in Hong Kong at the end of the 1970s and to portray an imperfect or unlikely hero is a common strategy in a kung fu comedy. However, due to the fact that before the early 1990s, Hong Kong films could hardly ever be officially released in mainland China,[9] the Mainland audiences of the day were more familiar with the *wuxia* films made in the 1980s in the Mainland (*Wu Lin Zhi* [Zhang Huaxun, 1983]; *Wu Dang* [Shu Sha, 1983]; *Shen Bian* [Zhang Zien, 1986]) in which a serious, magnanimous hero has to deal with the enemies of the country or the miseries of his family. It is therefore not difficult to understand why the carefree, funny Fong Sai-yuk won favour with the students when they saw the film. A similar reason could be used to explain why Hong Kong critics speak more highly of Li's essentially serene Wong Fei-hung than his vociferous Fong, since a more serious, 'deeper' hero might be preferable in the so-called 'postmodern' context of Hong Kong.

Apart from the *wuxia* films which they had watched before, the other films they were watching at the time also affected the military students' attitude to *Fong Sai-yuk*. Both Liu and Ren mentioned that this film stood out as an exceptional 'compulsory film'. As described above, under a compulsory viewing system, most of the films watched by the interviewees in the university were mainstream and politically correct. In the early 1990s, in contrast to the farces and parodies prevailing in Hong Kong cinema, the screens in mainland China were full of serious propaganda films. After the 1989 Tiananmen incident, the state reinforced its ideological control and invested heavily in so-called 'leitmotif films'.[10] As a result, quantities of *ju pian* (giant/huge films) came out. In the context of the early 1990s in the Mainland, *ju pian* specifically refer to two kinds of film: war films dealing with the CCP's revolutionary history, such as *The Decisive Engagement 1–3* (Li Jun, 1991), and biographical films portraying the founding fathers of the CCP and the Chinese People's Liberation Army, such as *Mao Zedong and His Son* (Zhang Jibiao, 1991). These movies are characterised by extreme length, large-scale military involvement, big budgets and government sponsorship, since as Chris Berry (1994) suggests, the government was aiming to launch new initiatives to reeducate the population and instil patriotism and nationalism. Although most revolutionary historical films did badly at the box office,[11] they occupied the screen in such places as military universities, where ideological control was extremely tight. *Fong Sai-yuk*, which shows much less interest than most in such issues as patriotism or nationalism, and, in Hunt's words, performs 'either a willful forgetting or a parodic de-Sinicisation of a local hero' (2003: 147), thus stands out for military students as a transgressive film. Bored with the clichéd preaching of overwhelming 'leitmotif films', the students showed unusual enthusiasm for this entertaining and de-politicised kung fu comedy.

While the students' film-viewing experience serves as an intertextual context for the consumption of the film, their military university constitutes another important contextual factor which contributes to the students' readings of the film. Students in my university all studied language and literature, while in our daily lives we had to endure rigorous, sometimes inhuman military-type training and surveillance, without complaint. Many of us innocent and passionate young people came to this university with romanticised and idealised views, but the reality brought us only restraint, oppression and disappointment. For many students who graduated from my university, their undergraduate experience, torn between the yearning for freedom and the bitterness of reality, is more like a traumatic memory. In fact, during my interviews, these military graduates often referred to their daily lives at university. Liu described his university life as 'gloomy' and confessed that watching *Fong Sai-yuk* brought rare joy to it. Ren asked, 'Didn't you feel repressed at a military university? Too many constraints, unkind cadres, injustice . . . I wished I were Fong Sai-yuk, with outstanding martial arts skills, so I could teach a lesson to those people who made me suffer'.

The students' responses to the film could be read as both an escape from and a resistance to the coercive environment. Both the military students and Fong can be seen as powerless sons, under the control of a strict 'father' (for the former, the army). While to question or challenge the authority of the 'father' is impossible and forbidden, a perfect mother-son relationship seems to offer a utopia, where with the mother's support and love, patriarchal repression can be escaped for a while. The students' strong identification with the mother-son bonding elaborated in the film betrays their desire for a more relaxed and unconstrained atmosphere in which they could freely develop their individuality.

On the other hand, the film depicts Fong as an anarchic, mischievous adolescent hero, who constantly entangles himself in trouble and pays little attention to the lofty causes to which his father is devoted, such as fighting against the Qing emperor and restoring the rule of the Han people. This image of the unconventional hero was strongly endorsed by the military students because its anti-authority implications correspond to their hidden and silent resistance to an over-strict militarised administration. As a symbol of escape and resistance, *Fong Sai-yuk* was perfectly in tune with the sentiment prevailing in a Chinese military university of the early 1990s, and was thus welcomed enthusiastically by the students. Of course, audiences in other places (such as students in a non-military university) might have had a similar response. Some interviewees suggested that the film had such a wide appeal because it catered to the taste and mentality of young people. However, the students in a closed, cheerless and restricted military university probably felt more sympathetic to and impressed by it.

From the accounts of the interviewees, I note that Jet Li's changing career and star persona also play a significant role in shaping the military graduates' memories of *Fong Sai-yuk*, an influence which might be termed 'double nostalgia'. I usually ended my interviews by asking the interviewees what impression they had of Jet Li as an actor. More than half the interviewees answered this question by talking about Li's film debut, *Shaolin Temple*. Chen Q. said, 'My first response to Li is *Shaolin Temple*. It was such a sensational event at that time. I have watched that film more than once'. Chen J. recalled, 'I still remember how I went to watch *Shaolin Temple* . . . I and two of my classmates from primary school travelled a long way by bicycle. It is really memorable and unsurpassable'. Many interviewees clearly expressed their adoration of Li's unaffected performance as Jue Yuan in *Shaolin Temple*. In their eyes, it is the little monk Jue Yuan, rather than the master Wong Fei-hung, who remains the most memorable character Li ever played, before Fong Sai-yuk. With this unfading image in mind, they tended to see Fong Sai-yuk as a kind of continuation of Jue Yuan, since both of them are boyish and funny. A nostalgia for Jue Yuan can partly explain why more interviewees identified with the comic Fong than the dignified Wong. For example, Liu thought that humour has always been a notable characteristic of Li's screen personality, ever since his earliest *Shaolin Temple* films. Jia admitted that she was not used to seeing Li in the role of Wong, as it was somewhat serious. By comparison, as already discussed, some Hong Kong critics, such as A Lisi and Yang Xiaowen, are not satisfied with Li's transfer from the unflappable Wong to the mischievous Fong, probably partly because it is Wong who makes Li a superstar in Hong Kong and is thus more memorable for Hong Kong audiences.

The other kind of nostalgia functioning in the interviewees' memory of the film results from the fact that since 1998 Li has re-located his career to the West. The interviewees were clearly not happy with Li's new identity as a Hollywood star. 'Li is labelled as purely a martial-arts star in Hollywood. It is a pity. He might have gone further if he hadn't left Asia' (Jia); 'Li's roles in Hollywood films are totally different from the ones he played in China, less heroic, less glamorous . . .' (Chen Q.). The typical attitude towards Li's crossover career is – 'I don't like any of his Western films!' (Ye, Chen J.), or 'I still prefer his previous hero image . . .' (Wang Y., Jia). The discontent with the screen persona which Li has built up in his Western films leads to a nostalgia for the heroic images he established in his past Chinese work, which undoubtedly help to reshape the military graduates' memories of *Fong Sai-yuk*. To some extent, their emphasis on their fondness for Li's Fong seems like a process of reclaiming Li's identity as a Chinese hero. When the students watched the film in 1994, it made them feel nostalgic about Li's first film role, Jue Yuan, which is related to their childhood memories; when in 2005/7, they recalled their experience of watching *Fong Sai-yuk*, the film itself becomes the object of their nostalgia.

Conclusion: 'mother's boy' as masquerade

My examination of the military students' reception of *Fong Sai-yuk* offers a different picture of the film from the critical responses to which I referred earlier in the chapter. While a comic 'mother's boy' image can be described as 'immature', thereby undermining the character's claim to serious masculinity within critical discourses, the military students thought that it represented a more homely, convincing and accessible, yet by no means less heroic, *wuxia* hero. While the popularity of the new *wuxia* films of the early 1990s is often interpreted by critics as a sign of anxiety among audiences, related to specific historical events such as the June 4 incident and the 1997 handover, no interviewee in my research ever mentioned either of these events. It therefore appears more appropriate to suggest a connection between their fondness for the film and their specific position as a student at a military university in mainland China in the early

1990s. My findings do not necessarily contradict existing critical opinions, but rather they raise some important issues in terms of understanding the relationship between screen images, contexts and audiences.

First, is it not over-simplifying to try to relate one or more films to a specific historical event? I do not intend to deny the far-reaching influence of the 1989 Tiananmen incident on Chinese cinema and on the shared state of mind of Chinese society. In fact, what I believe is that, as a historical trauma, it, to a large extent, destabilises and deconstructs the 'father' myth, thereby putting Chinese masculinity into anxiety and crisis. I cannot agree, however, that one should take this or any other historical event as a kind of shortcut to a simplified, homogenised interpretation of rich film texts and diverse audience responses. On the basis of my exploration of the military graduates' memories, I would like to suggest that, compared with public events and a 'collective memory' such as the Tiananmen tragedy, personal circumstances and memories could in some cases play a more significant part in shaping audience responses to a film.

Second, how can we avoid indiscriminately applying the discourses of one culture to that of another when we try to address the meanings of screen images for audiences in different cultural contexts? As discussed above, the mother-son bonding in the film is regarded as one of its main attractions. No interviewee used the term 'Oedipus complex' to describe this bonding, nor would they assume that becoming a man means severing maternal ties. According to Chinese morality, 'filial love' to parents (to father and mother equally) is a basic value, as well as one of the foremost qualities that a man should possess. Moreover, 'growing up with mother' is a common experience for many Chinese people, as for various reasons fathers are often away. This cultural background could partly explain why a 'mother's boy' image is welcomed and resonates with the interviewees.

However, although the comic 'mother's boy' image offered in *Fong Sai-yuk* is refreshing in that it stands for a depoliticised male hero, in contrast to the highly-politicised male representation in Chinese cinema tradition, it does not challenge or undermine the core male representation – 'father's son'. Instead, 'mother's boy' mainly functions as a masquerade to conceal the anxiety about being a true 'father's son', both on and off screen. In the film, as a mother's boy, Li/Fong does not need to be a superman: he can ask for help whenever he is in danger; he will easily be forgiven if he fails; he can commit mild transgressions with his mother's cooperation. Yet in spite of all this licence, as the interviewees noticed, Li/Fong does not challenge the authority of the father in any respect. To become a mother's boy could rather be seen as a male strategy for renegotiating with a powerful 'father' and veiling one's deep anxiety.

Similarly, the fondness for the 'mother's boy' image among the military students in my research masks their anxiety generated by the coercive environment. By identifying with a 'mother's boy' *wuxia* hero, the students feel empowered in the face of a repressive 'father' (the army), and able to escape (mentally) from his control, although not for long, as their accounts betray.

'Mother's boy' as masquerade could also be applied to the broader social context. As I discussed earlier in this chapter, the father-son relationship plays a key role in constructing and maintaining Chinese male subjectivity. When the belief in the 'father' is shaken and imposes frustrations, unimpaired and self-sufficient masculinity turns out likewise to be a myth. Chinese societies of the early 1990s are characterised by disillusion with the 'father' figure represented by the CCP government and scepticism towards accepted ideals of masculinity and male heroism. *Fong Sai-yuk*, by foregrounding mother-son bonding, to some extent redeems the traumatised mentality of the Chinese people in the face of a repressive but inescapable 'father'. This may partly explain its popularity across the three Chinas in the early 1990s. Hunt (2003) inspiringly describes Wong Fei-hung and Fong Sai-yuk as 'the father' of the Hong Kong kung fu film, with its eternal 'boy'. Indeed, despite his seemingly lighthearted mother's boy image, Li/Fong is still always a 'father's son'.

As mentioned earlier, Li declared that Fong was a role he could identify with most, probably because it is closest to the first screen character that made his name – the young monk Jue Yuan in *Shaolin Temple*, although father-son narratives are very different in the two films; Li/Jue's revenge for his father's death forms the central plot of *Shaolin Temple*. However, *Fong Sai-yuk* would be the last time that Jet Li played an adolescent hero in a *wuxia* film, a persona that suited him so well, and he would have no chance to reclaim it in his later transnational career.

Notes

1. They are *Once Upon a Time in China III*, *Fong Sai-yuk*, *Fong Sai-yuk II*, *Last Hero in China*, *Tai Chi Master*, *Kung Fu Cult Master*. While all these six films made profits of over HK$10 million in Hong Kong, five of them were placed among the Top 10 Box Office successes of 1993 in Taiwan.
2. Following *Once Upon a Time in China III*, *Fong Sai-yuk* was the second Jet Li film to be officially released in all three places.
3. This data comes from the Hong Kong Film Archive.
4. Within the last four years or so, I saw this film on UK television at least three times.

5. Jackie Chan's *Drunken Master II* (1993) also pays particular attention to the mother-son relationship, but it came out later than *Fong Sai-yuk*.
6. They are Jia J., Ye M., Li M., Wen H., Li L., Ren X., Sun M., Chen Q., Wang Y., Zan Q., Xie Z., Wang P., Liu K., Chen J., Cao H. Nine of them majored in Chinese literature and language, three in English, one in Vietnamese and two in Burmese. Nine of them had left the army and six were still serving in it at the time of my research.
7. *Wuda pian* is another name for *wuxia* films.
8. Among these four interviewees, three simply answered 'Yes' without further explanation, while Wang Y. still saw Fong as a hero but felt that his image as a mother's boy made him less manly.
9. These were usually available in the form of video-cassettes at the time.
10. 'Leitmotif film' refers to a movie which fits into or promotes the official state ideology.
11. According to Yingjin Zhang, 'in spite of mandatory viewing from schools and free tickets from work units, only five major revolutionary historical films (in the whole '90s) made it to the annual top ten list and the remainder failed miserably at the box office' (2004: 286).

Part II

Jet Li as transnational kung fu star

5

Villain/killer/child: crossover images and Orientalist imagination

In the first part of this book, I examine Jet Li's three classic *wuxia* hero images – scholarly master Wong Fei-hung, unbridled lover Ling Hucong, and adolescent hero Fong Sai-yuk – as constructed in the reception of different audience groups from Hong Kong and mainland China. In the early 1990s, Li also inspiringly reinterpreted other *wuxia* heroes, such as Tai Chi master Zhang Sanfeng who temporarily loses his mind due to the betrayal by his childhood friend but regains his identity with the help of Tai Chi; reflective and open-minded Chen Zhen, the disciple of renowned martial artist Huo Yuanjia (a role Li would play ten years later); and another southern hero, Hung Hei-kuan, whose relationship with his son rather than his heroic deeds is highlighted in the film. It cannot have been easy to portray these very different types of *wuxia* heroes, especially given that most of them had been successfully transferred to the screen before (Wong Fei-hung by Kwan Tak-hing and Jackie Chan, Chen Zhen by Bruce Lee, Fong Sai-yuk by Fu Sheng and Hung Hei-guan by Chen Guantai). Using his martial arts skills as a powerful means of enhancing his performance, Li approaches these *wuxia* heroes in a fresh way and contributes to the genre a number of memorable hero images.

With the output of period *wuxia* movies falling dramatically, 1994 marked the end of the new *wuxia* cycle as well as the decline of the Hong Kong film industry. As a result, Li shifted his focus to action-filmmaking. Between 1994 and 1998, Jet Li made six contemporary action films in which he plays a police or army officer from the Mainland (*My Father is a Hero* [Corey Yuen, 1995]; *The Bodyguard From Beijing* [1994]), a killer (*Hitman* [Stephen Tung, 1998]), a bodyguard (*High Risk* [Wong Jing, 1995]), or a science fiction hero (*Dr. Wai in the Scripture With No Words* [Ching Siu-tung, 1996]; *Black Mask* [1996]). Although less sensational compared to his new *wuxia* work, these actions films did fairly well at the box office and caught the eye of Hollywood film producers. While I believe Li's Hong Kong action films deserve more critical attention, this book does not have space for further discussion. I would just like to point out that it was these less visible action films that provided Li with a passport to Hollywood and prepared him for his subsequent transnational career. In the second part of my book, I turn to Jet Li's transnational career since 1998, to explore how his image has been rebuilt in his English-language films (and later on in his transnational Chinese films) and how it has been received by global audiences. In the current chapter, before considering the specific case of Li's transcultural reception, it would be instructive to examine the context of his transnational career by locating him within the history of the representation of the Chinese male on Western screens, and also in the pantheon of transnational kung fu stars.

Stereotyping or anti-stereotyping? Hollywood's Chinese kung fu bodies

A key issue which has frequently been raised in the discussion of the representation of the Chinese male on Western screens is stereotyping. As Lynn Pan observes, 'Almost all writing on the portrayal of the Chinese in Western film revolves around the notion of "stereotype"' (1992: 58). In his discussion of stereotypes of gay people, Richard Dyer defines stereotyping as the way in which 'dominant groups apply their norms to subordinated groups, find the latter wanting, hence inadequate, inferior, sick or grotesque and hence reinforcing the dominant groups' own sense of the legitimacy of their domination' (1980: 30) and asserts that stereotypes are 'characteristically fixed, clear-cut, unalterable' (ibid. 29). What Dyer argues is equally appropriate when put in the context of cross-cultural and inter-racial stereotyping. Chinese male stereotypes on Western screens have been created and disseminated since the early years of cinema.

In his article 'The Image of Overseas Chinese in American Cinema', Ng Chun-ming gives a vivid depiction of three well-known Chinese male images in early American films.

> [Cheng Huan] His performance, aided by slant-eyed makeup, shaven forehead and piggy tail, recoiling movements, was a classic depiction of an early Chinese immigrant. (1992: 83)

> [Charlie Chan] Forthright on the outside but smart on the inside, as well as his touch of Chinese simplicity and honesty. (Ibid. 85)

> Fu Manchu's bloodcurdling appearance, his head shaped like a snake with the eyes of a rat, his whole visage of evil, the long nails, garbed in the long robe of a mandarin

in the Qing court, inspire terror. The Fu Manchu image set the typical stereotype in the West of a Chinese character who is the devil incarnate. (Ibid. 88)

The above three characters have become prototypes for Chinese male representations in English-language films, or at least have offered a range of unchangeable traits for Chinese men, such as gentleness, asceticism, cunning, inscrutability and so on. From a different perspective, Shi Wenhong (1992) discerns two types dominating Chinese male images in Western films. One is that of the emasculated, submissive Chinese man, starting from the lonely 'yellow man' Cheng Huan in D. W. Griffith's *Broken Blossoms* (1919) and continuing in the effeminate 'last emperor', Pu Yi, in *The Last Emperor* (Bernardo Bertolucci, 1987). The other type is the kung fu performer, such as Bruce Lee or Jackie Chan, whose physical capability is exploited to produce sensual pleasure for Western audiences, similar to the stereotyping of black people as 'singers' or 'dancers'. In Shi's view, both types offer simplified, marginalised images of the Chinese male.

Indeed, the early stage of Chinese male representation on Western screens is full of stereotypes which result largely from die-hard racial politics and colonial ideology; but I cannot agree that crossover Chinese male stars such as Lee or Chan have simply continued or reproduced stereotypes, as Shi seems to suggest. Rather, their transnational careers are marked by 'anti-stereotyping' as well as 're-stereotyping'. The reason why these Chinese male stars could break through into Western markets lies partly in the fact that their images challenge long-standing Chinese male stereotypes. Compared to their predecessors in Hollywood, they are usually regarded as playing more positive on-screen roles. For example, Kwai-cheung Lo notes that, while Chinese males in the American media have long symbolised compliant and passive femininity, 'the Hong Kong stars now are mostly associated with the hard-fighting, gun-wielding, and muscular heroes of the action thriller and comedy' (2005: 147). In fact, a common tactic for these border-crossing male stars is to distance themselves from stereotyping by bringing in some new elements, while at the same time simulating 'the traditional clichés of Asians depicted by Hollywood, bringing the image as close as possible to the "original" stereotypes' (ibid. 136).

As mentioned in the Introduction, the significance of Bruce Lee's crossover success lies in his articulation for the first time of a tough Chinese masculinity. For example, Yuan Shu (2003) suggests that Lee tries to break away from 'the Asian soft body' represented in American popular culture and to remasculinise the Asian male body as tough, aggressive and competitive. However, for Stephen Teo, *Enter the Dragon* (Robert Clouse,

1973), a film often viewed by Western critics as Lee's greatest achievement, is his 'least interesting' film, because Lee is forced to submit to the West's perception of him as a mere action hero and performs 'a clichéd characterisation of the reserved, inscrutable and humourless Oriental hero so often seen in Hollywood movies' (1997: 117). Among critical discourses, on the one hand, Lee's crossover role is a breakthrough, in that it categorically dismantles the wimpy, passive Chinese male stereotype in English-language films. Yet on the other hand, it more or less reinforces such formulaic representations of the Chinese male as inhuman, mysterious and Superman-like and thus becomes simply another stereotype of Chinese/Asian men: 'the chop-socky, kung-fu fighting Asian American male' (Chan 2000: 372).

This conflicting process of anti-stereotyping and re-stereotyping also applies to another transnational kung fu star, Jackie Chan. The difference between them is that, when Chan sought his global presence, he had to cast off two kinds of stereotype of Chinese men: the effeminate Chinese male image and the tough, invincible Chinese man introduced by Bruce Lee.[1] Chan's Western success has therefore been built upon the negotiation between and re-definition of soft body and hard body. Chan's characters run away from any trouble and danger in the first place, get hurt easily and win their fights by luck. In comparison with Lee, Chan's on-screen image is undoubtedly softer, but not in the same way as the effeminised, passive Chinese male in the Western imagination. As Yvonne Tasker puts it, 'Chan's softness does not mean a lack of muscularity or an inability to fight, but suggests a more fluid masculinity, in refusing either to take the male body too seriously, like Lee, or to play the part of Oriental other' (1997: 334).

However, Chan does not escape from the foreign star's common fate of being typecast in Hollywood films. Mark Gallagher notices that comedy often places Chan in a submissive, masochistic position, thereby destabilising his character's control over the film's humour. In his view, while 'a narrative makes the protagonist a comedic foil, he becomes an inappropriate action hero according to Western conventions, and by association the type itself appears unviable as a model of identity' (1997: 24–5). Gallagher's argument is supported by the consecutive box office failures of Chan's Hollywood films after *Rush Hour 2* (Brett Ratner, 2001) and his three-year absence from Hollywood afterwards.[2] In *Around the World in 80 Days* (Frank Coraci, 2004), Chan even cedes the leading role to a less known British actor and becomes an out-and-out comedic foil. Uncontrolled self-deprecating humour and an overabundance of acrobatics not only turn Chan into an unlikely action hero, but also inadvertently (or knowingly?) create a clown-like Chinese male image which is becoming another stereotyped representation of Chinese men on Western screens.

Jet Li, like his predecessors, has had to face stereotyping in his transnational film journey. For example, he could easily have been put into the category of 'kung fu superman', not to mention his first American role as a villain, which offers another example of the 'Yellow Peril'. As a simplified, shorthand way of depicting the image of the 'Other', stereotyping often reflects the incomprehension between different cultures and races. To a certain extent, stereotyping and the concomitant distortion and prejudice are perhaps inevitable in the representation of the 'Other' in popular culture. Probably in this sense, Lynn Pan remarks that 'the cross-cultural theme is a difficult one for the cinema: it is only too easy to find yourself perpetuating stereotypes' (1992: 63). However, since a stereotyped construction of the Chinese male image in Hollywood films remains in force, it certainly deserves further exploration, especially considering that, Chinese/Asian stereotypes are often more negative and distorted than stereotypes of Europeans or Latinos in American films, and, in addition, often more complicated, in that they are closely related to the issues of Orientalism, racism and colonialism.

Yet, rather than simply recognising and decrying various stereotypes in Li's English-language films, it is more constructive to consider the careful construction of these stereotypes in relation to discourses of race, nation and gender, by both filmmakers and audiences, and the way in which stereotyping/anti-stereotyping has functioned in the transformation and reconstruction of Li's star image within a transnational context. While many studies of minority representation in Hollywood cinema either 'construct a typology of images, focusing on stereotypes as ideological phenomena', or 'examine the institutional aspects of racism' (Xing 1998: 53), the reception of so-called 'Orientalist films' amongst different audiences remains a much less discussed topic. In the Introduction and the first part of this book, I mentioned more than once responses from Chinese audiences to Li's English-language films as being characterised by disappointment and resistance. What particularly interests me here, however, is how Western audiences read these crossover films: do they share Chinese audiences' anti-Orientalist sentiment, or do they join Western institutions in producing Chinese male stereotypes? As we know, public prejudices are not created merely as a negative result of screen images, but also actively participate in constructing those stereotyped images.

The current chapter sets out to examine Western readings of Li's English-language films. Li has appeared in ten English-language films so far and the first six will be discussed here (*Lethal Weapon 4* [1998]; *Romeo Must Die* [2000]; *Kiss of the Dragon* [2001]; *The One* [James Wong, 2001]; *Cradle 2 The Grave* [Andrzej Bartkowiak, 2003]; *Danny the Dog* [2005]). I am aware that the term 'Western reading' is too broad to do justice to the complex dimensions of spectatorship, so to be more specific, I focus on Western critical discourses from a range of English-language newspapers and magazines.[3] Around one hundred reviews of Jet Li's English-language films published in fifteen different newspapers and fifteen different magazines (covering most of the important film press in the UK and US) between 1998 and 2005 will be considered in this chapter, to represent a range of Western critical opinions.

Western critical responses: villain, killer and child

Li's Hollywood debut was in the fourth and last episode of the long-running action blockbuster *Lethal Weapon* series starring Mel Gibson and Danny Glover. In the film, Li plays a ruthless triad boss who imports illegal immigrants to America as slaves in order to finance the release of his brother from a prison in China. Li explained that he accepted this role because the producer, Joel Silver, told him 'villain first, then good guy' (quoted in Rynning 2000: 83). After *Lethal Weapon 4*, Li played the leading role in his subsequent five Western films, two of them still with Silver as producer (*Romeo Must Die*; *Cradle 2 The Grave*), two of them in collaboration with the famous French filmmaker Luc Besson (*Kiss of the Dragon*; *Danny the Dog*) and one with the Chinese-American director James Wong (*The One*). Looking at 100 press reviews, it is intriguing that Li's villainous characters (in *Lethal Weapon 4* and *The One*) appear more stereotyped but get good reviews; whereas Li's hero images are clearly more anti-stereotyped but are poorly received.

Leon Hunt argues that *Lethal Weapon 4*'s 'mixture of xenophobia and Oriental-fetishism marks it out as the most interesting of the "crossover" films and an intriguing punctuation mark in kung fu's complex transnational career' (1999: 97). Indeed, unreflecting racism or stereotyping in the film can easily be picked up. Take, for example, the design of Li's costume. It is quite hard to imagine that Li's lethal triad boss, with his incongruous silk suits and a weird pigtail, lives in either the contemporary US or China. What matters for the film seems not whether or not this conforms to historicity, but whether or not it caters to deep-rooted Western perceptions of the Oriental. This perfectly attests to Jun Xing's observation that 'while it is difficult to describe inscrutability, some of the key elements are racial features (body shapes, facial features, and skin color), peculiar dress and hair styles, exotic eating habits, weird customs, and grotesque language accents' (1998: 66). Other examples are Gibson's making jokes about 'flied lice' in a Chinese restaurant, or trying to provoke Li by mocking him as 'enter the Drag Queen', both of which, in Hunt's opinion, could be from a scene in numerous 1970s kung fu films 'as the arrogant "foreigners" taunt the silent kung fu master who will settle accounts later' (1999: 97).

However, the film's xenophobic undertones appear not to have registered with Western critics. In contrast to Chinese responses to Li's portrayal of the villain, which exhibit vociferous anger, disappointment and regret, Western critics relish Li's evil character. Whenever Li is mentioned in the reviews of this film, the comments are positive and laudatory. According to Jeff Jensen, *Lethal Weapon 4*, as the subtlest demonstration of the furious charisma and supersonic fists and feet which made Li a star in Asia, 'earned him the most effusive praise' (2001: 44). Many reviewers suggest that Li actually 'stole' the film because his villain looks more attractive and charming than Mel Gibson's hero, as the following extracts illustrate:

> *LW4*, as a film, is really nothing more than a series of setpieces, strung together by director Richard Donner to showcase the buddy antics of Gibson, Glover and Pesci. The film springs to life, however, when Jet takes center stage. Li creates an aura of absolute cold-hearted menace as he takes on Gibson and Co. over a simple-minded story. (Ranaletta 1998: 22)

> But the series has sequel-fatigue syndrome, and the American stars – Mel Gibson, Danny Glover, Joe Pesci, Rene Russo – are looking bored and bloated. Only the Jet Man looks as if he's on the sunrise side of stardom: smooth, sexy, ready to rumble. (Corliss 1998: 72)

Undeterred by Li's character's inhumanity in killing innocent people, the critics have no hesitation in complimenting Li's presence. 'Although he hardly speaks in the film, his ample charisma is on display along with his balletic martial arts ability' (O'Hehir 1998: 46). 'With his sleek features and lightning-fast moves, it's no wonder Jet Li stole the show . . . leaving American audiences cheering for more' (Koseluk and Gennusa 2002: 17). In a word, Li is reviewed as an energetic, 'charismatic anti-hero' (Corliss 1998: 72) in *Lethal Weapon 4*. This 'charismatic villain' image also appears (though to a lesser degree) in the reviews of another of Li's villainous roles, in *The One*, where he plays both the good and bad guys. John Hazelton declares that 'Li has his moments as the evil Yulaw but his presence fades when he portrays nice-guy Gabe' (2001: 23). Similarly, Matthew Leyland admits that Li 'has fun as a villain' (2002: 51) in *The*

Figure 5 Jet Li as Gabe Law in *The One* (James Wong, 2001).
(Source: Kobal Collection.)

One. Despite its obvious Orientalist construction, Li's image as the evil foreigner captivates Western critics. But Li does not make an equally good impression in his leading roles and critical opinion is rather negative towards Li's performances as a hero.

In contrast to the critical acknowledgement of Li's charismatic villains, many reviewers describe Li as an unconvincing hero who lacks charismatic presence. The most notable comment is that Li exists only as a fighting machine without any acting skill, and one reviewer sums this up: 'Li's martial arts skills are as brilliant as his acting skills aren't' (Fair 2001: 38). The following five comments on each film illustrate this prevailing critical opinion:

> [*Romeo Must Die*] Jet Li, a newish arrival from Hong Kong's overrated action film industry, certainly kicks better than he acts and is not helped by a screenplay that unwisely requires him to get romantic as well as rough. (Bond 2000: 26)
>
> [*Kiss of the Dragon*] The action is fun and ultra-violent, the story is satisfactorily ridiculous and the acting is non-existent. (Som 2001: 17)

[*The One*] Li struggles to play two — actually three — characters . . . He winds up little more than two fighting machines. (Honeycutt 2001: 18)

[*Cradle 2 The Grave*] While Li continues to show little development as an English-language actor in his scant dialogue scenes, the star's precision foot- and fist-work remain superlative, barely breaking a sweat or altering his stoic expression as he flattens a series of adversaries. (Rooney 2003: 78)

[*Danny the Dog*] Perhaps Li has more in common with Danny than he would care to admit – both are fighting machines who are really interesting only when they are in action. (Fde 2005: 13)

From the above quotations, it is not difficult to tell that Western critics enjoy the visual spectacle created by Li's superior martial arts skills. As Haider (2002) suggests, physical expression, as well as being the principal draw of the film [*The One*], is Li's true forte in his attempt to break into the Western market. However, to Western critics, Li looks interesting and charismatic only when he is fighting. The action scenes seem to them to be the only redeeming feature in his English-language films (except possibly for *Danny the Dog*) since he is perceived as someone who does not know how to act. Apparently, these Western reviewers, unlike the Hong Kong critics I discussed in Chapter 2, do not see Li's physical skills as part of his acting. Moreover, in their view the former somewhat undermines the latter. Li has therefore suffered from the same accusation as that levelled at his Hollywood counterparts, Jean-Claude Van Damme and Stephen Seagal for instance, that – a true cliché in Western critical discourse – martial arts/action stars cannot act. Probably because of this prejudice, whereas for Hong Kong critics Li stands out as a dignified, prestigious kung fu master, for Western critics, Li can play only killers who use martial arts skills, and nothing more, to fulfil their mission. If in his successful Hong Kong career, Li has taken fighting beyond the physical dimension to gain cinematic and cultural significance, his crossover journey seems to have reduced him to a mere fighting machine, at least within the Western critical responses examined here.

Besides the critical consensus about Li's 'good martial skills but limited acting ability', other often-heard comments concern Li's limited command of language and diminutive size. As a crossover Chinese star, Li's inadequate English is apparently one of his greatest obstacles in the West. In his research on the Asian-American Internet reception of Jet Li, Julian Stringer (2003) also picks up on the issue of 'limited English skills' in Asian Americans' discussion about Li's Western performances. From the comments he quotes, we can sense the sympathy among

Asian-American fans, while by comparison Western critics do not show much lenience towards Li's language problem. Martin Hoyle sneers at Li's 'apparent inability to utter lines with clarity or comprehension' (2002: 16). Nigel Floyd complains about 'the Cantonese-speaking Li's awkward dialogue delivery' (2000: 81) [it should be noted that Li is actually a Mandarin speaker]. Robert Koehler writes, 'Li continues to struggle verbally in English, relying on his unflappable, hawk-like face and eyes to provide a movie star's confidence' (2001: 27).

Body size is another prominent issue in Western critical responses to Jet Li. In fact, it is a new topic in the discussion of Li's star image, because it was hardly raised at all in either critical or fan discourse on Li's Chinese-language films. Many critics like to highlight Li's small size in their reviews, as the following examples demonstrate:

> Barely 5ft 6in with a pock-marked face and bogbrush hair, he looks positively runt-like when not jamming a fist into a henchman's sternum. (Macaulay 2000: 22)

> Short (especially compared with his towering co-stars here), unassuming and sort of scruffy looking, Li has never been a particularly charismatic figure, and it remains to be seen how far he can go in American films. (McCarthy 2000: 25)

> The pockmarked and noticeably diminutive Li shares Van Damme's ability to kick ass, but acting – or even changing visual expression – does not come easy to him. (Tookey 2001: 48)

It is quite interesting to note that Western critics enjoy what Li's diminutive body can do (fighting) but not the body itself. This, on the one hand, further entrenches Li as a fighting machine without any personal charm, and, on the other hand, together with the comments on his scant English, helps to build up another image of Li to be found within Western critical discourse, that of the child.

After consecutively playing similar invincible cop/killer roles in five English-language films, Li unexpectedly took up a new persona – Danny the dog, a man treated as a dog and raised as a fighting machine, with the mind and personality of a young child. Similar to his first Western role as a villain, this role was also somewhat controversial, especially for Chinese audiences. Totally distancing himself from his usual superhero screen image, Li plays an abject, downtrodden Danny, which some Chinese see as insulting to their race. This, when Li is the acknowledged 'Emperor of Chinese kung fu', has led in part to its failure to be shown in mainland China (although its extreme violence is also to blame for this).[4] Within Western critical discourse, by contrast, *Danny the Dog* (also known as *Unleashed*) probably enjoys the most positive reviews of all Li's English-language films. Many reviewers agree that it contains Li's best performance in the West. For example, Lewis Beale writes, '*Unleashed* is of interest primarily because star Jet Li has an appealing screen presence' (2005: 37), while Gregory Kirschling remarks that 'if Li logged any research time hanging out at kennels, it's paid off. In non-attack mode, he lends the movie true heart' (2005: 53).

Significantly, both positive and negative reviews of this film try to draw comparisons between Li and Danny as a childlike character. As well as the one quoted earlier ('Perhaps Li has more in common with Danny than he would care to admit . . .'), Jamie Russell comments satirically, 'Li's puppy-dog eyes and blank expression are perfect for Danny, a man who . . . was brought up without the socialising influences of other humans' (2005: 78–9). Taking a different tone, Paul Zimmerman claims that 'Li comes off as the most gullible and loveable outsider since Daryl Hannah in *Splash*' (2005: 56). It is interesting to see Li is put into the same category as the unsophisticated mermaid Hannah. Besides identifying Li with mentally childlike characters, the above-quoted critical opinions concerning Li's 'small size' and 'limited language capability', can also be related to the attributes of a child.

From an examination of the press reviews above, three prevailing images of Li constructed in Western critical discourse are manifested: namely, the charismatic bad guy, the dispassionate killer, and the childlike Chinese man. None of these images resemble the personae which Li has built up in his Chinese-language films. A few questions then arise: why do Western critics enjoy watching Li as a villain but not as a leading man? Given that the career of an action star usually relies mainly on his heroic screen presence rather than his acting skills, why is Li's acting ability in his Western work attacked so vehemently, resulting in his being defined as a fighting machine? Even though there are a number of Western actors (such as Tom Cruise) who lack the ideal body size, but who have built successful careers in Hollywood, why is Li's diminutive stature such an insurmountable disadvantage? In the following section, I attempt to probe more deeply into the reasons underlying Western critical responses to Jet Li's English-language movies.

Orientalist imagination: Yellow Peril, the Asian as child and crossover politics

Although the above three screen images are fairly new for Li, they are nothing new in terms of Chinese male representations on Western screens.

In fact, no matter whether villain, killer or child, all more or less fit into the stereotypes of Chinese/Asian men in Hollywood history. Stereotyping in this context should be seen as part of Orientalist discourse. Since Edward Said broached the subject in 1978, Orientalism has become a powerful theoretical tool for examining representations of minorities in Western (especially Hollywood) cinema. In Said's argument, as a colonialist discourse which represents colonised Otherness, Orientalism is 'a Western style for dominating, restructuring, and having authority over the Orient' (1978: 3). As a result, it is often linked with cultural distortion and the misrepresentation of minority cultures in the West.

While many critics are keen from a variety of standpoints to disclose the constant practice in Hollywood films of perpetuating Orientalist discourse through generic formulas, narrative conventions and cultural assumptions, the concept of Orientalism has attracted some criticism in recent years. For example, Matthew Bernstein argues that 'simplifying films to a structured opposition between East and West cannot account for these films' specific articulation of power relations and even for their compelling appeal to audiences' (1997: 11). From another perspective, Rey Chow points out that critics of Orientalism often hold a nativist and essentialist standpoint by assuming the existence of an original, authentic national identity and claiming that cultural translation is 'a unidirectional, one-way process' and that 'the value of translation is derived solely from the "original"' (1995: 184). While I am aware of the limitations of the notion of Orientalism, I still see it as an efficient critical tool to uncover prejudice and the constraints heavily imposed on transnational Chinese stars.

As many critics agree, nothing is more ingrained in Western popular consciousness than the concept of the Yellow Peril in terms of perceptions of Chinese/Asians, which, in Xing's view, is theoretically and politically supported by the germ theory, 'intermixed with racial, anti-immigrant, and xenophobic rhetoric' (1998: 55). In her book *Romance and the 'Yellow Peril'*, Gina Marchetti incisively argues that Hollywood's depiction of Asia has been inextricably linked to the notion of the Yellow Peril that has contributed to the idea that 'all nonwhite people are by nature physically and intellectually inferior, morally suspect, heathen, licentious, disease-ridden, feral, violent, uncivilized, infantile, and in need of the guidance of white, Anglo-Saxon Protestants' (1993: 2–3). As mentioned earlier, in the early twentieth century, this deep-rooted notion found its perfect cinematic embodiment – Fu Manchu. Ziauddin Sardar and Frances Saunders rightly point out that Fu Manchu films have given the depiction of the cruel and evil Chinese 'an enduring and international form' (2000: 46).

Since then, the Yellow Peril narrative/Fu Manchu-like character has continued to feature in American films. Xing notices that, as a pervasively displayed stereotype, Chinese/Asian men are routinely portrayed as gangsters or rapists. Yvonne Tasker further suggests that the Yellow Peril formula has been perfectly played out in American action cinema as it is more visibly concerned than other Hollywood forms with discourses of racial difference and masculinity. According to Tasker, in a genre defined so much by physicality, black and Asian performers have had more opportunities to take on major roles. However, the opportunities offered by such roles inevitably 'reinscribe stereotypical definitions of the physical, often further positioning black and Asian characters within a fantasized marginal space of criminality or deviance' (1997: 318).

Against such a background, we could argue that Western reviewers' responses to Li's villain roles to some extent result from their Yellow Peril fantasy, which 'projects Euroamerican desires and dreads onto the alien other' (Marchetti 1993: 2), though they express fascination more than hostility – they find Li menacing but charming, even more attractive than Mel Gibson as the heroic opponent. If the film text of *Lethal Weapon 4*, as Hunt claims, 'encapsulates the paradoxical collision of Asiaphilia and Asiaphobia quite so spectacularly' (2004: 279), its reception among Western critics similarly incorporates this collision. While Western reviewers' fondness for Li's evil character indicates a kind of Asiaphilia, their ineradicable Asiaphobia is also betrayed by their attitude – comfortably and unreflectively welcoming a rather stereotyped and racist portrayal of an Eastern devil. Hunt insightfully sums up this point: '[T]his play between fascination and hostility – Chinese superman and Yellow Peril – has been an important part of the Western consumption of kung fu' (1999: 88). As the reviews show, as long as a Chinese superman (Li) is confined to the domain of villain, Western critics can enjoy both.

Yet, it would be partial to conclude that Western critical responses merely reassert the Orientalist imagination. A couple of reviewers I examine do recognise the stereotyping in *Lethal Weapon 4* and show sympathy to Li's character for the racist abuse he suffers. For example, Richard Corliss writes, 'with his Buddha-beatific closed-mouth smile, he [Li] endures a lot of jokey cross-cultural insults from Gibson' (1998: 72). Andrew O'Hehir points out that the film's injection of Eastern energy leads to 'some unsavoury onscreen stereotyping' (1998: 46). Furthermore, the critical acknowledgement of Li as a 'charismatic villain' carries some positive impact.

First, the critical view of Li as a charismatic villain adds 'charm' as a new element to the perennial Yellow Peril formula, which marks Li out as different from previous Yellow Peril images such as Fu Manchu. Second, it was through this role that Li found himself accepted by American audiences and was given the chance to star in his subsequent English-language films, hence establishing himself as a reliable star in medium-budget Hollywood action vehicles. Third, acting the part of a successful villain unexpectedly opened up a new path for Li, who had always been a hero on Chinese screens, and for crossover Chinese stars in general. After *Lethal Weapon 4*, not only did Li seem to develop a predilection for villainous roles – he plays another bad guy in *The One*, an apparently half-good half-evil character in both *War* (Philip G. Atwell, 2007) and *The Warlords* (2007), and a cruel emperor in *The Mummy: Tomb of the Dragon Emperor* (Rob Cohen, 2008) – but other famous Chinese stars, such as Zhang Ziyi (*Rush Hour 2*; *Horsemen* [Jonas Åkerlund, 2009]), Gong Li (*Memoirs of a Geisha* [Rob Marshall, 2005]) and Chow Yun-fat (*Pirates of the Caribbean: At World's End* [Gore Verbinski, 2007]) also started to play villains (or semi-villains) in Hollywood. This is a significant turning point in the Hollywood journeys of Chinese stars.

Zhang Ziyi, imitating Li, launched her Hollywood career by playing a villain, but Chow Yun-fat's acceptance of a villainous role is particularly worth noting given his previous objection to the idea of playing a villain in Hollywood. Only a few years earlier, his manager Terence Chang had declared that if Chow plays a real villain in America, 'his career in Asia will be over' (quoted in Chute 2001: 36). However, Li and Zhang's Asian careers prove far from over; indeed, their careers seem to have been bolstered by their Western experiences. Arriving at Hollywood before Li, Chow's crossover career is nevertheless not as eye-catching and viable as Li's, probably partly because he was too cautious to play out stereotypes in the Western imagination. While we have enough reasons to consider Li's 'charismatic villain' image as just another stereotype, we cannot deny that it has offered an effective way for Chinese stars to break through to the Western market, that is, to be flexible. Stereotyping may be unavoidable but it is not always unpleasant, especially if it can be bent to the advantage of transnational stars.

Li's second image among Western critical reviewers, that of the 'dispassionate killer', easily finds its prototype in the 'kung fu superman' originating in the early 1970s with Bruce Lee's ephemeral success and the first 'kung fu craze' in America. Words such as 'invincible', 'mysterious' and 'cold', which are frequently used to describe Li's screen persona, were also the characteristics of imported Chinese kung fu heroes thirty years earlier. No wonder Li is often called the 'new Bruce Lee' by Western critics. In generic agreement, when a Western audience watches an action film or a Chinese audience watches a *wuxia* film, they expect more of a heroic presence than a subtle performance. This is where an action/kung fu star differs from a dramatic actor. However, in Chapter 2, I commented on a holistic attitude towards martial arts performance among Hong Kong critics, and argued that by using martial arts as a means of portraying a character, Li proves that kung fu stars can act. Indeed, through 'impersonating in fighting', Li has created one memorable *wuxia* hero after another on Chinese screens. Yet, in his English-language films, as discussed above, his acting abilities become the target of most of the adverse criticism. While Li's command of English does him no favours in developing a character, and different cultural evaluations of the 'acting' of kung fu/action stars do exist, I would attribute Li's typecasting as a killer mainly to Hollywood's crossover politics, that is, the politics which allow a Chinese action star to survive in the West only as a fighter and not as an actor.

Given the fact that almost all the film talents which Hollywood has imported from Hong Kong are working in the martial arts/action area, including action stars, action directors and martial arts choreographers, it is not difficult to work out that the intentions of Hollywood filmmakers are to use Hong Kong action to make a profit. In an interview, producer Joel Silver says that, because he was annoyed by seeing nothing fresh or original in American action films, he decided to make *Romeo Must Die*. But Silver's search for the 'fresh and original' is obviously confined to the domain of action scenes only. He proudly mentions one new element tried out in the film – a scene in which Li's martial arts fighting is presented in X-ray – commenting, 'When we played that scene in America the audience went out their fuckin' minds' (quoted in Freer 2000: 10). Elsewhere, Silver neatly sums up the way in which Li is used in the film: 'Jet is our special effect' (quoted in Macaulay 2000: 23).

Indeed, in kung fu stars' transnational careers, the emphasis has been exclusively on physical capability, as their main selling point. This is the case not only in the films these transnational kung fu stars made in Hollywood, but in their Hong Kong work repackaged for American distribution, such as Jackie Chan's *Rumble in the Bronx* (Stanley Tong, 1995) in which, as Steve Fore (1997) notes, Chan was sold primarily as a physical performer, while the less 'universal' aspects of his star persona were played down. As a result, the careful build-up of these actors' star personae and sophisticated characterisation in their crossover films both become insignificant and largely neglected. All that is required of Li and others therefore is to stick to their astonishing stunts. This is no doubt why Richard Corliss comments on Li's Hollywood films: 'Since his mission is not to learn American ways but just to catch the damn villain, a Li movie can get down to basics: punch, kick, pummel, kill' (31 March 2003).

On the one hand, these crossover politics resonate with a long-standing practice of casting Asian actors in Hollywood; as Jun Xing argues, 'Very rarely are the Asian roles fleshed out as fully developed characters. This system of stereotypical delimitations has successfully prevented dimensional development and aesthetic continuity in the creation of Asian characters on the screen' (1998: 78). On the other hand, they uncover a characteristic of transnational image-flows; 'goods mean more and people mean less, a "dystopia" of appropriation and marginalization' (Hunt 2004: 279–80). In their Hollywood films, Li and other Chinese action stars have been transformed into commercial signifiers – the Chinese martial arts equivalent of black stars as symbols of hip-hop culture. Of greater concern to the studios is how these stars can fulfil their function of signifying; they are less concerned with making them look appealing to audiences. We might conclude that, although crossover Chinese stars have finally gained leading man status after decades when Asian actors were cast in the Yellow Peril role, they never got the chance to build their career in Hollywood as actors. This could partly explain why Chow Yun-fat, with good acting skills but limited martial arts skills, seems to have become stuck in his Hollywood adventure, or at least is less successful than the more athletic Li and Chan.

While the identity of these transnational Chinese stars as actors is mainly being impoverished by Hollywood's film production and distribution machinery, this impoverishment is also based on the industry's understanding of its consumers. According to Lo, 'the characterizations of Hong Kong actors in Hollywood films rely predominantly on many American presuppositions of what an ethnic Asian should be like than on the specific symbolic values that these actors could offer' (2001: 471). In order to secure a crossover success, Hollywood filmmakers have tried to come as close as possible to the stereotyped portrayal of the Chinese male as the emotionless kung fu superman. Yet, as seen from overwhelming complaints about Li's acting in press reviews, Western critics are obviously not satisfied with Li's appearance in English-language movies only as a fighting machine. They require more than stereotyping.

Hollywood's crossover politics are touched upon in a number of reviews: 'Considering the quiet charm that diminutive martial arts champion and actor Jet Li has shown himself capable in such films as *Once Upon a Time in China and America* [1997], his latest vehicle, *Cradle 2 the Grave*, is remarkably cold' (Etherington 2003: 42); 'But as he showed last year, Li may need a Chinese director to bring out his own regal steeliness. In the Zhang Yimou hit *Hero*, he was more than a solemn killer' (Corliss, 31 March 2003). Despite these sympathetic comments, most Western

Figure 6 Jet Li as Danny and Morgan Freeman as the piano tuner, Sam, in *Danny the Dog* (Louis Leterrier, 2005). (Source: Kobal Collection.)

critics tend to blame Li's poor acting ability instead of the film's simplified characterisation for his image as a 'dispassionate killer'. This betrays the deep-rooted Orientalist outlook with which the West consumes Chinese kung fu/action stars, that is, enjoying their spectacular physical performance whilst belittling them as people who only know how to kick. In this respect, Western critics also play an active role in maintaining and reinforcing the old stereotypes of the Chinese male.

Li's third image, that of the 'child', is less noticeable as a stereotype than his 'villain' and 'killer' archetypes in academic accounts, but no less visible on Western screens. In Hollywood films, Asian ethnicities have an enduring representative, who is coded as very young. For example, Li's Danny in *Danny the Dog* can find an earlier counterpart in the *Jungle Book* (Zoltan Korda, 1942) character of the teenage Mowgli (played by Sabu, a young actor of India/South-Asian origin), who was raised by wolves in the jungle and tries to learn human behaviour while keeping jungle ideas. In addition, like the black buddy construct, the friendly 'Asian boy sidekick' exists as another racial foil for the white action hero. An earlier example is the character Short Round from *Indiana Jones and the Temple of Doom* (Steven Spielberg, 1984), a tough streetwise child who is rescued by Jones and loves him as a father figure. This character is again echoed by Li's role as Danny, who is rescued by and gets fatherly care from the black pianist played by Morgan Freeman.

The latest 'Asian boy sidekick' is perhaps embodied by the Chinese actor Qin Shaobo, who plays The Amazing Yen in the three *Ocean's* films (*Ocean's Eleven* [Steven Soderbergh, 2001]; *Ocean's Twelve* [Steven Soderbergh, 2004]; *Ocean's Thirteen* [Steven Soderbergh, 2007]). Even smaller than Li, Qin never speaks English in the films but seems always to be understood. Although China and India have a much longer history and a much older culture than America, their people are often represented in Hollywood as 'child', which helps to define Asian people as simple, uneducated and unthreatening. Well-known for his portrayal in his Chinese period of the prestigious patriarch Wong Fei-hung, Li nevertheless plays out the 'Asian as child' stereotype in his English-language films, such as a teenager in *Romeo Must Die* and a childlike man in *Danny the Dog*. This is especially ironic if we consider Li's actual age when he played these roles: in the former, he was thirty-seven years old; in the latter, he was forty-two.

Apart from industry practice, as discussed above, Li's image as a childlike Chinese man is also constructed within Western press reviews. What cannot go unquestioned is why Western critics show more generosity to Li as Danny than to his other leading performances. When they make fun of Li's diminutive body, are they uncomfortable with the fact that 'Hollywood's latest action hero is small' (Macaulay 2000: 22–3), or with the fact that Hollywood's latest action hero is Chinese? In order to answer these questions, it is worth considering the three transnational kung fu stars – Bruce Lee, Jackie Chan and Jet Li – together. Mark Gallagher suggests that conventional action heroes display a range of character traits associated with traditional Western definitions of masculinity, including 'physical size, strength, charisma, pronounced facial features, the ability to generate action, and facility with aggressive behavior' (1997: 23). Obviously, the physiques of these three stars do not fit in with Western archetypes of maleness. On this precise point, Gallagher points out that Chan's comic body 'manifests both his characters' power and limitations: the gift of nearly superhuman athletic prowess and the hindrances of body size and social position' (ibid. 37). Similarly, the issue of body size is also central to the understanding of Li's crossover star persona, as seen in the above discussion of Western critical responses. Indeed, his body size, along with his nationality, has become the important ground on which Western critics view Li as a childlike man.

Furthermore, Western responses to the crossover action films of Chinese kung fu stars cannot be separated from the general reception of kung fu films in the West. In his widely-accepted and often-quoted generic definition of the kung fu film, Stuart Kaminsky proposes that 'the kung fu hero . . . is invariably a lower-class working figure . . . Bruce Lee, and others, by their size and nationality, are metaphors for the downtrodden. The Hong Kong Chinese laborer is certainly a disdained member of society from Japan to Europe and has never been considered hero material before' (1982: 142). Kaminsky reveals an important fact here, that is, in the West kung fu stars are read as representative of the downtrodden. Similarly, in his study of the initial reception of kung fu cinema in North America in 1973, Desser suggests that kung fu film is a genre of the underdog of colour fighting against colonialist enemies and white culture, and hence offers 'the only nonwhite heroes, men and women, to audiences alienated by mainstream film and often by mainstream culture' (2000: 38). These kung fu stars, as the embodiment in the Chinese context of such Chinese heroic principles as self-sacrifice, chivalry, brotherhood and patriotism, become in their translation to the West, the heroes of the underdog.

The English-language vehicles of these transnational kung fu stars continue to reinforce this Orientalist construct. By blurring his overt and distinctive cultural nationalism into a generalised 'reaction against racism', argues Teo (1997: 113), Lee's only Western film, *Enter the Dragon*, transfigures and tapers down a Chinese kung fu hero to an angry underdog in the Western world. Chan is reconstructed in a slightly different way. By toning down both racial politics and nationalist sentiments, and by undercutting or even parodying Chinese heroism, Chan's Hollywood films portray him as a clown-like Chinese lead, thereby offering inoffensive entertainment to global, and in particular, Western, audiences.

Clearly, neither Lee nor Chan has been seen as a conventional action hero within Western critical discourse. The reason for their popularity in the West to some extent stems from the fact that they fit into the category which Western audiences can accept and enjoy: the representative of the underdog. By comparison, Jet Li's Western performances cannot be easily categorised into either Lee's angry underdog or Chan's funny underdog. Without these familiar transnational Chinese male representations as a reference, Western critics seem to have difficulty in identifying with Li's hero image in his first four English-language star vehicles. By contrast, they are more willing to accept Li's role as the childlike, downtrodden Danny, probably because it is closer to such common Western perceptions of Chinese men as 'Asian as child' or 'kung fu hero as underdog'.

Western critical readings show Chinese stars can be accepted in the West only if they conform to Western expectations, which confirms once again the logic of 'cultural translation', that is, exchange between East and West always means 'the demand on non-Western people to conform to Western standards and models but not vice versa' (Chow 1995: 176). Yet, despite being negatively typecast, Li's Danny is regarded by both Western critics and fans[5] as his best Western performance. Like the choice he made to play villainous roles in Hollywood, Li's decision to take on a childlike role conveys the newly-gained confidence of a transnational

Chinese kung fu/action star, the confidence to overthrow a previous hero image and try something different and new. Ella Shohat and Robert Stam (1994) insightfully point out that the demand for 'positive images' from minority cultures sometimes betrays a lack of confidence and becomes a sign of cultural anxiety. It is probably only by conquering this anxiety and focusing on delivering good performances rather than producing 'positive images', that transnational Chinese stars can start changing the Orientalist imagination so deeply rooted within both Western filmmakers and critics.

Conclusion

Corey Yuen, Li's long-term collaborator, talks about Li's star appeal: '[He] embodies the term "heroic". He has that charisma and heroism when he's on screen' (quoted in Ferrante 2001: 47). Yuen's comment may be applicable only to Li's Chinese career. Western critical responses to Li's English-language films show that with his Western roles his heroic presence has disappeared. Instead, Li exists in critical discourses as a charismatic villain, dispassionate killer and childlike Chinese man. Whether or not Li is able to play a convincing hero in an English-language film might be arguable, but apparently Western critics are more willing to appreciate Li as a villain or childlike man and correspondingly more reluctant to accept him as a hero. While in *Lethal Weapon 4*, Li's quiet and imperturbable screen presence is seen as charming and appealing, in the reviews of his English-language star vehicles this is turned into evidence of his scant acting skills and language ability, making him seem expressionless and unable to deliver dialogue. As such, in *Lethal Weapon 4*, even with no romantic interaction at all, Li looks 'sexy' to some Western critics; but when he does have romantic potential with the female lead in his starring roles, he is defined as 'sexually unattractive'. I further explore this issue in the next chapter.

It is therefore safe to conclude that Li, and transnational Chinese kung fu/action stars in general, survive in the West at the price of having their heroism toned down or even denied. As this chapter has made clear, Li has been demonised ('villain'), marginalised ('killer') and caricatured ('child') in his English-language films, due to deep-rooted Yellow Peril imaginings, current crossover politics which debase Chinese kung fu/action stars to inhuman fighting machines, and the fact that kung fu stars have always been related to the image of the underdog in Western critical discourse.

It appears that the influx of Chinese film talent into Hollywood and the growing Western audiences for this talent since the late 1990s have not changed long-standing Orientalist discourses, either in terms of cinematic representation or cross-cultural reading. This is not to say, however, that they have not been challenged in any aspect. My research on Western critical responses to Jet Li's English-language films demonstrates that, on the one hand, stereotyping is often accompanied by anti-stereotyping, and on the other hand, that biased perceptions always coexist with antiracist discourses. Gina Marchetti has named this new strategy 'postmodern Orientalism' (1993: 203), while some might prefer to call it neo-Orientalism. No matter how the concept of Orientalism is defined and transformed in the context of increasing West-East exchange, transcultural reception is undoubtedly a complex and conflicting process. Negotiating between stereotyping and anti-stereotyping, Li has not been able to repeat his success as a prestigious Chinese *wuxia* hero in his English-language films. However, his newly-gained screen identities – charming villain and childlike man – not only enriched his star persona and brought him new global fans, but opened up a broader range of roles for Li as an actor. Li would win his first acting award in the Hong Kong Film Awards a few years later for his semi-villainous role as General Pang in *The Warlords* (2007), which attests to the fact that his crossover experience is not all negative, even though the reception of his English-language films seemed discouraging at the time.

Notes

1. Chan's failure in crossing over to Hollywood in the first half of the 1980s (for example, *The Big Brawl* [Robert Clouse, 1980]; *The Cannonball Run* [Hal Needham, 1981]), largely resulted from American filmmakers' intention to make him the second 'Bruce Lee' without endowing him with any unique screen persona.
2. These commercially and critically unsuccessful films starring Chan are *The Tuxedo* (Kevin Donovan, 2002), *Shanghai Knights* (David Dobkin, 2003) and *Around the World in 80 Days* (Frank Coraci, 2004).
3. These include *the Daily Mail, The Independent on Sunday, New Statesman, Empire, The Sunday Times, Evening Standard, Time Out, The Financial Times, The Times, The Guardian, The Sun, The Daily Telegraph, The Sunday Telegraph, Time, Daily Variety, Sight and Sound, Film Review, Variety, Screen International, Total Film, Village Voice, Asian Age, Cinefantastique, Premiere, Asian Cult Cinema, Post Script, Entertainment Weekly, Hollywood Reporter, Film Journal International* and *Video Business*. Most of these are based in the UK and US, and a couple are from Australia. I collected research material mainly from the British Film Institute National Library in April 2005 and May 2007, and also from the EBSCO Film and Television Literature Index in July 2007.

4. The poster for the film, in which Li's neck is being trodden on by an unknown foot, has stimulated angry responses in China's media.
5. Lots of positive comments on Li's performance in *Danny the Dog* can be found on the fan sites such as *The Internet Movie Database*.

6
Asexual Romeo? Male sexuality and cultural perspectives

In his research on the Asian-American Internet reception of Jet Li's English-language roles, Julian Stringer observes that the 'kiss on the big screen' has taken up most discussion space on the websites which he visited and many Asian-American movie fans are baffled by the fact that Li has never kissed any of his interracial female screen partners. According to Stringer, even though 'being in a unique position to possess and project healthy and good Asian sexuality' (2003: 284), which represents both a reversal and a reinvention of one of the key continuing stereotypes of Asians in the US media – the sexual deviant – Li is perceived as not actually possessing sexuality of any kind. Asian-American audiences are certainly not alone in viewing Li as a sexless leading man. When examining Western press reviews of Li's English-language films, I notice that 'lack of sexual attraction' stands out as one of the main charges brought against him, as the following reviews demonstrate:

> Sadly, Li's lack of charisma is cruelly exposed in the more dramatic or intimate scenes, especially those involving the film's nominal romantic interest, hip hop singer Aaliyah. (Floyd 2000: 81)

> The connection that Jet Li's ascetic supercop makes with Bridget Fonda's abused hooker is central to the plot, but is at best amusingly gauche and at worst excruciating, as when Fonda relates to Li her garbled backstory. During this supposedly pivotal scene, acting and dialogue are both negligible and only alternating close-ups of the actors' eyes convey any sense of a growing attachment between the two characters. (Leyland 2001: 51)

Such criticism of Li is not at all surprising; it reveals one of the most enduring Western myths about Chinese masculinity, namely, 'asexual Chinese men', and should be discussed in relation to the representation of male sexuality in Hollywood cinema.

Desexualised Chinese men on Western screens

There are three principal ways in which male sexuality is made visible in mainstream Hollywood films: the body as sexual spectacle, genital acts of love with women, and homosexual implication. In his article on male sexuality in the media published in 1985, Richard Dyer points out that the symbolism of male sexuality is 'overwhelmingly centred on the genitals, especially the penis' (1985: 29). He also argues that popular film and television often place women as objects of a 'natural' male sexual drive, therefore reinforcing a notion that women represent what 'male sexuality is ostensibly there for' (ibid. 41). Dyer's accounts reveal the most common imagery of male sexuality at the time – equating male sexuality with the penis – and its most popular media representation – having sex with a woman.

Since the publication of Dyer's article, the representation of male sexuality in the cinema has incorporated some new elements. First, it has become almost commonplace within academic accounts to argue that the (white) male body is displayed as the spectacle and as the object of an erotic look (Tasker 1993; Cohan 1997),[1] especially in certain genres such as the musical or action cinema. Second, the formerly 'displaced' or 'repressed' male-to-male relationships (both on screen and off screen) have been explored in great detail in the light of homosexual desire. Erotic feeling between male characters (though understated in most cases) or between male audiences and male characters on screen has therefore become a noticeable way of defining male sexuality in the cinema. Despite these new means of defining male sexuality, physical intimacy with women remains the predominant way of representing male sexuality on screen. It seems to be the most prevalent norm by which to judge male sexuality, especially where non-white male sexuality is concerned. For example, many Hollywood films are keen to portray African men as obsessed with sex, in line with the clichéd image of 'black hypersexuality'. In contrast, the stereotype of the 'asexual Chinese male' is to a large extent based on a film tradition that tends not to associate the Chinese male with 'the act of love' with women on screen.

If we look at the sexual representation of those early Chinese male images on Western screens – Cheng Huan, representing effeminacy; Charlie Chan, the asexual; Fu Manchu, the sexual deviant – it is not difficult to conclude that, no matter whether they are 'good guys' or 'bad guys', they are without exception characterised by weak bodies and sexual impotence. With his tough kung fu hero image, Bruce Lee remasculinised the Chinese male body in the early 1970s, yet he has not been able to redeem the common asexual screen presence of Chinese men. Both Yvonne Tasker (1997) and Jachinson Chan (2001) point out that Lee's only Hollywood work *Enter the Dragon* (1973) helps to perpetuate this asexual Asian male stereotype, given that Lee's character is reluctant to choose a girl to spend the night with, something his white and black counterparts are certainly happy to do. Indeed, as Richard Fung neatly sums up, an Asian man is either an 'egghead/wimp' or 'the kung fu master/ ninja/samurai', who is 'sometimes dangerous, sometimes friendly, but almost always characterized by a desexualized Zen asceticism' (1991: 148).

Though in a stronger position to control their star persona, more recent border-crossing Chinese male stars have been viewed as continuing to play 'asexual' roles. Like Lee's crossover film, Jackie Chan's Hollywood films involve hardly any romantic sub-plot, instead pairing him with a black buddy. Mark Gallagher reads Chan's image in his American films as that of a 'sexless loner', an image which exists partly because 'major studios do not yet view Asian couples as commercially viable and Western cultural taboos still forbid a white woman's attraction to an Asian man' (1997: 33). An American sociology professor's question precisely conveys Chan's sexual image on Western screens: 'He's a funny martial artist, but are you going to sleep with him?' (quoted in Pan 2000: 50) Chow Yun-fat, the 'sexiest Asian man' – an image built up in both the action films and romantic dramas which he made in Hong Kong – has been viewed as 'desexualised' in his Hollywood roles, due to the fact that he has never made love to a woman on screen. In his discussion of Asian influences in American popular culture, Leo Ou-fan Lee mentions that the local press in Hong Kong finds Chow's Hollywood work rather disappointing and wonders: 'Why doesn't Chow Yun-fat go to bed with Mira Sorvino, as any white male hero would do with a non-white heroine in a typical Hollywood movie?' (1999: 30)

When judged by whether or not they have physical intimacy with women, Chinese men on the Western screen are hopelessly 'desexualised', as the above comments show. However, it is worth noting that different opinions on the sexuality of Chinese men – transnational Chinese kung fu stars in particular – do exist, when other norms about sexuality such as body as sexual spectacular are applied. Some find that Bruce Lee is very sexy in terms of the way he displays his body, for example when he takes off his jacket to fight, or practises martial arts half-naked in front of a mirror. While Stephen Teo (1997) proposes narcissism as a key characteristic in defining Lee's male sexuality, Jachinson Chan (2000) suggests that Lee's character encourages an (homo)erotic desire for his body from both male and female characters. Jackie Chan's obsession with exhibiting, in outtakes, his physical injuries incurred during filming action scenes can be read similarly; glorifying one's vulnerable but extremely resilient body is no less narcissistic than showcasing one's muscular and invincible body.

Compared with Lee and Chan, Jet Li probably has more reasons to be viewed as 'asexual'. Although Li is famous for his physical capability, his body per se has never been in any way highlighted in his films. He hardly ever exhibits a damaged and suffering body as his Western counterparts tend to do; he never takes off his shirt to fight, as Bruce Lee often does; he exhibits no penchant for showcasing his real wounds outside the character, as Jackie Chan seems to enjoy doing. To be sure, Li's body is not an effective location for playing out the discourse of sexuality. Li's Western work also offers little space for a homosexual interpretation, since Li does not bond with male characters in any significantly homosocial way.[2] Consequently, Li's sexuality has to be represented solely through romantic interplay between Li and his female screen partner, but the fact that in his Western roles Li has never done anything more than giving his female lead a hug has led to a firm view of Li as 'sexually unattractive'.

However, if we compare Li's sexuality as portrayed on the Western screen with his sexuality represented in his Chinese films, and especially if we consider the cross-cultural reception of Li's sexual image, some interesting questions emerge. First, with an invariably chaste sexual persona, Li 'has worked perfectly well as a romantic lead of sorts' (Hunt 2003: 176) in his Hong Kong films (and his early *Shaolin Temple* films made in the Mainland). Why, then, in his English-language films, does this turn into evidence of his having no romantic feelings and a handy way to place him in the tradition of 'sexless Chinese men'? Is Li's 'sexless male lead' mainly a textual construction, functioning as a strategy to confirm the sexual dominance of the white hero, or is it also constructed by the interpretation of audiences? Does 'sexual unattractiveness' really represent a dominant perception of Li's sexuality on the Western screen, as my survey of Western critical reviews seems to suggest?

Second, while Hunt appears to suggest that it is Western critics who have commented on Li's 'lack of chemistry' with female leads (ibid. 176), Hong Kong journalists and Asian-American fans also feel unhappy with their hero's Platonic relationships with interracial romantic partners, as referred to above. Does this indicate that the 'asexual Chinese man' is no longer entirely a Western construction, but also a reflection of Chinese men's self-definition which has unconsciously taken shape through a complicated process of resistance and identification in the age of globalisation of film production and distribution?

Third, in the Chinese context, Li's sexuality is never an eye-catching topic, partly due to a film tradition in which male sexuality has always been downplayed, as I discuss later, and also because Li's status as a heterosexual male hero in his Chinese work is so far from being challenged that there seems no need to discuss his sexuality (even when his character is involved in a homosexual relationship; see Chapter 3). In contrast, as a minority actor in Hollywood, Li's sexuality is frequently foregrounded in the discussion of his Western screen persona, though this sexuality is often defined as 'asexual'. Does the global dissemination of Chinese male sexuality simply reinforce the Western cliché of the 'asexual Chinese man', or does it also offer a chance to build up a new 'transnational Chinese male sexuality', therefore unexpectedly bringing to the fore Chinese male sexuality, which has long been understated or even repressed on Chinese screens? With these questions in mind, I explore in this chapter how Li's sexuality in his Western roles has been constructed by looking at another category of audience on which my book focuses – the fans. More specifically, I examine users' comments from *The Internet Movie Database* (*IMDb* hereafter) on the relationships of Li's characters with women in four of his English-language films: *Romeo Must Die* (2000), *Kiss of the Dragon* (2001), *The One* (2001) and *Danny the Dog* (2005) (a total of 1,075 at the time of my research).[3]

First of all, I should offer an explanation about my choice of the *IMDb* as the site on which to conduct this reception study. What is the *IMDb*? Why choose it? Based in the UK and the US, the *IMDb* is arguably the world's biggest collection of movie information and provides full details about a movie 'from who was in it, to who made it, to trivia about it, to filming locations and even where you can find reviews and fan sites on the web'. Given its self-definition as 'something by movie fans for movie fans',[4] and given its statistics of over 42 million visitors a month from all over the world, the *IMDb* is an ideal location to investigate fans. This raises another important question: who are *IMDb* users?

This is a tricky question because in a virtual world, Internet users can never be reliably identified. Hence, I can give only a rough description of *IMDb* users, based on rudimentary information. First, they are movie fans, hardcore or casual. After all, who would bother to publish a posting unless they were fond of movies? Second, they are based all around the world, although the majority are in the US, UK and other European countries. This is known from the locations marked by users under the title of each posting. It is quite difficult to decide whether to call the *IMDb* fans Western fans or global fans. While the term 'Western fans' obviously leaves out fans from other parts of the world and seems unnecessarily to reinforce boundaries which are quickly disappearing in an era of globalisation, calling these users 'global fans' risks exaggerating their diversity, especially considering that the language used on this site is English, which excludes fans who cannot use English, for example, most fans from China. Therefore, in this chapter I choose not to apply either the term 'Western fans' or 'global fans', but instead to refer to '*IMDb* fans', although I still want to draw attention to their largely Western background. Third, while many *IMDb* users examined here clearly show they are Jet Li fans (by confessing 'I am a Jet Li fan', or by expressing their fondness for Li's Asian films), most of them may not be particular Jet Li fans, but general action fans who show in their postings some interest in and knowledge of Li's films. Only a few users declare that they are not action fans or that this is the first time they have watched a Jet Li film.

'Asexual Romeo': Hollywood product or cultural perspective?

Before looking at the ways in which *IMDb* fans talk about Li's relationship with his female lead in these four films, a brief introduction to the plot of each film will give some idea of how this relationship is placed in the narrative of that film. Among the four films, *Romeo Must Die*, the first English-language film in which Li starred, has been discussed most in terms of its romantic dimension, since the film title indicates a modern version of *Romeo and Juliet*. Li plays an ex-cop who escapes from a Hong Kong prison and goes to America to investigate the murder of his brother. Li meets and falls in love with Aaliyah, the daughter of a black gang-leader whose followers seem to have been involved in his brother's death. After her own brother is murdered, Aaliyah joins Li in the hunt for justice. *Kiss of the Dragon* revolves around Li and the female lead Bridget Fonda, but there is only a potential romance between them. As an undercover agent from China, Li comes to Paris to help the French police arrest a Chinese criminal but unexpectedly gets trapped in a conspiracy headed by Richard, the police chief. By chance, Li meets Fonda, a US farm girl who is forced to become Richard's hooker to keep her daughter safe, and they have to help each other to fight against the evil police inspector. Less discussion has been devoted to Li's romantic relationship in *The One*, since Carla Gugino is Li's wife from the beginning of the film. As a sci-fi film in which Li plays a double role, the film focuses on good Li's defeat of bad Li, leaving Carla more or less a romantic foil. *Danny the Dog* portrays Li as a childlike man who is treated like a dog and raised as a fighting machine throughout his entire life. After an accident, the

Figure 7 Jet Li as Liu Jian and Bridget Fonda as Jessica Kamen in *Kiss of the Dragon* (Chris Nahon, 2001). (Source: Kobal Collection.)

wounded Li is sheltered by the blind piano tuner Morgan Freeman and his stepdaughter Kerry Condon, who treat him like a family member and start to humanise him.

Probably because of their identity as action fans or Jet Li fans, the attitude towards Li in the *IMDb* user comments is quite different from that found in the Western press reviews I examined in the previous chapter. While the critics are generally harsh and hypercritical, *IMDb* fans are friendlier towards Li, regardless of whether they like or dislike the film itself. For example, in contrast to the critical consensus that Li is a fighting machine without any acting skills, several typical opinions can be observed in the *IMDb*: (1) Li is a good actor; (2) Li is not used properly – his performance is let down by the script and the directing; (3) Li is not a great actor, certainly, but remember this is an action film. Generally speaking, sympathy and understanding characterise the *IMDb* user comments whenever Li is referred to.

When it comes to fan readings of Li's romantic relationships, predictably, different opinions emerge from the several hundreds of comments posted. While some do find a strong on-screen chemistry between Li and his female partners, more postings express dissatisfaction with the underdeveloped romantic plots in Li's English-language films. Here, I give four exemplary comments, on four films respectively.

[*Romeo Must Die*] Another thing that really turned me off was the way the relationship between Li's and Aaliyah's characters is portrayed. I thought that the intent of showing an interracial love story was pretty courageous. Therefore I was extremely disappointed when they ended up holding hands. How can this happen in a movie which is supposed to be based (however loosely) on the greatest love story of all times?! (Bahrom1, 27 March 2001)

[*Kiss of the Dragon*] I also expected some romance between Li and Fonda [which would've been a nice touch] but the 'knock-em-up' writers can only think about the action sequences to actually make more of a plot. (Movielover-9, 23 November 2001)

[*The One*] Carla Gugino plays Li's wife TK who, aside from being a female presence, is just there. Perhaps the writers, including writer/director James Wong, should do actual research for the right formulas to brew chemistry between a Caucasian woman and a Chinese man, because there obviously isn't any between Li and Gugino. (L'Apprenti, 23 November 2001)

[*Danny the Dog*] When the girl had taken off Jet Li's collar and was about to kiss him on the lips, she suddenly changed her mind and kissed his neck. Why the change of mind? . . . They had been spending quality time together and at least it seemed she had developed an attraction to Jet Li's character. Perhaps the director did not want the romantic development to go any further than just very good friends for whatever reasons (?) (Gambino1-1, 22 October 2005)

It is notable that a large number of *IMDb* fans share the critical view of 'lack of chemistry between Li and his screen partner' or 'unconvincing romance', but blame the director/writer/producer instead of Li himself for the unsuccessful romance, as the above quotations and many other similar ones demonstrate. Hollywood's reluctance to portray an interracial romance is seen as a serious hindrance to creating a convincing love story. For some fans, the approach to interracial romance in Li's English-language films is often ambiguous: 'I thought the movie was cowardly in remaining ambiguous to Li and Aaliyah's relationship in the film, never outwardly showing them as more than close friends' (Skubrick-5, 18 December 2000); 'Two build a friendship that climaxes into one can only guess into a couple relationship – the film's [*Kiss of the Dragon*] ending is ambiguous' (Charlie_062497, 5 December 2001).

Stringer's observation concerning Asian American fan sites also applies here: 'no kisses' is a much-discussed issue. The lack of physical intimacy, for many fans, undoubtedly precludes any emotional development between Li and his female screen partners, as seen in the following two postings: 'I cannot believe he didn't get to kiss Aaliyah . . . These two were supposed to be falling in love and he did not get to kiss' (Cills, 29 March 2000); 'The relationship between Li and Bridget Fonda goes nowhere. Doesn't Li ever KISS anyone in these movies?' (Bob-45, 23 July 2001). Again, this lack of physical intimacy is attributed to Hollywood's biased representation of interracial romance: 'It seems as if the filmmakers themselves look down on this interracial romance. The closest they get to intimacy is a hug and even that looks like a hesitant move' (Li-1, 5 April 2003); 'Of course, this is Hollywood in full Interracial Mode, where characters are only permitted a brief embrace at the end and perhaps a quick peck on the cheek if they're lucky' (BlueNeon-2, 7 April 2000).

Responding to the rumour that Joel Silver, the producer of *Romeo Must Die*, cut the final scene in which Li and Aaliyah actually kiss,[5] a fan points out that 'Contrary to what others were saying, there was a definite chemistry between ever-gorgeous Aaliyah and Jet Li. Joel Silver's decision to cut out the kiss scene between them can only be seen as a racist move if not economical' (Misterkim-2, 25 March 2000). Many fans admit that they do not expect a Jet Li film to be a romantic drama, but they do wish they could see a bit more romantic development between Li and his female leads: 'It was clear that the movie needed more romantic scenes. I mean it was crystal clear that both Aaliyah and Jet Li had a crush on each other, but I can remember no scene where they said it, or even looked in the eyes!!' (Mohsen, 4 August 2001); 'I'm not one for love stories but I would have liked it if they had Jet Li and the girl have a better love story and a sequence [*Danny the Dog*]' (sexcnessim, 20 September 2005).

From the *IMDb* user comments quoted above, two points are of interest. First, if 'asexual sexuality' has become part of Li's Western screen persona, for the *IMDb* fans, it is the politics of interracial representation rather than Li's lack of sexual appeal that should be held responsible for this. The fans appear to presume that, in the face of the powerful Hollywood system, Li does not have much choice except to play the expected role – a stereotyped sexless Chinese male. This raises further intriguing questions. For example, to what degree do transnational Chinese action stars (and transnational stars more generally) have control over their Hollywood roles? A typical dilemma that transnational stars often have to face is: if they are less successful than they were at home, they are regarded to have been misused by Hollywood, thereby losing their own strength and distinction, but if they do become successful in Hollywood, they could be accused of having compromised in order to cater to Hollywood tastes. However, in Li's case, while he may not have the same power as he does in Asia, neither is he as vulnerable as the fans assume. While I agree with the *IMDb* fans that Li's screen romances have to a large extent been manipulated and restricted by Hollywood's interracial politics, I also suspect that it may partly be Li's own preference not to kiss his female leads, given his screen persona as a conservative and shy male hero, which he has built up throughout his Chinese career.[6]

Second, while filmmakers and the industry still dwell on the imaginary 'asexual Chinese male', the *IMDb* fans are showing obvious signs of weariness with this long-standing cliché and a desire to see a more humanised Eastern hero with a more visible sexuality. However, while the fans express dislike for the disturbing pattern in interracial romances presented by Hollywood, which does not allow the Asian hero to develop a real romance with women and to express his sexuality, they at the same time impose Western notions of romance and sexuality onto a Chinese male lead. A popular opinion here is that there is no chemistry, no well-developed romance, because there are no kisses or sex scenes. This perspective once again confirms accepted ideas of what comprises male sexuality in the cinema (Hollywood cinema in particular), as Dyer defined it in the 1980s – that the sexual is centred on an act (of love) and represented visually by scenes involving physical intimacy, such as kissing or sexual intercourse.

Action cinema, as many fans note, is not a perfect genre for showcasing love stories. American action films, in Gallagher's view, generally imply 'the incompatibility of combat and heterosexual romance' (1997: 33). Yet, this does not mean that they lack romantic action. In fact, 'the hero bedding the heroine' has become one of the indispensable formulae within action film narratives and a scene rarely omitted in most Hollywood action films. Through physical consummation, not only is male sexuality made 'present', but the audience is reassured about the male hero's heterosexual identity in reaction to a homosexual anxiety triggered by the predominance of homosocial relations in action films. Probably due to this 'horizon of expectation', the *IMDb* fans, who are familiar with action genre conventions and the Hollywood code of representing romance, are unhappy with Li and Aaliyah's ending up 'holding hands' instead of 'sharing a kiss', or feel confused to see that Condon kisses Li's neck and not his lips. However, is physical intimacy the only approved way to represent romance in cinema? Does a romance have to be consummated through a kiss or sexual intercourse? Does a male lead such as Li have to kiss or bed a woman to claim his sexuality on screen?

As mentioned in the Introduction, Kam Louie proposes to conceptualise Chinese masculinity in light of the *wen-wu* paradigm. In Louie's definition, *wu* heroes in Chinese traditional narratives do not have romantic relationships with beauties as a *wen* scholar would do, because they need to attend to their social obligations and remain incorruptible both morally and sexually. Louie points out that, in contrast to Western 'real men' who always get the girl, the *wu* hero must reject women, because the 'containment of sexual and romantic desire is an integral part of the *wu* virtue' (2002: 19). Armed with this understanding, Louie argues that Chinese notions of *wu* masculinity have been transformed by Western (Hollywood) constructions of masculinity, as exemplified by the careers of three border-crossing male action stars, Bruce Lee, Jackie Chan and Chow Yun-fat. One of the main changes is that in their Western roles they form romantic attachments to women. Yet at the same time, Louie notes a common charge against these Chinese male personae: that they are wooden and lack sex appeal. Louie suggests that the lack of explicit sexual intercourse associated with the screen personae of Lee, Chan and Chow should be seen in light of the conventions of the traditional Chinese hero, as well as the public morals of Chinese audiences. For audiences raised in such a cultural and historical context, Louie writes, 'there was no question that the looks in the actresses' eyes demonstrated a desire for Lee's body just as strong if not stronger than the Bond girls' flirtations with 007', and Lee, far from being wooden, 'exudes much sexuality' (ibid. 147).

I cannot agree with Louie that the heterosexual desire of a Chinese male hero is a kind of Hollywood reinvention of Chinese masculinity, given the fact that 'hero+beauty' is a long-standing and exuberant narrative prevalent in Chinese culture, and that the *wu* heroes on screen do have romantic relationships with women, even though they hardly ever consummate them in an explicit manner. Nevertheless, I appreciate two points that Louie makes in his work. First, 'the lack of an act of love', characteristic of the sexual representation of Chinese male heroes on both Western and Chinese screens, apart from being seen as a stereotyped portrayal, should also be understood within the context of Chinese culture and morality. According to Cheng Yu, traditional Chinese folk morality regards sexual activity as detrimental to the body and the corrupter of moral standards, so 'not only must the ideal hero abstain from sexual indulgence, he has to be practically celibate' (1984: 25). For Chinese men, showing affection to women publicly and directly is considered inappropriate and shameful, in particular when it is judged to conflict with other greater causes. As Sek Kei observes, 'In times of crisis, love and romance is not a priority and is indeed, incompatible with the prevailing mood. Heroes should be celibate and have nothing to do with women' (1991: 63). This cultural influence can partly explain why, in both the Mainland and Hong Kong film traditions, when male heroism or dignity needs to be highlighted, in such genres as *wuxia* film or action film, women have to be sidelined and male sexuality has to be minimised. Rather than simply taken as a manifestation of sexlessness, Chinese men's reluctance to have physical intimacy with their screen partner is also an exhibition of cultural personality.

Louie is also correct in indicating that the star persona is constructed by different cultural perspectives in different reception contexts. In Jet Li's case, we hardly ever see him kiss or have physical intimacy with the objects of romance in his Chinese films, but this does not stop Chinese critics and fans from regarding Li as a charismatic, attractive male hero (as discussed in the first part of this book). Indeed, throughout his screen career most characters Li has played have hardly felt comfortable with women. But it is precisely through this hesitant, shy screen persona that he offers audiences such memorable romantic stories as the covert but lasting love between Wong Fei-hung and Aunt Thirteen in the *Once Upon a Time in China* series. When Li transfers to the Western screen, the way in which many *IMDb* fans define on-screen romance – as something which must end in physical intimacy – has made them see Li's portrayal of romantic relationships as unconvincing, or 'lacking chemistry'. This clearly demonstrates that different norms and traditions of the on-screen representation of romance and sexuality lead to different readings of star performance.

When some *IMDb* fans complain about a love story without kisses, they are showing intolerance for a representation of romance and sexuality which is different from the one they are used to. Thus, if they find that Hollywood's interracial politics are deliberately trying to deprive Li of his sexuality, these fans inadvertently choose to disavow Li's sexuality by willing him to kiss, or, better, have sex with his female partner in order to create the desirable chemistry. To some extent, this betrays a kind of Western cultural hegemony – a Chinese man can be regarded as sexual only if he conforms to Western standards of what constitutes male sexuality and how it should be shown. In this sense, the sexless Chinese male, one of the most enduring myths in the West, is not only produced by Hollywood but also by its audiences.

Li therefore has to face a double castration in his crossover career: while Hollywood's racially conservative narratives, such as the inviability of miscegenation, leave little space for his characters to develop any romantic feelings, his low-key sexuality, characteristic of a traditional Chinese hero, is viewed by many fans (especially Western fans) as no sexuality at all. It was somewhat ironic to try to reinvent Li as a modern Romeo in his first Western leading role, given that the star persona which Li had built up in his Chinese films is a far cry from Shakespeare's Romeo. But the title '*Romeo Must Die*' is quite prophetic: when judged from a Western perspective, Li as a modern version of Romeo does indeed die in regard to his romantic or sexual image in the film.

Women's friend: alternative model of male sexuality

I have argued that cultural perspective plays a crucial role in constructing Li's on-screen sexuality. However, I do not intend to treat either Chinese or Western audience as a homogenous and isolated whole. In fact, a few *IMDb* fans do express their objection to the way in which Hollywood represents heterosexual desire:

> [*Kiss of the Dragon*] The chemistry that clicks between her and Li is strong and even sometimes sweet and touching. Some see the lack of an actual romance blossoming between them as another sign that Hollywood isn't much for interracial couples (much like in *Romeo Must Die*) but I think it's better this way. Plus, I'm getting tired of seeing the hero bed the heroine in an impulsive moment of passion. Fonda and Li's quiet communication and toned-down feelings are more effective than a kiss or love scene would be. (Jiangliqings, 23 September 2001)

> [*Danny the Dog*] Kerry Condon as Victoria is sweetness, innocence and unbridled love for Danny but it [sic] comes across as a sister for a long lost brother. The idea of sexual tension between the two of them almost never raises its head and that is one of the best things about this movie. It shows a 'love interest' that Hollywood has lost over the years. That a man and woman can be together and a relationship formed and strengthened without the two of them jumping into bed. (Stanley, 14 May 2005)

The first user has a Chinese name and the second one appears to be a Westerner. But it hardly matters whether they are Chinese or Western. The important point is that they offer another opinion on the representation of romance and male sexuality in the cinema. This is that a kiss or love scene is not the only or necessary way to deliver romantic feeling; 'quiet communication' or 'toned-down feelings' can also make a male hero look attractive in certain circumstances.

Moreover, for many *IMDb* fans, male stars do not have to have a love relationship with a woman in order to display their sexuality. As I discussed above, when some fans focus on the love story in Li's English-language films, they often express their disappointment at finding no chemistry. Interestingly, other fans who read the relationship of Li and his female counterpart as 'friendship' and not 'romance' often perceive a strong on-screen chemistry. It would be remiss not to mention the latter, a no less compelling perception at the *IMDb*, as the following quotations exemplify.

> [*Romeo Must Die*] Most endearing was the emerging relationship between Trish (Aaliyah) and Han (Jet Li). It wasn't a ridiculously sappy express ride to love, if [sic] the story had clung to the events of 'Romeo & Juliet.' Instead, a more platonic and time/place-feasible friendship develops between the two characters. (Shadows-8, 31 March 2000)

Figure 8 Jet Li as Han Sing and Aaliyah Haughton as Trish O'Day in *Romeo Must Die* (Andrzej Bartkowiak, 2000). (Source: Kobal Collection.)

[*Romeo Must Die*] Both Jet Li and Aaliyah give it their best and while there is no real conception of romance, there are a lot of small, warm, pervading impressions of friendship which I found to be quite charming. (Deepcheck, 28 March 2000)

[*Danny the Dog*] The bond Jet shared with Morgan and Kerry Condon was excellent as they had great chemistry together . . . he really gets to be extremely likable once he meets Freeman and also develops a cute relationship with his daughter. (Callanvass, 28 February 2006)

[*Kiss of the Dragon*] What makes the film special is Bridget Fonda's role. She plays a prostitute who teams up with Li to identify and catch the real villain . . . The bond of trust that develops between the two is very absorbing to watch and looks convincing. (Gatsby2244, 24 April 2005)

Indeed, 'friendship', 'buddy', and 'bond' are more frequently mentioned among the *IMDb* postings than 'romance' or 'love' when it comes to the relationship between Li and his female screen partner. This is rather surprising, given the usual expectation that there must be some romantic interaction between the action hero and his love interest. Why do these fans prefer to see Li and his female lead as buddies and not lovers? To answer this question, consider the following users' comments first: 'For fans of Hollywood-love stories, the movie is a late disappointment because who might have thought Aaliyah and Li will fall in a great emotional ending-love serenade is eventually not satisfied with the ending scene. To me it was a relief that this love serenade did not happen which would have fulfilled another stereotypical moment in this movie' (Thome, 27 March 2005); 'It has comedy and a good friendship between Jet Li and Aaliyah characters . . . I'm happy that Joel Silver did not make a romantic story line between Li and Aaliyah, because it would have been the same old predictable story line' (Blew12, 16 December 2001); 'The girl was pretty good too, I was worried she would be used solely as a romantic foil, but instead she was there for him as a friend' [*Danny the Dog*] (Kyrat, 31 May 2005). Clearly, it is the 'predictable story line', 'stereotypical moment' and convenient 'romantic foil' often seen in Hollywood action films that make the fans long for a refreshing relationship between the hero and heroine.

In many action films, the woman usually exists as either a powerless victim who is waiting to be rescued by the male hero in line with a hackneyed model of rescuer/rescued, or as a romantic foil who establishes the male hero's sexuality and gives an emotional dimension to the story. Alternatively, the woman represents a troublesome presence who adds some comedic elements to the film, as in Jackie Chan's action comedies. In each of these cases, the male hero dominates and controls the relationship.[7] By constructing woman as an object to be gazed at, desired and possessed, the male hero exhibits his aggressive male sexuality. In terms of heterosexual representation, Li's English-language films are distinct from most Hollywood action films. Li's character and the female protagonist usually build up a bond to help each other in the face of difficult situations, and they do not then 'fall into the melodramatic tiger trap' (Robotman-1, 7 August 2001). In *Romeo Must Die*, Li and Aaliyah work together to find their brothers' killers; in *Kiss of the Dragon*, Li and Fonda team up to fight against the common enemy, the corrupt French police chief; in *The One*, the film shows how Li and Carla support one another in defeating the villain, rather than their family life as a couple; in *Danny the Dog*, Condon teaches the savage Li about human life and love while Li protects her from danger at the end of the film.

Furthermore, unlike the usual Hollywood narrative, in which the male hero will eventually get his romantic interest, these films give audiences little idea about where Li's relationship with his female friend will go. As some fans note, the films often end in an ambiguous way. Look at the final sequence of each film where the female lead appears together with Li's character: Aaliyah comforts the exhausted Li with a hug after Li's showdown with his wicked father and the two of them walk away together holding hands (*Romeo Must Die*); Fonda kisses Li's hand to express her gratitude for getting her daughter back, but Li looks away embarrassedly and then both of them turn their gaze to Fonda's sleeping daughter (*Kiss of the Dragon*); Li goes to the concert and finds, to his surprise, that the friend to whom Condon dedicates her performance is actually himself (*Danny the Dog*). For the *IMDb* fans, the female lead in Li's films is not a woman to be rescued or conquered, but instead is treated as an equal by the male lead; as a friend, a buddy. Probably because of this, the fans frequently use terms such as 'sweet', 'endearing', 'cute' and 'touching' to describe the chemistry between Li and his female screen partners.

On the basis of the fans' comments, it is reasonable to suggest that Li's Hollywood work introduces an interracial male-female buddy narrative into the action film. This new model is refreshing, not only because it rejects the hero/beauty formula, but also because in a male-oriented genre, buddies are almost exclusively represented by men. On the one hand, interracial male-female buddydom challenges a male-dominated genre by portraying a more equal, reciprocal relationship between the hero and heroine. On the other hand, it transgresses the racial boundary by forming a firm bond between two leads who come from different races. It is worth pointing out that the interracial male-female buddy model does not present the same construction of power and subservience as seen in interracial male buddy films (for example, the white hero and his black helper).[8] This is perhaps because both sides (non-white male, female) have been previously repressed in the white, male-centred action genre and are therefore able to build up a relatively equal, less power-based relationship. In various aspects, the interracial male-female buddy narrative provides the possibility of deconstructing stereotypical representations of race, gender and sexuality in action cinema.

By portraying a buddy relationship with his female lead, Li also offers a different image of male sexuality, as the following *IMDb* user comments imply. 'The hero is [sic] likable guy played by Jet Li. Despite his martial arts penchant for violence, he has a soft, boyish look to him and doesn't seem to fit the type. He's always the gentleman in [sic] here, with no profanity either' (Ccthemovieman-1, 15 July 2006). 'Jet Li is all about earning the viewers respect. Jet isn't ripped or massive but he manages to be menacing, in fact he is small and subtle – modest and humble, even Bruce Lee didn't have that quality' (Tai, 1 July 2001). 'Jet Li is vulnerable, had decent chemistry with Carla Gugino and was very likable!' (Callanvass 25 May 2005) 'It is still a touching film which manages to show everything Jet has to offer from his likable, shy persona to his impressive physical grace' (Ryan, 5 August 2005). According to these postings, Li is tough, menacing, duty- and honour-bound, like a typical male hero, but at the same time humble, subtle, gentle and vulnerable, characteristics which are not normally those of action heroes, either Western or Eastern. For the fans, Li is undoubtedly physically strong, given that he is a superb martial artist and that he has never been beaten up in any of these four films, but at the same time, he is emotionally vulnerable because he is 'unsure of himself around women in an intimate situation' (Frost, 25 August 2001) and because his befriending of women puts him on an equal footing with his female counterparts.

It is, of course, nothing new for action films to portray male heroes as physically vulnerable. However, even physically vulnerable male heroes are emotionally powerful; they always take control of relationships with women, or simply exclude women. By refusing to treat women conventionally as romantic interests, by showing more care and respect for his female partner, Li introduces a boyish, soft sexuality into action cinema. Among *IMDb* user comments, the words used most frequently to define Li's unique screen presence are 'shy', 'modest', 'boyish', 'innocent' and 'likable'. When not defining Li's relation with the leading female character as romantic interplay, many fans admit that Li has real charisma on screen and good chemistry with the female star. If male sexuality in the cinema is not simply equated with the manifestation of libidinous desire, if sexiness can also be revealed in a star's performance and charisma, then Li is undoubtedly sexual in the view of many *IMDb* fans.

Perhaps because they have grown tired of the arrogant, pompous white heroes of Hollywood, who have never hesitated to showcase their sexuality on screen by getting women easily, the *IMDb* fans find Li's soft sexuality extremely charming and appealing. However, the reason for this may also be that a modest, sexually non-aggressive Eastern male hero is less threatening and thereby more easily accepted. This proposition can be supported by comparing Li's sexuality with the sexuality of teenagers and women. On the one hand, Li's sexuality is being constructed on Western screens in a way which closely resembles the 'teen idol' – immature, boyish – which may be not so much asexual as completely non-threatening to mainstream (Western) audiences. On the other hand, Li's sexuality within its Western construction bears similarities to what Louie observes is the 'ideal man' created by Chinese women writers in the twentieth century, featuring such qualities as 'youthful innocence, sexual naiveté, tenderness and exotica – characteristics which traditionally have been associated with femininity' (2002: 99).

Conclusion

In Stringer's case study of Asian American Internet responses to Jet Li, he notes that the main concern is whether or not Li's star image is adequate to represent Asian/Asian American masculinity, and he comes to the conclusion that Li is revealed as 'no "perfect" Chinese man' or 'emasculated Asian American man' in the discussions among Asian American fans. (2003: 282–3) My research into *IMDb* fans' responses to Li's relationships with his female protagonists offers a slightly different picture, identifying three broad interpretations of Li's sexuality. First, many fans hold similar perceptions to those of the Asian American fans or Western critics, such as 'lack of chemistry' or 'unconvincing romantic lead', but they show more sympathy for Li's perceived 'asexual image' by pointing to Hollywood's restricted representation of interracial romance. Second, some fans do find a strong chemistry between Li and his female partners and argue that physical intimacy is not the only way to represent romance in the cinema. Third, many fans put aside Hollywood's compulsory heterosexual model and enjoy Li's interaction with women as buddies as well as his modest sexuality. The *IMDb* user comments show a more open-minded and diverse approach to Li's sexuality on Western screens and demonstrate the possibility of non-sexual representations of romance and male sexuality in the cinema.

However, as I argue throughout this chapter, when *IMDb* fans criticise the representations of interracial romance and Chinese male sexuality in Li's English-language films, they actually in some ways help to reinforce those stereotypes: for example, wanting him to kiss the female lead in order to get rid of the 'asexual' image, as if this were the only way to create chemistry and erotic feeling; or calling Li's sexuality 'boyish', 'innocent', or 'likable' which reflects a common strategy in defining an unthreatening sexuality for the sake of safeguarding the dominant categories (white/male/adult). Thus, on the one hand, Li's Western roles continue to perpetuate the 'asexual/emasculated Chinese male' myth, in the light of a deliberately-constructed discourse of race, gender and sexuality; on the other hand, he has started to introduce a soft, Eastern-flavoured sexuality into Western films, which seems to respond to what Dyer twenty-five years ago called a version of male sexuality 'that is not nasty and brutish, silly and pathetic, but varied, sensuous, langorous, warm and welcome' (1985: 42).

While risking the stigma of asexualisation, Li's Western performances nevertheless provide an alternative model of male sexuality, which has been gradually changing Western perceptions of Chinese men and probably Western notions of male sexuality as well, albeit in a less dramatic way. In fact, this process started with Bruce Lee's crossover persona of almost four decades ago, which similarly refused to exhibit an aggressive heterosexuality. In this regard, Louie might not be over-optimistic in declaring, '[I]t seems that Chinese masculinity has succeeded in becoming part of the global consciousness of masculinity' (2002: 154). However, Li's transnational star image is not only constructed in relation to the discourse of gender and sexuality; national identity is another notable issue often raised in the discussion of Li and other transnational kung fu stars, a topic to which I now turn in Chapter 7.

Notes

1. This discussion was sparked off by Steve Neale's article 'Masculinity as spectacle', published in *Screen* in 1983.
2. *Danny the Dog* portrays a father-son relationship between Li's Danny and Morgan Freeman's blind piano tuner, but it by no mean invites an erotic interpretation.
3. All the postings I quote in this chapter were accessed in October, 2006. All quotations preserve original punctuation and spelling.
4. Both quotes are from the *IMDB*, 'What is the Internet Movie Database?', http://imdb.com/help/show_leaf?about
5. Li confirms this rumour in an interview (with Val Sinckle at Medium Rare TV) by admitting that two versions of the ending were shot – one with a hug and one with a kiss and in the end the studio decided which to use. In the same interview, when asked how he felt about the downplaying of the romance between him and Aaliyah in *Romeo Must Die*, Li offered the interesting explanation that there was no room for physical romance, as the story takes place over a short time period.
6. See my discussion in Chapter 8.
7. There also exist some strong female images in the genre, but I do not think they have ever changed the male-dominated model. As Yvonne Tasker describes in her *Action and Adventure Cinema* (2004), these action heroines portrayed in the movies like *The Mummy* (Stephen Sommers, 1999), *Charlie's Angels* (2000), *Die Another Day* (Lee Tamahori, 2002) are physically strong and independent but emotionally vulnerable.
8. For relevant discussion, see Yvonne Tasker, 'Black buddies and white heroes', in her *Spectacular Bodies: Gender, Genre and the Action Cinema* (1993).

7
National hero/spectacular body: national and transnational identities

Desinicising transnational kung fu stars?

As many critics note, the construction of male images in Chinese-language films, especially in the male-dominated *wuxia* genre, has always been accompanied by a strong nationalist overtone. In his article discussing Chinese identity in Hong Kong cinema, David Desser explores the way in which the heroic, masculinised male body in martial arts films embodies, highlights and stabilises a Chinese nationalism and identity, thereby creating a global audience and solidifying kung fu stardom. Desser suggests that this muscular, nationalist masculinity, exemplified by Bruce Lee, Jackie Chan and Jet Li, is expressed in two noticeable ways. The first is by anti-Japanese/anti-imperialist sentiments, which contribute to the assertion of a pan-Chinese identity. The second is through a body of Chinese knowledge, most remarkably, the mastery of Chinese martial arts and other knowledge such as Chinese medicine, the motif of secret scrolls and the Shaolin Temple, which together mark a specific Chinese identity and are central to the masculinisation of the Chinese cinematic hero. According to Desser, by packaging muscular masculinity within specifically Chinese cultural dimensions (martial arts in particular), Hong Kong cinema successfully exported not only an image of China, but also masculinised Chinese men, the latter to some extent accounting for 'the Asianisation of Hollywood' (2005: 295).

Desser rightly reminds us that, across the Hong Kong careers of these three stars, 'Chineseness' strikingly exists as an indispensable part of their star persona and largely contributes to their star appeal. Chinese nationalism has been commonly seen as Bruce Lee's incontestable brand and legacy. Many critics comment that Lee uses his body as a location to build political ideals and ethnic pride. For example, Yuan Shu suggests, 'Bruce Lee appropriates nationalism as a matter of physical strength and connects the body with individual dignity, family responsibility and national honor' (2003: 54). Yvonne Tasker discerns that the discourses of masculinity and nationhood are in complex ways bound up together in Lee's star image. She argues, 'This assertion of nationalism is very clearly inscribed through the revelation of Lee's body' (1997: 318). Jackie Chan is regarded as picking up the overtones of nationalism in Lee's kung fu films. For Stephen Teo, 'Chan's movies in the '80s were practically alone in preserving Bruce Lee's tradition of kung fu as an instinctive but disciplined art linked to a cultural and national identity' (1997: 122). Steve Fore believes that Chan's longstanding popularity among Chinese audiences comes partly from his ability to build a screen and public persona over a network of traditional Chinese values and character traits (2001: 116). Gina Marchetti goes further to call Chan 'an emblem of authentic "Chineseness", chauvinistically celebrating the superiority of Chinese culture and the power of Chinese kung fu' (2001: 154).

However, Desser's claim, that the exportation of masculinised Chinese men accounts for 'the Asianisation of Hollywood', may be over-optimistic, for the transnational careers of these stars often suggest the precise opposite – their desinicisation. Indeed, the desinicisation of their Western screen persona has been a visible debate surrounding these transnational Chinese kung fu stars. Salient evidence here is provided by the fact that the nationalist theme often found in their Hong Kong work has been dissolved or replaced in their Hollywood films. Leon Hunt sees *Enter the Dragon* (1973), Lee's only English-language film, as 'something of a compromise' (1999: 90), in that Lee's super-patriot image and anticolonialism are decidedly toned down. Teo also notes in this film that 'the theme of Chinese pride and dignity vis-à-vis the prejudices and humiliation of foreigners' is almost untouched (1997: 117). He thus concludes that the film 'conveys the West's antipathy towards Lee's nationalism, and it shows a sullen and sulking Lee forced to submit to the West's perception of him as a mere action hero' (ibid.).

The success of Chan's crossover action comedies (*Rumble in the Bronx* [1995]; *Mr. Nice Guy* [Sammo Hung, 1997]) is often seen to have 'shifted away from his "Chineseness" in concession to the forces of late transnationalism' (Teo 2005: 197). Similarly, Shu suggests that Chan's success in the US should be attributed to his 'embracing of multiculturalism (2003: 51). For Shu, Chan's sense of 'multiculturalism' has nothing to do with nationalist consciousness or cultural diversity, but aims to accommodate the tastes and needs of the middle class worldwide. Chan's Hollywood films (for example, *Rush Hour* [1998]), by further downplaying the issues of racial politics and national identity and making everything comic, perfectly fit him into the multicultural rhetoric of the US.

If Lee's passionate nationalist persona is repressed in his Hollywood work and Chan is allocated the identity of a 'world citizen' for global circulation, is there a similar negation of masculine nationalism in Jet Li's transnational career? Though not as uncompromising as Lee's, nationalist sentiment has always underlined Li's Chinese-language films, from his early xenophobic role in *Born to Defense* (1986), through the patriotic patriarch figure in the Wong Fei-hung films, up to his modern-day incorruptible Mainland cop image in his later Hong Kong action films (*The Bodyguard from Beijing* [1994], for example). Since he moved to Hollywood, Li has played Chinese men from different parts of the world: Hong Konger (*Romeo Must Die* [2000]), mainland Chinese (*Kiss of the Dragon* [2001]), Taiwanese (*Cradle 2 the Grave* [2003]), Chinese-American (*The One* [2001]), and Chinese-European (*Danny the Dog* [2005]). Probably no other Chinese male star has played out such a flexible Chinese identity as Li has in his English-language films. However, Li's pan-Chinese identity bears no significance to narrative or characterisation in his English-language films. None of these films bothers to provide any more information on the background of Li's role than simply designating him as a Hong Konger, a Taiwanese or a mainland Chinese. His character in *Romeo Must Die* even speaks Mandarin, although he is supposed to be an ex-cop from Hong Kong.

Therefore, while Li's body becomes an omnipotent signifier of Chineseness, the richness and significance behind it are emptied and erased, so that Li's national/cultural identity in his English-language films appears to be rather vague and expendable. As Lo observes, 'Hong Kong stars in Hollywood films are generally portrayed either as foreigners from China or as generic Chinese whose cultural origin has no significance to the plot of the film' (2005: 134). By doing so, Chineseness in these films is 'converted into a given that can hardly be modified and vigorously reshaped', thus serving as a 'static ethnicity that American society assigns to the other in order to consolidate its dominant self' (ibid.). This indeed reflects a common practice in assimilating foreign actors in Hollywood; that is, using imported stars as all-purpose ethnic and eliminating their distinctive cultural characteristics.

If Li's English-language films have tried to label him with a simplified and static Chinese identity in order to rebuild him as a star in the West, the actor himself appeared to have made some effort to reclaim masculine nationalism by starring in Zhang Yimou's ambitious pan-Chinese production *Hero* (2002), Li's first Chinese-language film after he transferred to the West. As a film which carries a strong nationalist message but is aimed at the global market, *Hero* turned out to be a sensational hit both in China and around the world.¹ It has been commonly regarded as ushering in an era of Chinese blockbusters. This is particularly meaningful considering that before the North American release of *Hero* (2002) in 2004, only one of Li's English-language films (*The One*) had been released in mainland China. To a large extent, *Hero* can be seen as Li's first truly 'transnational' work, in which his transnational identity begins a vivid dialogue with his Chinese identity. In terms of Li's career trajectory, *Hero* is as important as his film debut in *Shaolin Temple* (1982), his Hong Kong debut in *Once Upon a Time in China* (1991) or his Hollywood debut in *Lethal Weapon 4* (1998). What particularly interests me about it, though, is how Li was repositioned in a nationalist narrative, after having gained a transnational identity by making films in the West, and the ways in which audiences from different cultural contexts read this complex national/transnational construction.

Hero: a romantic homecoming

Hero is 'a return to one of the oldest foundation myths for the country' (Berry and Farquhar 2006: 195) – the story of the king of Qin, who later became the first emperor in Chinese history (221–210 BC). The king of Qin is notorious for his cruelty because he had countless people killed in order to consolidate numerous small kingdoms into one 'unified' China. Jin Ke, a *xiake* from Yan, one of the kingdoms conquered by Qin, tried to assassinate him in order to repay the trust of the prince of Yan. He failed and was killed, but his ideal of valuing friendship and righteousness more than life has become an exemplar of Chinese heroism and inspired endless *wuxia* stories ever since. When Zhang Yimou came to adapt this old story for the big screen, he presented it in a number of new ways.

First, the well-known assassin Jin Ke is here displaced by a low-ranking Qin official called Nameless (Jet Li), whose forebears were actually from the kingdom of Zhao. In order to get close to the king of Qin (Chen Daoming), he claims that he has killed the king's three most feared enemies, Broken Sword (Tony Leung), Flying Snow (Maggie Cheung) and Long Sky (Donnie Yen). Second, the whole story is narrated through a conversation between Nameless and the king of Qin. Nameless kneels before the king and recounts how he has defeated these three assassins. The stories of their deaths are seen in flashback and revisited in three versions, from Nameless's lie to what the king surmises happened and finally the truth. Third, and probably the greatest departure from the original tale, Nameless finally gives up his mission to kill the king of Qin because he is persuaded by the king's belief (which is also Broken Sword's belief) that unifying the kingdoms by force can bring permanent peace, and therefore the assassins from other kingdoms should renounce their personal hatred for the good of the masses and the state. At the end of the film, Nameless is executed by a hail of arrows from the Qin army.

Talking about his motivation in making this film, Zhang Yimou says, 'I want Western audiences to see the Chinese ethos in *wuxia* films apart from their captivating martial arts . . . Many contemporary *wuxia* movies overemphasise fighting and they lack the Eastern spirit within' (quoted in *Cause* 2002). Indeed, the film shows an attempt to delve more deeply into Chinese culture, rather than focusing on a simple revenge plot and endless physical violence. On the one hand, *Hero* tries to explore the cultural connotations of Chinese martial arts, such as their close relationship with calligraphy, through depicting Nameless's struggle to understand two pieces of calligraphy written by Broken Sword, 'all under heaven' and 'sword' – meant to persuade Nameless to give up his assassination attempt for the supposed benefit of the majority. On the other hand, the film attempts to foreground the *xia* part of *wuxia*, the essence of 'the hero' in *wuxia* culture, namely, fighting and self-sacrifice for the sake of friendship and righteousness, through inventing two self-sacrificing storylines, those in which Long Sky and Flying Snow consign their lives to Nameless in order to assist him in his mission to assassinate the king and Nameless' belief that he is sacrificing his life for the peace of the masses.

While *Hero* provides a perfect vehicle for discussing a range of issues around the national and the transnational, in this chapter I intend to focus on the key issue of national/transnational identities and to examine the way in which they are constructed in the film in relation to transnational star image and cross-cultural reception. More specifically, I attempt to explore how Jet Li's Chinese identity and transnational identity are brought into conflict, negotiated and constructed by the film's audiences from different cultural contexts. Noticeably, Li's enthusiasm for *Hero*, as articulated publicly in various occasions, seems to have surpassed that for any other film he has made. For example, Li confesses, '*Hero* is a film of my dreams. When I read the script, I cried twice. In my 22-year career of making movies, this is the first script that made me weep' (quoted in Pollard, 15 August 2004). Li declares that he has no regrets about giving up a role in the hugely successful sci-fi action film *The Matrix* (1999) in order to make *Hero* (quoted in Hahn 2003). Even after the film was vehemently criticised for its political message, and Zhang Yimou started to deny his initial intention of using this film to ponder what it really means to be a hero, instead foregrounding his commercial and artistic considerations, Li still consistently reveres the heroism embodied in the film and insists that *Hero* is 'one of the most important action films' (ibid.). While Li's comments on the film could easily be seen as part of its marketing strategy, his passion for *Hero* is worth further discussion.

Before *Hero*'s official premiere in China, a three-hour documentary entitled *Cause* (Gan Lu 2002) was aired on television in mainland China and functioned as an effective promotion tool. This was made up of selected footage from 400 hours of material gathered during a four-year record of the production of the film. First-hand information provided by *Cause* helps us trace Li's emotional investment in the film, especially when it comes to a conversation between Li and Zhang Yimou at an early stage of filmmaking, which revolves around such important issues as definitions of the *wuxia* spirit, approaches to notions of heroism and discourses concerning the concept of Chinese culture. *Cause* propagates the view that the film has come about as a result of a primary creative dialogue conducted between director Zhang Yimou and star Jet Li. In other words, Li not only stars in this film, but contributes to the formation of its story and theme. This provides an opportunity to look at the way in which Li is posited (and posits himself) in a narrative of cultural nationalism and how this nationalist sentiment is closely related to Li's status as a returning crossover star.

For example, when Li is shown meeting Zhang for the first time in 2000 to discuss the idea of making *Hero*, Zhang tells Li, 'I hope this film can become one of the most important movies in your career. We will tell the audience what makes a person a real hero is not his excellent martial skills, but his unsurpassed insight' (quoted in *Cause*). Li apparently agrees with Zhang, although he speaks about the issue in a slightly different way:

> Only people born in the yellow earth will aspire to seek it [the essence of the hero]. Fighting does not attract us at all. The most alluring is the core of the *wuxia* spirit, namely the mutual respect and trust beyond life and death. For Chinese, the feeling of having a soul-mate touches the heart so intensely that you will try your best to do something for the other, even paying with your life, without thinking twice about it. (Ibid.)

The inescapable implication here is that such 'unsurpassed insight' and 'essence of the hero' cannot be found in the action films which Li made previously in Hollywood. When Zhang talks about why he has invited Li to take part in this film, he frankly admits that he hopes Li can attract a wide audience. 'One of the reasons why I cast Jet Li was because I needed a star, a big star, to lock in the Chinese market' (quoted in Eagan 2004: 18). On another occasion, he says that Li brought *Hero* into at least 2000

American cinemas (quoted in Zeng 2003: 10). By contrast, Li explains why he accepted the part as follows:

> Director Zhang wrote me a letter after sending me the screenplay. After I read it, I surely knew that I would present myself in this film. It is only because of one word, a Chinese word...'soul-mate'...He [Zhang] is such a passionate and unfettered person underneath his scholarly appearance. I know it is the blood born in the yellow earth that is running in his veins. (quoted in *Cause*)

It is interesting to note that although in the above quotations Zhang and Li seem to agree with each other, they actually present very different expectations of the film *Hero*. While Zhang harbours the ambition to exhibit the essentials of *wuxia* culture to Western audiences in order to change the latter's supposed fixed opinions of Chinese martial arts movies, Li is presented as eager to go back to 'the yellow earth', the symbol of the Chinese nation, by making a film which will please Chinese audiences. While Zhang is seemingly very practical-minded in his desire to use Li's star appeal to ensure box-office success at home and abroad, Li appears to be propelled by romantic feelings such as the notion of repaying someone for placing their trust in him (as Jin Ke did for the prince of Yan in the old story of assassinating the king of Qin). In short, Zhang Yimou – a director who won fame at Western film festivals in the 1980s but suffered a decline after the mid-1990s – intended to revive his popularity in the West through making a very Chinese *wuxia* film. By contrast, Jet Li – a star who built his initial *wuxia* hero image in the PRC in the early 1980s, then spent fifteen years making films in Hong Kong and America and had only recently returned to China – wanted to portray a homecoming *wuxia* hero whom Chinese audiences will both recognise and embrace and also to revitalise his star image, believed by many to have been tainted by his 'Orientalist' Hollywood roles.

Was Li's endeavour to reclaim his title as a 'Chinese hero' approved by audiences on both sides of the Pacific Ocean? In the rest of the chapter, by investigating mainland Chinese and American critical reviews of *Hero*, I attempt to reveal the complex construction of national and transnational identities within the film's cross-cultural reception and, above all, its significance to Jet Li as a transnational Chinese star.

Whose hero? Mainland Chinese and American critical responses to *Hero*

Hero is the most profitable film Li has ever made.[2] Despite *Hero*'s being surprisingly audience-friendly both in mainland China and the US, many mainland Chinese critics found fault with it. By contrast, it won nearly unanimous critical praise in the US. This is not the first time Li has stirred conflicting responses in different cultural contexts. His performance as a villain in *Lethal Weapon 4* won him many Western fans but was strongly attacked by Chinese audiences for its Orientalist representations. However, the critics' disagreements over *Hero* more intensely reveal the tensions and contradictions in a Chinese star's transnational career.

Accompanying the film's huge box-office success, heated discussion of it flooded newspapers, magazines and websites in the Mainland, from the end of 2002 to the beginning of 2003. Chinese films had not brought so many people into the cinema for a long time and the Chinese media had never given so much attention to a film before. On the one hand, watching *Hero* became a fashion amongst the Chinese public; on the other hand, websites and the press were deluged with angry condemnation and derision. Most notably, many film scholars, who usually keep some distance from low-brow popular culture, were also involved in this fervid debate. All of this constituted a unique and significant '*Hero* phenomenon' on the cultural map of contemporary China.

Amongst numerous critical reviews and articles, I focus on those published in influential film journals, such as *Film Art*, *Contemporary Cinema*, *Movie Review* and *Film Literature*.[3] The authors of these articles, who are either film scholars or senior film critics, may be labelled Chinese intellectuals, thus distinguishing them from film fans or ordinary audiences. Looking through about forty articles, one finds that, although there is a critical consensus regarding the film's artistic achievement, the critics agree that the expression of the *wuxia* spirit and the construction of the *wuxia* hero image in *Hero* are questionable and unsuccessful. While its contribution to the industrialisation and transnationalisation of Chinese cinema has been widely acknowledged, *Hero*'s ideological message and historical perspective are largely rejected.

Chinese critics strongly challenge what they see as the film's confounding of the *wuxia* spirit with power worship. They find it difficult to justify the notion of *tianxia* (all under heaven), as articulated by both the king and the assassins in the film. In their view, *tianxia* is a justification of despotism and a packaged hegemonic discourse. Shang Ke vehemently attacks 'the concept of hero from the standpoint of dignitary' conveyed by the film. He points out that the core of the *wuxia* dream lies in its anti-authoritarian stance, and hence 'in a *wuxia* film, letting the King of Qin instruct the assassin to submit to power in the name of peace is a big joke' (Shang and Gao 2003: 28), which represents 'the idea of a hero from the perspective of authority rather than that of the masses' (Shang and Gao 2002: 18).

Figure 9 Jet Li as Nameless in *Hero* (Zhang Yimou, 2002). (Source: Kobal Collection.)

Shang Ke's articles resonate strongly amongst many critics. While Hong Xiu (2004) is surprised that the biggest hegemonist in Chinese history is exalted as a great hero, Wang Dong (2003) laments that the spirit of resistance which is central to the story of assassinating the king of Qin has been represented as 'reactionary' in *Hero*. Guo Yuelian goes even further, calling *Hero* 'a story about slaves'. She writes, 'It is ironic that a group of people who are seeking enthrallment are worshiped as the heroes in this film . . . The film extols power politics in the name of national interest, astonishingly ignoring cultural diversity and individual rights' (2003: 9).

In the eyes of many Chinese critics, *Hero* is an anti-*wuxia wuxia* film. Consequently, the hero image which Li tries to build up in the film is regarded as unconvincing. Huang Shixian claims, 'the eulogium of "*tianxia*", "peace" and the imperialism of the king distorts and erases the heroism of Nameless which a hero assassinating the King of Qin should have, thereby frustrating the audiences' expectation of identifying with him' (2003: 19). Huang insists that *Hero* subverts the notion of *xia* and deconstructs the *wuxia* film genre. Similarly, Jia Leilei argues that Nameless's heroic assassination is transformed into a rite, that of surrendering to the king. 'The opposition between the righteous and the wicked, between *wuxia* hero and tyrant, which are fundamental to a *wuxia* film, is therefore dissolved' (2003: 22). Jia points out, 'Nameless's final resignation breaks his promise to Flying Snow and Long Sky, who offered their lives to him, not to mention betraying his mission of revenge for his family and country' (ibid. 21). Judged from this, Nameless has lost his raison d'être and dignity as a Chinese *xiake*. Jia concludes that what is killed and honourably buried at the end of *Hero* is not only the character Nameless, but the Chinese *wuxia* spirit.

For some of the above reasons, Li is accused by many Chinese critics of portraying a 'pseudo hero', 'weak hero', 'soulless hero' or 'mute hero'. Zhang Ying suggests that a *xiake* such as Nameless, who would sacrifice himself for so-called 'grand righteousness', the logic of the king, has been 'emptied and transformed into a hero without emotion or humanity' (2003: 15). Zhang claims, 'We prefer to see the heroes in Hong Kong *wuxia* films because they have vulnerable feelings and hearts' (ibid.). Interestingly, several critics draw comparisons between *Hero* and Li's *Swordsman II*, in order to demonstrate how the rousing *wuxia* spirit and charismatic *wuxia* hero in the latter are missing from the former.

As for Li's performance, it is commonly criticised for being overshadowed by excessive conceptualisation of the film. Zhou Xing (2003) suggests that Jet Li's Nameless should be a profound role but the film does not allow Li actually to play this character, instead letting him deliver such abstract concepts as *tianxia*. Zhang Hongqiu (2003) complains that Li stays impassive and cool from beginning to end, without demonstrating any ancient chivalrous ethos. Hai Yin bemoans the misuse of Li in the film: 'It is a pity that despite his good acting skills and heroic blood, Li finally becomes a pseudo hero' (2003: 13). In short, while the critics think that Zhang Yimou should be held chiefly responsible for this 'retrogressive *wuxia* film', Jet Li (and other co-stars) are seen as puppets who implement the director's ideas, and in so doing are deprived of personality and charisma. Shang Ke's nostalgic remark may represent a widespread disappointment at Li's long-awaited return to the Chinese screen: 'After watching *Hero*, I really miss Li's Wong Fei-hong, Fong Sai-yuk and Ling Hucong, even the monk Jue Yuan' (Shang and Gao 2002: 18).

Having examined Chinese critical reviews of *Hero*, let us now take a look at the response of American critics to the film. I draw here upon material to be found at *Rotten Tomatoes*, a film resource website based in the US. As stated on the website, 'With more than 127,000 titles and 644,000 review links in its ever-growing database, *Rotten Tomatoes* offers a fun and informative way to discover the critical reaction on movies from the nation's top print and online film critics'.[4] The *Rotten Tomatoes* reviews can therefore be considered to be an ideal indication of American critical response. There were altogether 183 reviews of *Hero* in *Rotten Tomatoes*' collection, mostly published around the time of the film's

American release in August and September 2004. With 173 fresh tomatoes (good reviews) and only 10 rotten tomatoes (bad reviews), *Hero* scored 95 per cent on the Tomatometer, but its average rating is 8.2/10. This means that while most critics apparently enjoyed the film, its overall quality, based on an average of individual critics' scores, is not as impressive as its popularity. A line representative of critical consensus offered under the title of the film neatly summarises *Hero*'s American appeal – 'a sumptuous movie that'll excite your eyes if not your heart'.

From around 150 critical reviews,[5] I discover that American critics hold many similar opinions on *Hero* to their Chinese counterparts regarding the film's unsurpassed visual style (this is indeed the film's common selling point both at home and in overseas markets), its lack of sentiment ('*Hero* is visually deep, but emotionally shallow' [Berardinelli, August 2004]; 'Ultimately, *Hero* is a film of images, not emotions. We remain distanced from the characters' [Gillespie, August 2004]), its total lack of character development ('Character development is almost non-existent, acting is mute' [Berardinelli, August 2004]). Yet, there are also noticeable dissimilarities between American and Chinese critical responses.

First, their critical tones are quite different. Chinese critics clearly do not feel that *Hero*'s visual strength can make up for its seriously problematic theme and unconvincing story. In contrast, despite their awareness of the film's numerous flaws, American critics unreservedly embrace its visual beauty and exalt the film as 'visual poetry', 'the most beautiful film ever made'. For example, Bill Clark declares that the film is proof positive that it is possible for a film to triumph on style alone, with the actual story taking a back seat. 'To watch *Hero* is to watch visual poetry . . . the film shows us the story through action, not dialogue . . . *Hero* is a visual, emotional and poetic masterpiece' (Clark, 23 December 2004). Susan Tavernetti refers to the controversy which *Hero* has stirred up in that it urges individual sacrifice for the greater good and veers from the historical record to propagate a legend of the emperor and the assassin, but she insists that the criticism does not alter one fact – 'No current release can rival the visual splendor and cinematic poetry of this historical epic' (27 August 2004).

Second, Chinese critics and American critics exhibit different concerns over the picture. Unlike Chinese critics, who attach great importance to genre conventions such as the embodiment of the *wuxia* spirit and the portrayal of the *wuxia* hero, American critics simply marvel at its stunning fight scenes while paying little attention to the philosophy of Chinese martial arts or the essential meaning of the term 'hero' which the film seeks to emphasise. As a consequence, compared with Chinese critics,

American critics feel much more comfortable with what the film has achieved – the innovative and captivating fight choreography – and much less disappointed by what the film does not seem to achieve – the exhibition of *wuxia* spirit and heroism, as the following quotations demonstrate:

> A film of unsurpassed beauty and inspired action choreography, Zhang Yimou's first stab into the world of balletic violence is as poignant and invigorating as any of the Fifth Generation Chinese dramas that preceded it . . . What's remarkable about the fight scenes in this film . . . is that they are presented in a largely nonlinear fashion, emphasizing the emotional weight of the choreography rather than the visceral impact of haphazard but cool-looking sequences of kicks and punches. (Gilchrist, 30 August 2004)

> Flying swordsmen, beautifully orchestrated cast-of-thousands shots, even a fight among carefully selected leaves of fall contribute to this breathtaking film . . . For those like me who lack the background to judge martial arts action, the stunning beauty of the film will be enough to captivate. (Lowerison, August 2004)

Intriguingly, though showing less interest in finding deep meanings in this *wuxia* film, some American critics give more sympathy to the film's attempt to inject philosophical and historical themes into a revenge story. Carla Meyer observes that the film tries to complement the action with a serious examination of the nature of heroism. 'Not as profound as it is pretty,' Meyer comments, '*Hero* nevertheless gives us something to ponder . . . *Hero* takes a wide-angle view of heroism, one in which dying for a lost cause is just as noble as killing for a winning one' (27 August 2004). Similarly, Connie Ogle acclaims, 'Despite jawdropping action, this glorious film thrives on a concept rare to martial-arts films, namely that violence may not always be the proper course, even when it is wielded in the name of justice' (August 2004).

The third main discrepancy between American and Chinese critics lies in their commentaries on Jet Li's performance. While almost none of the Chinese critics seem to be satisfied with Li's endeavour to rebuild his hero image in *Hero*, American critics speak highly of Li's presence in the film: 'Jet Li and all of the actors turn in great performances and blend well with the startling camerawork' (Cooper, 30 August 2004); 'I really enjoyed seeing Jet Li allowed to do what comes naturally. His performance is very good – and very subtle, as it should be' (McGranaghan, August 2004). These good reviews are not only in contrast with Chinese critical responses, but also with the constantly negative reviews of Li's Hollywood films in Western critical discourse (see Chapter 5).

While Chinese critics find that Li's Nameless is overshadowed by the charismatic heroes whom Li has portrayed in his previous Chinese *wuxia* films, American critics compare Nameless with Li's Hollywood roles, thereby coming to the conclusion that *Hero* is one of the best Jet Li films. For example, Peter Lowry compares *Hero* to Li's previous American films such as *Kiss of the Dragon* and *The One* and claims that it 'stands head and shoulders above them all, despite being made with likely smaller means' (22 August 2004). Jules Brenner remarks, 'Jet Li's composure is magnetic in a role far more compelling than his *Cradle 2 the Grave* appearance' (August 2004). In the eyes of American critics, after starring in a depressingly mediocre series of American films, Li 'makes a triumphant return' (Knight, August 2004) to a Chinese hero in this film, in contrast to Chinese critics' accusation that Li is humiliating the *wuxia* hero by portraying a cold, soulless assassin. Interestingly, while Chinese critics lament that Zhang Yimou has misused and abused Li's talents, American critics use Li's performance in *Hero* to justify their criticism of American filmmakers who do not know how to use him effectively.

National hero versus body of spectacle

From the above examination of mainland Chinese and American critical responses to *Hero* and Jet Li, we notice that critics from both countries are largely in agreement with each other in terms of artistic evaluation of the film, including its visual style, fight choreography, storyline and characterisation, but have different opinions on the moral, historical and political message of the film, and above all, on its portrayal of a *wuxia* hero. While most American critics seem to enjoy, even to revere the film, the majority of the Chinese critics tend to show their uncomfortable mistrust of it. I would like to suggest that Li's different identities – as a 'national hero' in China and as a 'body of spectacular' in the West – offer an effective way to understand this critical discrepancy. I also argue that Li's double identity as constructed in two critical discourses should be understood in relation to the wider cultural and cinematic context in each country.

First of all, consider this account from Zheng Xiaotian's 'Aesthetic value of the movie *Hero* and the view of the nation-state as supreme':

> Jet Li earned his overnight fame by starring in *Shaolin Temple* (1982). This influential film could be read from two perspectives. First, it is Scar Literature[6] in Chinese cinema. By developing a traditional moral narrative – both good and evil will be paid back one day – it largely lays to rest the traumatic memory of the Chinese masses during the post-Cultural Revolution period. Second, it is an 'Eastern national fable' in contemporary China. By displaying dizzying martial arts, it announces that China can catch up with the West not only through a process of modernisation, but also through its own great tradition, which greatly satisfies the national self-esteem of

Chinese people. By watching a Jet Li film, Chinese audiences find a perfect chance to give full vent to their long-repressed emotion. (2004: 22)

Zheng suggests that for mainland Chinese audiences, Li functions as an 'avenger' in the domestic context and an 'Eastern hero' in the transnational context. In his view, although Li has worked in Hollywood for a few years, he continues to exist in the imagination of mainland Chinese audiences as a 'national hero', and becomes the main selling point of *Hero*. Zhang concludes that, without Li functioning as an effective symbol of the 'Eastern national myth', *Hero* would have failed at the box office in the Mainland. Zheng's illuminating comments reveal Li's identity as a 'national hero' which to a large extent constitutes his star appeal among home audiences. It is precisely the inappropriate positioning of this 'national hero' in a controversial nationalist narrative that frustrated the expectations of *Hero*'s Chinese critics.

Earlier in this chapter, I discussed *Cause*, a documentary which suggests that *Hero* should be understood as an expression of Chinese nationalist thinking, as implied in the statements made by Jet Li and Zhang Yimou throughout the documentary. With a national hero used to embody nationalist ideas, no wonder Chinese critics tend to read *Hero* as a cinema of national parable. It is nothing new for the *wuxia* narrative to be woven into the discourse of nationalism and, as mentioned at the beginning of this chapter, male heroes have often been used to build a national myth in *wuxia* film. However, mainland Chinese intellectuals' *wuxia* imagination and their view of Li as a 'national hero' are certainly different from the way in which Bruce Lee's cultural nationalism is identified by overseas Chinese or Jackie Chan's nationalist image is read by Hong Kong audiences, and hence deserve further discussion in relation to specific social and political circumstances.

If, as Benedict Anderson (1983) insightfully points out, the nation is an imagined political community, China has been imagined in a quite different way since the 1990s. Before 1990, in mainland China, the concept of the nation was mainly interpreted through official ideology. With the advent of the 1990s, and with a rising consumer culture and the ubiquitous dominance of the media, popular culture, outside state indoctrination, started to play an increasingly important role in constructing a secular Chinese nationalism. In this sense, Zhang Xudong remarks, in China in the 1990s, 'a discerned overlap between the state and the mass cultural reinvention of the nation indicated a broader and more complicated space for national imaginings than that which is sanctioned by state discourse' (1998: 111). Chinese intellectuals' involvement in the process of re-imaging the nation can be clearly observed from the academic re-evaluation of the place of the *wuxia* genre and its cultural significance.

Popular *wuxia* novels had traditionally been dismissed by Chinese academics for their supposed lack of merit, but the situation began to change in 1992, when Beijing University scholar Chen Pinyuan published his groundbreaking book *The Xiake Dream of Chinese Literati for Centuries: Genre Studies of Wuxia Novels* – the first systematic and theoretical engagement with the *wuxia* genre and the '*wuxia* complex' to be found among Chinese intellectuals. Two years later, Beijing Normal University professor Wang Yichuang listed Jin Yong, the well-known Hong Kong *wuxia* author, among the ten best novelists in modern Chinese literature, igniting a heated debate concerning the nature and value of *wuxia* culture within academia and in the media. In their controversial book *China's Road under the Shadow of Globalisation*, Wang Xiaodong, Pang Ling and Song Qiang (1999) similarly eulogise the *wuxia* spirit, but from a different perspective. They propose a cultural strategy to fight against American hegemony and to deal with a perceived cultural crisis in contemporary China. This strategy is to build a form of nationalism which resembles the *wuxia* spirit. According to them, if China fails to construct this nationalist *wuxia* spirit so as to dispel the spiritual desolation of the Chinese people, it will prevent China from surviving in the modern world, not to mention establishing and maintaining a powerful country (Wang, Pang and Song 1999). It is intriguing that Chinese intellectuals started to identify with traditional *wuxia* culture and ground their pronouncements on Chinese nationalism firmly within the *wuxia* imagination in the early 1990s.

As discussed above, Zheng Xiaoping sees Li's *Shaolin Temple* as 'Scar Literature' in cinema. In a similar vein, Chinese intellectuals' fascination with *wuxia* culture can partly be seen as a reflection of their dissatisfaction with domestic politics and their longing for freedom and justice after the Tiananmen tragedy in June 1989. If Li's 'avenger' image in *Shaolin Temple* (1982) was extremely popular in early 1980s' China because it embodies the theme of 'good defeats evil', thus largely laying to rest the traumatic memory of the Chinese masses after the Cultural Revolution, it is no surprise, twenty years later, to see Li's Nameless being disdained as a shameful submission to autocracy. Nameless renounces his mission of assassinating the king of Qin and changes from a determined resister against despotism into a resolute defender of it; this flies in the face of Chinese critics' expectations of Jet Li as an angry and uncompromising avenger. Chris Berry incisively relates Chinese intellectuals' rejection of the film to their political sensibility: 'With *Hero*, not only is submission to the patriarch lauded, but the audience too, is encouraged to understand the strategic necessity of his cruelty and brutality. For all the rethinking of the Tiananmen Democracy Movement and its viability, few from that era are prepared to turn their thinking around quite this far' (2003: 24).

The yearning for *wuxia* culture among the Chinese intelligentsia can also be explained as a response to an underlying worry alongside the blessings of China's economic and cultural globalisation – how to build an independent, unique cultural identity and counteract the homogenising global ideology of Westernisation and Americanisation. *Wuxia* narrative, the most indigenous Chinese cultural form, offers a forceful means to build up an independent and dignified male subjectivity, thus defying any threat to Chinese national and cultural identity. *Hero*, however, promotes a new hegemonic discourse – 'all under heaven', which, as many Chinese critics discern, is the symbol of the current global order dominated by the US, while the greater righteousness which Nameless finally accepts alludes to the undoubted righteousness of anti-terrorism (Zhang 2003:13). In the view of Chinese critics, the seemingly open-minded Nameless actually bends to the logic of power politics, namely, the will to erase difference by violence. Exactly in this sense, *Hero* is interpreted as flattery, toadying to the US, and Li is regarded as a 'dead hero'.

In conclusion, in contemporary China, the *wuxia* narrative can be absorbed as a reflection of cultural nationalism, but in the meantime it also functions as a spiritual resistance to the officially-constructed discourse of nationalism and globalisation. Li, as a 'national hero', is expected to be a firm resister to both domestic authoritarianism and Western hegemony, thus preserving an unbroken Chinese masculinity and appeasing the anxiety among Chinese intellectuals in the face of internal oppression and external threat. However, when Li chooses to forsake his previous *wuxia* hero image and sacrifice himself for the greater power as Nameless, in the eyes of Chinese critics, he is unable to continue functioning as a 'national hero', and to address their complex nationalist sentiment shot through with the spirit of resistance. Despite his intention to reclaim his title as a Chinese hero, Li inadvertently exposes himself to ideological appropriation in a problematic retelling of the story of the nation's birth, and thus suffers from intensive condemnation from Chinese critics.

If Chinese critics' rejection of Li's Nameless is understandable in the light of China's particular political and cultural context, it is somewhat surprising to see that American critics are not disturbed by the film's obvious nationalist, even totalitarian message, but instead praise it as one of the best Jet Li films. It is instructive to read the following quotation from *Rotten Tomatoes*' collection of *Hero* reviews:

> I don't think it's going too far to say that the martial-arts film has virtually become today's musical, especially as the former genre has become reliant on effects and wire-work to a degree that any pretence of realism has long since vanished. And with the highly stylized approach of breaking set-pieces up in terms of design and color, the line between the musical and the martial-arts film is even further blurred ... Regardless of its underlying ideology, *Hero* is, first and foremost, a nonstop excursion into *style*; that, I believe, is its raison d'être ... this is a film that exists for its sheer visual beauty – and in that, it's nothing short of breathtaking. Style rules here; thematic concerns and plot are just the icing on the cake. (Hanke, 1 September 2004)

Martial arts performance in Chinese *wuxia* films has often been likened to dance in Hollywood musicals. Accordingly, Jackie Chan and Jet Li are frequently mentioned in the same breath as Fred Astaire or Gene Kelly. The author of this review goes further when he defines martial arts films as 'today's musical'. This review is thus representative in that it precisely summarises how *Hero* has been received among US critics and audiences, that is, as a cinema of spectacle. This observation is supported by a number of American critical reviews. James Berardinelli believes that 'few who see *Hero* will be there for its thematic content. They will be there to enjoy the spectacle of wire-fu battles' (August 2004). Josh Bell suggests, 'In spite of people who want to view it as an example of a martial arts movie with depth, it's actually best appreciated on the surface' (26 August 2004). Shelly Kraicer applies the phrase directly in her review: 'Rather than narrative tout court, *Hero* offers pleasures more rarified, more abstract and profound: a cinema of spectacle allied to a philosophical program . . . Spectacle, rather than storytelling, teaches *Hero*'s philosophy' (2003: 9). With this kind of horizon of expectation, American critics could hardly have been more satisfied with what the film offers – incredibly beautiful scenery, dreamlike fight sequences, masterly use of colour and highly innovative cinematography. For a cinema of spectacle, convincing stories, strong characterisation or thoughtful themes are not as important as visual excitement.

Just as *Hero* is read as a cinema of spectacle, Jet Li exists in American critical discourse mainly as a body of spectacle, an identity built in the West since his first Hollywood film *Lethal Weapon 4*, in which he is offered as 'dynamic spectacle' (Hunt 2003: 158). American critics' warm reviews of Li may not have been earned by the quality of his performance (a common belief is that Li benefits greatly from a sterling supporting cast), nor because of his convincing portrayal of a hero (in fact, US critics hardly even mention this point), but are based on a comparison made with Li in a number of disappointing Hollywood action film productions, and above all, on the match between him as a body of spectacle and *Hero* as cinema of spectacle.

The view of Li as a body of spectacle is closely related to a wider action tradition in which the male body is displayed as spectacular, as well as the fact that Chinese martial arts films have always been consumed in America in terms of their visual spectacle embodied in the physical performance of kung fu stars. Leon Hunt (2003) sees Chinese martial arts films as an example of what Tom Gunning calls the 'cinema of attractions', along with Hollywood musicals and the theme-park spectacle of contemporary Hollywood blockbusters. In Gunning's definition, the 'cinema of attractions' refers to an earlier conception of cinema which 'sees cinema less as a way of telling stories than as a way of presenting a series of views to an audience, fascinating because of their illusory power . . . and exoticism' (1990: 57). Indeed, Chinese martial arts films, consumed in the US mainly as a 'cinema of attractions', always incite visual curiosity and supply 'pleasure through an exciting spectacle' (ibid. 58). Kung fu stars, with their marvellous martial arts skills, undoubtedly become the centre of this spectacle. Unlike the early kung fu films imported to the US in the 1970s, which are often dismissed as 'chopsocky', *Hero*, alongside Ang Lee's *Crouching Tiger, Hidden Dragon* (2000), has been called 'martial art-house film' in English-language critical discourse. However, with its breathtaking natural beauty and stylish fight choreography, it does not change so much as reinforce the rhetoric that American audiences go to watch a Chinese martial arts film for its visual spectacle. Jet Li, as a symbol of spectacle, in the view of American critics, finds his best place in this ravishing visual feast offered by a most Chinese genre film.

The film's desinicised American marketing also contributes to the reading of *Hero* as a cinema of spectacle and Li as a body of spectacle. The film's American release came two years after its premiere in China. Reportedly, this unexpected delay was due to squabbles over whether to recut it for US audiences or to dub the film in English; Miramax was concerned about its nationalist message, which had already stirred up controversy in China, and felt that it might be too Asian for American audiences to understand. As a result, promotional campaigns in America studiously avoided all traces of *Hero*'s Chineseness. For example, both on US theatrical movie posters and for the DVD release, *Hero* is advertised as 'a visually stunning martial arts epic' and paraded under the banner, 'Quentin Tarantino presents'. It is also branded as 'Jet Li's *Hero*' but no reference is made to Li's status as a Chinese star; the only two of the actor's previous titles to be name-checked are the Hollywood hits *Cradle 2 The Grave* and *Romeo Must Die*. The promotion of 'a visually stunning martial arts epic' and 'Jet Li's *Hero*' foregrounds visual spectacle as the picture's main appeal, given the generic expectations of a 'martial arts epic' and

Jet Li's star image as a symbol of spectacle in Hollywood. As Geoff King suggests, spectacle 'tends to translate more easily than other dimensions across cultural and language boundaries' (2001: 2). Despite the lack of emotional resonance or a deep understanding of the film, American critics are conquered by the exotic spectacle provided by *Hero* and its star, Jet Li.

Conclusion

According to the documentary *Cause*, when the filming of *Hero* came to an end, Jet Li wrote on his sword the line 'A hero plays a hero'. Clearly, the first hero refers to Li himself and the second one is his character Nameless, and this sentence could be understood as meaning 'a transnational hero plays a national hero'. Li's confident declaration offers this rhetoric: after many years away from his homeland and half a decade away from the *wuxia* genre that made him a star, Li returns in glory from the West, having conquered Hollywood and now appears in a big *wuxia* epic to reclaim his title as a Chinese hero. However, this romantic homecoming is fraught with instability and conflict, as seen in the critical responses to *Hero* in mainland China and America. Chinese critics' rejection of Nameless and the notion of the hero whom he embodies makes Li's glorious return less triumphant, just as he has never really conquered Hollywood, given the overwhelmingly negative Western reviews of his Hollywood performances. Li's predicament, as indicated in *Hero*'s transcultural reception, offers a metaphorical commentary on the careers of transnational stars: although they have had to make countless compromises in order to survive in a new land, it is equally difficult for them to go back to their mother culture. They constantly have to negotiate their new identity with the old one in order to be accepted by both sides.

In spite of this dilemma, Li's career as a transnational Chinese star is promising, in that it is strategically built upon the transnational imagination of audiences from different cultural contexts. Though Li's reconstruction of the *wuxia* hero was seriously criticised by Chinese commentators, his supposed 'triumphant return to the Chinese film industry' in the Western view makes *Hero* commercially and critically the most successful Jet Li film to date in the US, thereby offering enough reason for him to remain in Hollywood, not just as a Hollywood action star, but as a transnational star with strong career flexibility and huge commercial potential in world markets. At the same time, while Li has always received poor reviews from Western critics, his perceived 'conquest of Hollywood' among Chinese audiences and *Hero*'s huge success in the US have meant that the Chinese film industry views him as the key star to break the US market, and this has brought him many opportunities to star in important projects and work with prestigious Chinese directors in subsequent years. Li's filmmaking in each cultural and industrial context supports his work in other contexts. To sum up the argument of this chapter, while *Hero* marks Li's controversial 'return' to the nationalist politics of the PRC after a long absence making movies elsewhere, it was also the ideal vehicle for consolidating his status as a transnational Chinese movie star. By making *Hero*, Li achieved what a transnational star always dreams of achieving, coming home while remaining in Hollywood.

Finally, I would like once again to emphasise that Li's national identity and transnational identity are not clear-cut and mutually exclusive. I have argued that the different opinions on the film *Hero* and Jet Li's character and performance in it among mainland Chinese critics and American critics partly result from Jet Li's double identity – as a 'national hero' for the former and a symbol of spectacle for the later. This 'national hero' and 'symbol of spectacle' may be taken as suming up Li's national and transnational identity respectively. However, these two identities are interdependent and transferable. 'National hero' marks Li's Chinese identity, but it also constitutes part of his transnational appeal – Li does to some extent exist in Hollywood as a Chinese kung fu hero, apart from existing as a more universal symbol of spectacle. Conversely, when Chinese directors capitalise on Li's image as a 'national hero', they also try to make good use of Li's physical capability in order to attract a broader audience, as Zhang Yimou has done with *Hero*. Hence, in a globalising era there is no such thing as a fixed national or transnational identity. If there ever existed a 'transnational Chineseness', it should have been built upon a constant negotiation between changing national and transnational identities. It is in this contradictory and at times conflicting process that Li's appeal as a transnational Chinese movie star resides.

Notes

1. *Hero* set a new record in the domestic market and an equally extraordinary record in East and Southeast Asia. It also enjoyed the second-biggest US opening of all time for a foreign-language film and became the second-highest grossing Chinese film in the US.
2. This record seems to have been rewritten by Li's later film, *The Warlords* (2007), at least for its Asian box office.
3. I collected these research materials during my research trip to Shanghai in the summer of 2004. They include ten reviews in *Xin dianying* (New cinema) (9, 2002; 10, 2002; 11, 2003), four in *Dianying yishu* (Film art) (2, 2003), five in *Dangdai dianying* (Contemporary cinema) (2, 2003), eight *in Zhongguo wenyijia*

(Culture and art of China) (4, 2003), four in *Dianying wenxue* (Film literature) (2, 2003), three in *Yingshi yishu* (Movie and television art) (3, 2003), two in *Dianying xinzuo* (New films) (2, 2003), one in *Dianying pingjie* (Movie review and introduction) (4, 2003), one in *Dazhong dianying* (Popular cinema) (4, 2003), one in *Dianying pinglun* (Movie review) (3, 2003), one in *Kexue zhongguoren* (Scientific Chinese) (2003).

4. Quoted from *Rotten Tomatoes*, 'About Rotten Tomatoes', http://uk.rotten tomatoes.com/pages/about
5. All articles were accessed in October, 2007. Since then, some reviews may have been removed. As a result, the pages are sometimes unavailable for some of the links given here.
6. Scar Literature is a famous literary movement popular at the end of the 1970s and the beginning of the 1980s in mainland China. These novels focus on the 'injured generation' after the Cultural Revolution, who vent their anger and hidden grief in public.

8
Borderless icon: star construction and Internet fandom

In the last six chapters, I have examined Jet Li's star image constructed in the reception of his on-screen personae among audiences from different cultural locations. Yet, as many academic writings elaborate (Dyer 1979; Allen and Gomery 1985; Geraghty 2000), it is the duality of the image that makes a star, a duality composed of on-screen performance and off-screen existence, publicised through gossip columns, celebrity interviews, fan magazines/sites/clubs, and so on. The discourses around stars therefore include not only how their films are promoted and consumed, but also how their life stories are distributed and received. The circulation of information concerning the star's 'real' life, according to Christine Geraghty (2000: 189), should not be seen as secondary to the film itself, in that it plays a crucial role in understanding the meanings of the star. This final chapter focuses on Li's star image as constructed in his off-screen personality.

Despite his various striking titles, such as 'the first film star in the PRC', 'Hong Kong/Asian kung fu superstar' and 'Hollywood star', Li is famous for his low-profile off-screen life,[1] especially compared with his Hong Kong or Hollywood counterparts. Li's early stardom in mainland China in the 1980s was characterised by a trait common in socialist stardom, that is, that a star's off-screen life did not receive much media attention and stars might establish their stardom entirely through their professional life,[2] but Li's extra-filmic life also remained inaccessible in his Hong Kong career in the early 1990s. The Hong Kong media noticed that Li purposely avoided talking about his private life in public, as a headline in *Ming Bao* (3 October 1994) – 'Jet Li's Three Secrets: Family, Money and Romance' – indicates. What Li says in various interviews always focuses on his films, his experience in martial arts and in recent years his Buddhist beliefs and charity work. Probably on this basis, Leon Hunt sees Li as a 'diffident celebrity', 'as though "Jet Li" does not exist outside his films and martial arts' (2003: 141).

However, it would be wrong to assume that Li has no off-screen personality, or that this personality has not been mediated by his publicity. During his thirty-year screen career, Li's name has hardly ever appeared in gossip columns. He was once divorced, but it was little reported. All the public is aware of is Li's long-term relationship with his current wife, Nina, and that he is a happy father of four daughters (two from his first marriage). Li's personal image outside film seems wholly stable, yet mysterious, which, to some extent, is due to the media construction.

In terms of the construction of a star's image, two kinds of industry strategies have been identified – one emphasising conflict, and the other coherence, between the glamorous screen presence and the private life of the star. In his seminal publication *Stars*, Richard Dyer (1979) proposes that there are always contradictions and tensions between the screen image and the star's personal life. Judith Mayne takes this argument further – that the very appeal of stardom comes from 'constant reinvention, the dissolution of contraries, the embrace of wildly opposing terms' (1993: 138). Some critics, however, discern another strategy for constructing the star image: that is, to highlight an integration, consistency and mutual support between the screen persona and the private life. Exploring the early years of the film star system in America, Richard DeCordova (1991) observes that a performer's off-screen life was mostly represented as a reflection of his or her on-screen roles. Summing up the above two viewpoints, Paul McDonald suggests that the public image of on-screen appearances and the publicised private image of the star's off-screen image either 'seamlessly correspond to one another, or antagonistically conflict' (1995: 83).

Both strategies of juxtaposing the picture personality with the off-stage image take effect only when they work on the audience. As Geraghty puts it, in the construction of the celebrity, 'it is the audience's access to and celebration of intimate information from a variety of texts and sources which are important here' (2000: 189). This audience is best typified by the fan, 'whose knowledge comes from a wide variety of sources and who reworks the material in the interests of working through contradictory questions of identity' (ibid. 185). As a special category of audience who are equally interested in the star's on-screen and off-screen presence, the role of fans in the complex process of forming and transforming the star's persona should not be underestimated. However, while many writers analyse how the star's off-screen personality is contrived and controlled by the industry through various publicity methods, not much attention has been paid to date to the fans' active participation in star-making. Over the years, fans have formed their own networks of communication, such as fan magazines and fan clubs, to circulate star discourse. Nowadays, with the popularising of the Internet, the discourses of stardom have proliferated at an amazing speed. It may be said that the fan site has replaced the fan magazine to become a central location for fans to engage with the star and rework materials as a basis for their own social identification and cultural exchanges.

In the previous chapters, I have looked at *Dingding Studio*, a mainland Chinese *wuxia* fan site (Chapter 3) and *The Internet Movie Database*, one of the biggest movie fan sites in the world (Chapter 6). In this chapter, my focus is *The Official Jet Li Website*. Among numerous fan sites, the star's official website deserves particular attention. Stars' official websites may appear to be different from one another, yet they share a common function of satisfying fans' curiosity by feeding them with anecdotes from behind the scenes or related to the star's personal life, which are supposedly more authoritative than information available in the entertainment press or on other unofficial fan sites. Another important function of the official website is for the star to communicate with fans directly and to help maintain the fanbase. Many stars visit their official websites regularly and leave messages for their fans. In short, the official website serves as another effective arena within which stars can build up their image.

The Official Jet Li Website is just such an arena, where rich discourses of stardom and fandom are constantly emerging. Li's low-key public presence, referred to earlier, predictably increases the appeal of his official website to his fans, in that it offers Li's own remarks about his life, films and outlook, as he promises in his on-site greetings. Given the lack of similar information in other media, for example, the press or television, *The Official Jet Li Website* stands out as an important place for Li to construct his off-screen image and for his fans to engage with this construction. In what follows, I examine the construction of Li's star persona through his publicity on his official website and the ways in which his fans make sense of this publicity, thereby effectively participating in the process of star-making.

Everybody can get close to Jet: an introduction to *The Official Jet Li Website*

Initiated by a team from Design Reactor[3] (later on taken over by *Rotten Tomatoes*), *The Official Jet Li Website* tries to distinguish itself from other stars' official sites by emphasising the idea of 'learning'. In its opening message of March 1999, Li, calling himself 'your fellow student', writes, 'I hope that this website will not only satisfy your curiosity, but also awaken your thirst for new knowledge. Take responsibility for your own learning.

Keep striving – there is always more to learn'. It seems that Li (and the people who created and maintain this website) seek to give the website a more serious look, in place of the entertaining or commercial appearance that usually characterises fan sites. This effort may be discerned from its unostentatious layout, its total rejection of commercial advertisements and the educative tone permeating Li's presentation of his life story and film career as well as his answers to fans' questions. A fan's comment indicates the site's style and character: 'I want to say that this is one of the best "fan" sites I've ever seen. None of that silly celebrity stuff, but plenty of food for thought. Great!' (Trish Maunder, 4 August 1999).[4]

The website is divided into two general categories: 'Jet Li' and 'Fans'. Under 'Jet Li', five sections – 'life', 'body', 'work', 'spirit', and 'mind' – respectively address Li's personal life, identity as a martial artist, film career, identity as a Buddhist and the website itself. Each section consists of 'essays', 'articles', 'biography/*wushu*-ography/filmography', 'questions' and 'media'. While the 'essays' are allegedly written by Li himself, the 'articles' and 'media' reflect Li's media exposure. In the 'questions' section, Li answers questions put to him in fan mails or chats during the period 1999–2002 (this was restarted in July 2007). The original website was presented solely in English but a Chinese version, which is simply the translation of its English version, has been added since mid-2007 to accommodate the increasing flow of Chinese-speaking visitors. A bilingual official website nicely reflects Li's status as a transnational Chinese star.

The other part of the website – 'Fans' – is the most lively section and the one to which I give most prominence. It comprises a long-running fan forum and the star's blog established in December 2006. On 26 March 2007 (the day I researched the site for this study), the site had 176,936 registered users, a much higher number of visitors, and a total of 138,096 postings had been published. The forum was divided into nine sub-forums in nine different languages (Chinese, English, French, German, Japanese, Polish, Russian, Hmong and Filipino) to accommodate the diverse language backgrounds of fans. This indicates Li's far-ranging fanbase, although more than ninety per cent of the postings were in the English forum. In its current version, the language forums have been reduced to three – 'English', 'Chinese' and 'Japanese' – but the English forum remains as the most active. Who, then, are these Jet Li fans on *The Official Jet Li Website*?

I would like to follow two threads to help trace the fans' identities. The first thread comes from a Chinese fan's suggestion that Li could open his blog on a popular Chinese website (JetLiang, 23 December 2006). Webmaster Mark responded by saying, 'It is not a viable solution' because

75% of the traffic on jetli.com comes from North America and Chinese fans make up only 1.7% of the traffic on this website (23 December 2006). It is a little surprising that the people visiting Li's official website are mostly North American fans, when Li has such a huge following in Hong Kong, Taiwan, mainland China and other Asian countries. Apart from the difficulty for the fans in these places of having to use English, the fact that Li had mainly made movies in the West between 1998 and 2006 probably led to a faster increase of the fanbase from the West than from Asia.

The second thread, entitled the 'First Jet Li experience' (FongSaiYuk319, 31 March 2005), attests to this proposition. Asked 'What was your first Jet Li movie?' and 'How old were you when you first watched it?', most of the fans answered that they were in their twenties and had begun to know Li and become Jet Li fans because of the appeal of his roles in *Lethal Weapon 4* (1998), *Romeo Must Die* (2000) or *Kiss of the Dragon* (2001), not his earlier Chinese work. Therefore, we can roughly identify Jet Li fans on his official website as a new generation of North American fans, distinguishing them from the fans of the 1990s from Hong Kong, East Asia and South-East Asia who were enthralled by Li's new *wuxia* masterpieces in the early 1990s and also from the fans of the 1980s from mainland China who were impressed by Li's debut in *Shaolin Temple* (1982).

What kind of off-screen image has been constructed through Li's publicity, in particular at *The Official Jet Li Website*? Is it consistent with, or contrary to, Li's on-screen persona? How does the interaction between Li and his fans help to establish and reinforce his star persona? Emphasising two-way responses and construction, my research focuses on four sections of the website: namely, fan mails and answers; Li's essays; the fan forum; and the blog entries and discussions. Reading through thousands of messages at Li's official website, what strikes me is that three key issues – authenticity, sexuality and cultural identity – which are often raised in the reception of Li's on-screen image and have been discussed in detail in the previous chapters, continue to be noticeable in, and sometimes dominate, the construction of Li's off-screen personality.

I am a normal guy . . .

As discussed in Chapter 2, the authenticity of his or her martial arts skills is one of the main criteria to define a martial arts star. It is also the subject of a long-standing debate surrounding Li's screen persona, among (mainly Western) critics and fans alike. Andy Willis points out that 'the idea that martial-arts performers can actually perform the actions we see them do on screen is their mark of authenticity' (2004: 182). Yet the intervention of cinematic technology and application of stunt doubles in martial arts films make it difficult to judge the authenticity of on-screen fighting. Therefore, 'a great deal of effort is spent in the creation of an authentic persona through other related media texts' (ibid. 183). This observation is true in terms of the off-screen constructions of Bruce Lee, Jackie Chan, or Stephen Seagal, who all try to deliver the same message – that the star can do as well in reality as on screen, if not better. But Li's case is certainly more complicated. While Li's status as a five-times national martial arts champion provides incontestable proof of his authentic martial arts skills, Li shows less interest in authenticating his hero image through publicity. Moreover, he often adopts an opposite strategy of deconstructing the authenticity of the martial arts star by distancing himself from the on-screen superhero image and instead emphasising his ordinariness in real life.

It is almost a cliché for Li to confess in interviews, 'I am not a hero', 'I am just a regular guy, boring. . .', 'He is a lot stronger than me', and so on. Similar statements can be found easily in his replies to fan letters on his official website. For example, concerning a fan's question 'What do you think is the biggest misconception the public has about you' (Dragonfly Dreams, 13 October 2001), Li answers: "Most people think that I'm this tough, strong martial artist but in reality I'm just a normal guy who likes to stay at home (whenever I have a chance)'. Unlike Bruce Lee, who is narcissistic towards his own body, Li always underplays the significance of physical prowess. In his reply to a fan's curiosity as to whether there is a specific reason for his unwillingness to 'expose' himself (literally, to take off his shirt) (Marc A, 12 August 2002), Li attributes this to purely physical reasons: 'I'm short, only 5'7" and my muscles don't really look that great. I think that if you looked at 10 people walking down the street, probably half of them have a better physique than mine'. Asked how he adjusts to the fame-induced changes in his life (Chill Imperial, 10 November 2000), Li gives a complete account of his general attitude, namely, thinking of himself as a normal guy.

> The most important thing, one that many people in the business overlook when they plunge head-in, is never to lose sight of yourself, never to forget who you are. I always think of myself as just a normal guy. A guy who was lucky enough to experience what he did, to have trained in martial arts at such a young age, to have, by chance, landed a career in the movie business and made the choices he did. Anyone can become a star, if the circumstances are right. And this star label, in my opinion, too often distorts the real being beneath – the human being, the person who is just like any other.[5]

As the above responses to fan mail indicate, Li tries to dismiss both the fetishism of his body/physical capability and the worship of his star status, by understating his identity as a 'real' martial artist and highlighting his drawbacks as a normal guy in off-screen life. In this respect, Li is an interesting contrast to Jackie Chan, who often plays an unlikely hero on screen, but tries to reclaim his hero status by disseminating a Jackie Chan myth through his off-screen publicity, that is, 'Chan does all the stunts by himself' or 'only Chan can do this stunt'. How do the fans react to Li's refusal to authenticate his star persona? First of all, compare the following postings. 'I like Jet because of the sense of integrity and honour he seems to project both on and off screen' (Taiji Kid, 5 September 2006); 'He's humble, respectful and honest' (AJ, 1 September 2006); 'JET's honest, wholesome and generous in a kick-ass sort of way . . . JET doesn't let his ego get in the way, either' (JRS, 30 August 2006); 'His manner in all the interviews and speeches I've seen is so sincere and polite – attentive and focused, intense but not overbearing' (Flagday, 30 August 2006).

In the praise from these fans, 'honest', 'humble' and 'sincere' emerge as the key words characterising Li's personality, which, to a large extent, results from his self-deprecating attitude in off-screen publicity. Given his established 'superhero' screen image and undisputed titles as martial arts champion, Li's claim to be ordinary, on the one hand, adds an unpretentious quality to his star persona and constructs Li as a sincere celebrity, and on the other hand, shortens the distance between Li and his fans. While stars' private lives as disseminated in the media often seem to be beyond the imagination of ordinary people, Li's confessing to be a 'normal guy' who loves to stay at home whenever he can sets him apart from most stars and presents him to fans as more like a familiar person, as the following message shows: 'I find out the man is a real worthy man, not perfect but a man whose beliefs and practices are honourable and then I'm totally hooked . . . I really feel like he's a fellow traveler' (Flagday, 30 August 2006). Furthermore, the embrace of Li's 'normality' speaks to a fantasy within fans: a normal guy/woman like me could be as successful as Li. JRS admits that Li appeals to him because 'he's humble and he's achieved the "American Dream" (for lack of better wording) – from rags to riches through good and honest hard work' (30 August 2006).

Although Li's off-screen 'normality' seemingly contradicts his screen image, it by no means denies it. The emphasis on the ordinariness of the celebrity is not the same as the ordinariness of what Jon Dovey (2000) calls the 'ordinary celebrity'. In the context of television docusoaps which make celebrities out of ordinary people, Dovey argues that celebrity has become accessible to anyone as the distance between the famous and the rest has been diminished. The construction of Li's stardom clearly does not work in this way. Li takes the side of ordinary people, yet he stands as an ideal man incorporating the ordinary and the extraordinary at once and is a hero whom his fans look up to. As Dyer (1979) proposes, the extreme ambiguity/contradiction of the phenomenon of stardom lies between the star-as-ordinary and the star-as-special and the combination of ordinariness and specialness is always a key element of stardom.

Li's statement, 'I am a normal guy', can therefore be regarded as a clever strategy of building his star persona on the contrast between the glamorous film world and the ordinary domestic life of the star. It is through this strategy that the superhero and the humble man, two seemingly contradictory images, are perfectly unified in Li's star personality. The responses of Jet Li's fans to this construction are a good indication of the mechanism of star discourses, that is, to preserve at once the accessibility and inaccessibility of the star. To put it simply, he is normal whilst he is also inaccessible. Li's 'superhero-next-door' image clearly reveals how the star persona is carefully constructed in relation to ordinariness and specialness, accessibility and inaccessibility. A posting from Mark, the webmaster of *The Official Jet Li Website*, interestingly attests to this construction:

> He's just a normal guy. He just happens to have a bazillion fans all across the world. But other than that, fairly normal.
>
> Oh and he's a super crazy amazing wushu athlete. But still – just a normal guy.
>
> Oh, and ridiculously rich and wealthy. But deep down . . . totally normal.
> And a huge movie star with over 35 films under his belt . . . but aside from that he's pretty much just your average joe. (5 February 2006)

Shy man versus sex icon

As discussed in previous chapters, sexuality is always an intriguing topic in terms of Li's screen persona. Since Li's shy – or, from another point of view, sexless – screen presence seems immutable, even a little mysterious for his audiences, both the media and his fans, in the West and East, take a great deal of interest in it. For example, Hong Kong's entertainment reporters were keen to uncover the reasons why Li held back in all romantic scenes after his breakthrough role as Wong Fei-hung in *Once Upon a Time in China* (1991) (*Wenhui* 1994a, 1994b). And Western critics, as discussed in Chapter 6, often complain about the lack of chemistry between Li and the female lead, viewing Li as 'sexually unattractive'. The task of handling this kind of curiosity and criticism thus becomes inevitable for Li in his off-screen publicity. Li's most notable strategy is to frankly admit that he is not good at expressing romantic feeling and to skillfully relate this to his shy, introverted personality. For instance, a few times in his blog, Li mentions his experiences in filming romantic scenes:

> To me, filming a love sequence is much harder than filming action sequences. I remember that when I was filming *Swordsman II* in 1992 there was a love scene. I remember Tsui Hark put a lot of effort into filming that scene and tried many ways to capture it. But no matter how hard he tried, he couldn't capture the scene he wanted. He said to me, 'How come filming you in a romantic scene feels like you are being assaulted?' (5 February 2007)

> As I've said before, I'm horrible at filming love scenes . . . The best actors in the world are probably very flexible expressing themselves emotionally and able to forget 'the self' when acting. But I am certainly not one of them. When I read the script [of *The Warlords* (2007)] and came upon the lines 'they could no longer hold back their true feelings, they embraced passionately. Fervently kissing, stroking and removing clothes . . .' I started sweating profusely because I had no idea how to do this! Later on, the director and I had conversations to discuss how to handle this sequence. But I still feel uncomfortable with it. I'm not sure how I'll pass this test tonight (1 February 2007).[6]

While highlighting his 'discomfort' in filming romantic scenes, Li at the same time tries to attribute this discomfort to his 'real' personality: his shyness, which he explains as a result of his conservative, puritanical upbringing. To the question 'Why do your characters avoid physical intimacy?' (Cassaundra Huskey, 3 April 2002), Li responds:

> To be honest, I'm not a very good actor – especially when it comes to romantic scenes. Even in my real life I'm not that familiar with these situations. I think the writers or directors know me and realize that it is a part of my personality and a limitation of my abilities. I think they create characters with that in mind.

Moreover, Li uses episodes in his life to reinforce the perception of his shy personality. Regarding another question, 'How does Jet Li meet girls, actually, how did Jet Li have the courage to speak to Nina when you guys first met?' (Angel, 13 October 2001), Li simply answers, 'I was pretty shy, so I did a lot of talking with my eyes.'

Apart from foregrounding his off-screen image as a shy man who always feels nervous with women and has little experience in dealing with them, Li also portrays himself as a traditional, responsible 'family man' by telling some off-screen stories on his website. The most famous one is that he turned down the main role in *Crouching Tiger, Hidden Dragon* (2001), which proved a huge success later, because he had promised to stay with his pregnant wife, Nina.

How do Jet Li fans on his official website respond to Li's shy personality, constructed as it is both on-screen and off-screen? Generally speaking, most fans regard it as part of Li's unique star persona and express their appreciation of it, as seen from the following postings: 'I love . . . his shyness as well. The way he behaves in front of a girl is cool' (Goodgoingish, 31 August 2006); 'It is very cute that a love scene is what makes Li uncomfortable' (Christicr4, 4 February 2007). For some fans, it is precisely this 'shyness' that makes Li attractive. JRS suggests that Li is such a babe-magnet 'for the simple reason that he's "forbidden fruit". You can see, but you can't have!' (12 September 2006). Elsewhere, JRS writes, 'lack-of-kissing will always leave his fans longing! Cool!' (13 August 2006). Spookie's comment confirms this 'longing' for Li in a love scene: 'An interesting trivia question for Jet Li fans – Jet Li has always turned down love scenes in the movies he has done but in what movie did he do his first actual love scene?' (4 February 2007) Similarly, Flagday thinks that Li should remain an on-screen virgin as 'the SEXIEST screen romances NEVER had anything but smouldering glances, surreptitious touching and suggestive after-scenes and most without nudity' (17 May 2005).

The most intriguing finding from my research on *The Official Jet Li Website* is that, in spite of his shy screen presence and the complaint about his 'lack of sexuality' often heard in Western critical discourse, many fans see Li as a sex icon. A poll on 'What makes Jet so unique and compelling to you?" was conducted in the forum (KL70, 30 August 2006). Stargazer234 (female) admits frankly, 'I'm very shallow, I just like JET's appearance. You know eyes, lips, smile, hair, etc.' (30 August 2006); GATSU (male) writes, 'I'm saying this in a non-gay way, but his boyish charm combined with his resolute persona are what I find appealing' (30 August 2006); Flagday (7 September 2006) confesses that although she likes Jackie Chan very much, he just does not have the 'sex appeal' which she feels Li has. While Li seems to appeal to both genders, female fans in particular find Li very sexy.[7] Some female fans in the forum are keen on discussing Li's charismatic effect on women by talking about his killer smile, his artless but appealing demeanour towards women, and his unconsummated romantic ventures.

Concerned that his marketing experts were not paying enough attention to women fans, who make up a huge section of the Jet Li market at present as well as a potential target market, one female fan, Flagday, a frequent visitor to the site, designed a poll entitled 'Marketing Jet . . . who are you?'

(7 September 2006). Of the fans who voted, 55 per cent were male fans and 45 per cent female fans. Interestingly, while there were no male fans aged over 40 in this poll, 20 per cent of the female fans were 'beautifully over 40'. A thread posted in the forum entitled 'The cover story – why use pink?' supports Flagday's assumption. Gene Ching, associate publisher of *Kung Fu Magazine* explains why they unusually used pink for Jet's cover image – 'Jet has a lot of female fans (including my own wife). So we figured just this once, we'd use a little pink, just for the ladies' (11 September 2006).

In fact, since his screen debut in the early 1980s, Li has always been admired by female fans from China, other Asian countries such as Japan and Korea, and all over the world. Anecdotes about Li's popularity with female fans can be found in the press. For example, it was reported (and confirmed by Li on his official website) that one young girl continued to send letters to Li for eight years. According to Xiao Zi (1984), after the release of *Shaolin Temple* in 1982, Li spent almost six months replying to letters containing marriage proposals. *Kuai Bao* (28 March 1995) reports that a female fan pursued Li backstage in a cinema in Shanghai and even injured herself in order to express her adoration to Li. Li's universal appeal to female audiences is further confirmed by the following fact: although *People* and *E!Online* often reach different verdicts on who the sexiest men are (probably because the former has a majority of middle-aged female readers while the voters on the latter are mostly younger women), Li was lucky enough to enter both lists – he was voted the 'Sexiest Foreign Man' by *People* magazine in 1998 and also ranked among the '25 All-American Sexiest Men in 2001' at *E!Online*.

Given that women are believed to be not particularly interested in action cinema, Li's popularity among female fans is worth noting. Moreover, why do his fans take views opposed to those of his Western critics of Li's shy or sexless screen image? Even though critics are usually more fastidious and fans more devoted, another important reason may be that fans pay a similar amount of attention to Li's on-screen and off-screen presence whilst critics mainly focus on his screen persona. For critics, 'no kisses' is simply evidence of Li's 'asexual' screen image. But fans tend to conflate Li's screen character and his 'publicised' private life and interpret 'no kisses' as a manifestation of Li's 'real' personality. When Goodgoingish asks, 'I've never seen JET kissing a girl in any film I've watched. What do you think the reason is? Is he saving his kisses for NINA?' (13 August 2006) JRS replies, 'I think it goes against his grain . . . goes against his beliefs' (13 August 2006). Stargazer234 writes, 'Well the JETster must do something right to make Nina wait for him for 10 years and to have 2 kids with him' (8 July 2006). Obviously, the consistent construction of the off-screen Li as a shy but reliable 'family man' contributes to his sexual appeal among many fans, especially female fans, as Daniels Girl's comment neatly summarises: 'You definitely ARE SEXY, always have been and even more so in the future because of your ability to keep yourself dedicated to your family and friends. That is EXTREMELY SEXY' (25 April 2007).

It seems that Li's star image satisfies the need of many female fans to 'have a good man to look up to', thereby making him sexy and appealing to them. This, according to John Fiske (1992), could be called a 'compensatory fantasy' for female fans who take the consumption of Li as an opportunity to find meaning in their social identities, experiences and desires. Unlike the apparent contradiction of the superhero/normal guy construction, when it comes to sexuality, Li's publicised private image seamlessly corresponds to his on-screen persona, thereby effectively blurring the line between the cinematic world and reality, at least as far as the fan is concerned. This coherent construction of the star persona not only makes up for Li's weakness in performing romantic scenes but also successfully constructs the persona of the 'shy but reliable man' as Li's unique trademark, which has won him immense female loyalty all around the world.

Non-violence versus violence

If the two aspects of Li's publicity discussed above are more or less common strategies of star-making, another noticeable off-screen construction into which Li seems to have put much effort has more to do with his specific identity as a transnational Chinese kung fu/action star; he strives to redeem his on-screen 'fighter' image by acting as an advocate of non-violence off screen. From very early on in his career, Li always declared that his aim in making films is to popularise Chinese martial arts as a wholesome form of athletics (Yang 1991), thereby clearly locating himself in the category of martial arts star. Yet, in recent years, this aim seems to have been slightly modified, in that Li has been trying to foreground the cultural rather than the physical side of the martial arts. In interviews and on his website, Li frequently claims that the deeper meaning of *wu* (martial or military) in Chinese is actually to stop fighting, and takes pains to promote the idea that 'violence is not the only solution'. On the one hand, Li made three so-called 'anti-violence' films (*Hero*, 2002; *Danny the Dog*, 2005; *Fearless*, 2006) in a row in order to realise his intention of using the form of violence to deliver his belief in non-violence. On the

Figure 10 Jet Li as legendary Chinese martial artist Huo Yuanjia in *Fearless* (Ronny Yu, 2006). (Source: Kobal Collection.)

other hand, Li often mentions his wish to retire from the action genre (for example, announcing that *Fearless* would be his last martial arts film) and expresses his aversion to the violent characters he plays in Hollywood (for example, talking about his reluctance to take on his role in *War* [2007] due to its extreme violence).

Other noticeable aspects of Li's recent publicity in relation to his advocacy of 'non-violence' are his confession that he is a pious Buddhist and his devotion to charitable work. In December 2006, Li announced the launch of the Jet Li One Foundation, an international relief agency. It is funded by the gift of one yuan/dollar a month from each supporter and aims at helping those affected by natural disasters. Since then, *The Official Jet Li Website* has become an ideal place for Li to pursue his philanthropic mission. On the website's homepage, the logo and the link of the Jet Li One Foundation are in the foreground, and half of the news headlines are about Li's charity activities. Soon after the inauguration of the One Foundation, Li started his blog and called on his fans to support this project. The One Foundation is undoubtedly a central topic in Li's blog, as he appears to relate everything else to it. For example, Li foregrounds his shy personality and enthusiasm for philanthropic work at the same time in the following blog entry written during the filming of *The Warlords*:

> At the start of every film production I really don't know how to break the ice with the lead actress. I'm more introverted and don't know how to communicate well with them. But for the sake of the foundation, I broke my 26-year-long habit and took the initiative myself to ask Jinglei to help spread news about the foundation on her blog. I hear that Jinglei has the most viewed blog in China. (29 December 2006)

It is not difficult to sense that Li has been trying in all possible ways to distinguish himself from his screen character, who must often fight and kill. While his reasons for drawing this distinction, such as his Buddhist world views, are manifold, the most important one may be that he is unhappy with the screen image built up for him in his English-language films since his crossover to the West – no longer a hero but a killer, not a martial artist but a fighting machine.

In *Heavenly Bodies* (1986), Richard Dyer pays attention to the stars' revolt against the lack of control they felt within the Hollywood industry and under capitalism. He cites Paul Robeson and Marilyn Monroe as protesters encapsulating the situation of black people and women, respectively. Similarly, Li's off-screen activities, whether they are to promote the philosophical and cultural meaning of Chinese martial arts, namely, non-violence, or to construct his off-screen image as a person who cares about public welfare, indicate Li's struggle and negotiation with Hollywood's racist discourse and commercial oppression. More specifically, unsatisfied with the fact that only his physical capability has been exploited and showcased on Western screens, and with being labelled as one among many martial arts performers, Li tries to reclaim his cultural identity within a film industry that tends to blot out any stamp of culture or individuality, especially where imported film talents are concerned. Thus, off-screen construction of himself as a tireless advocate of non-violence or a zealous philanthropist reveals to a large extent Li's intention to challenge Hollywood's stereotypical preconception that Chinese kung fu stars are people who only know how to fight. Again, how do Jet Li fans respond to Li's endeavours to mediate his star persona?

Corresponding with Li's publicised dislike of violence, fans often raise such topics in the forum as 'Jet Li in a movie without fighting', 'Jet says he will give up martial arts films', or 'Should Jet try comedy/drama for a future movie?' Three typical attitudes can be discerned in fans' discussions: down-to-earth, sceptical and sympathetic. The fans with a down-to-earth attitude think it would be good to see Li in different types of role, but that it is unrealistic for Li to want to give up action films altogether. Paulwardphoto feels that 'if he does do a movie without martial arts in it, it will be a commercial failure' (22 March 2006); Nightbird points out that martial arts are what Li brings to a film: 'There are plenty of actors.

Few great martial artists who do films. Jet's cutting out his best asset' (22 March 2006). The sceptical fans see it as ironic, or simply a promotional gimmick that while Li has always been an advocate of non-violence, he still participates in movies where violence is the only solution: 'I don't even listen to him anymore on the subject of retiring or whatever" (Dragonseeker, 22 September 2006); 'This makes me wonder why Jet Li even accepted the role in the first place if it contradicts everything he has ever preached for . . . He must've been offered a ton of money to do the film' (Gqxsensazn, 24 April 2006).

Yet, in spite of the above scepticism/criticism, most fans show sympathy for this contradiction embodied in Li's star persona, as the following postings demonstrate. 'As a martial artist who also embraces Buddhism etc. he no doubt feels strongly about the image of *wushu* and martial arts and that particular aspect of misrepresenting the spirit of the art' (thatguymark, 24 September 2006); 'I feel like Jet is caught in the middle of his beliefs, philosophy and his career . . . He wants people to know and understand the real meaning behind the Martial Arts and at the same time he has to feed his family . . ." (Solar Stanze, 22 September 2006). In fan discourse, the contradiction of violence/non-violence in Li's personality is read as an inevitable consequence of the conflicts between marketability and the cultural significance of Chinese martial arts, between Li's two identities as a martial artist and a Buddhist and between his unstable positions as a Chinese superstar and a minority actor in Hollywood.

As to Li's devotion to philanthropy (the One Foundation in particular), the fans respond ardently and unanimously. JRS comments:

> When people follow celebrities and their 'lives,' it's remarkable how many fall by the wayside. They're too busy partying, breaking the law, doing drugs and sleeping around like whores . . . It is such a breath of fresh air to hear about celebrities who want to give back to society . . . to use their status for the good of others . . . JET, you continue to nurture my belief that there is still some humanity left in our world! (5 February 2007)

Longhu writes, 'Jet Li, you are my hero. In a world which lacks good role models, I admire you for starting the foundation and using your talent for good causes that serve all people!' (17 March 2007). Apart from complimenting Li on his kindness and compassion, the fans show their support for him by donating to the One Foundation, helping to extend the One Foundation project in their own way, or offering suggestions for developing the project.

It is not rare for a martial artist to be a Buddhist – monks are often trained in fighting skills in temples (such as the famous Shaolin Temple)

– but it is quite unusual for an established martial arts star like Li to openly challenge his own screen image with his off-screen identities. It is nothing new to hear that a star is doing charity work, but it is surprising that Li puts it at the centre of his life,[8] and that his fans are so zealously involved in his philanthropic endeavour. The case of the One Foundation proves yet again that the meanings of the 'film star' have gone beyond the entertainment industry and entered the sphere of political and social life. This is especially noteworthy within the Chinese context as, throughout Chinese film history, stars have usually had poor reputations in the domain of morality. For his fans, Li is certainly not merely a fighter or a killer as depicted on the Western screen, but also a martial artist, Buddhist, cultural defender and moral model. This multiple star persona is built upon the construction of on-screen violence and off-screen anti-violence, while at the same time the contradiction thus entailed has been neatly turned into part of Li's star appeal.

Conclusion

In the preceding pages I have investigated three key aspects of Li's off-screen star construction. While Li's superhero image is widely recognised, off screen Li reveals himself as a normal guy who became a martial arts star by luck; while he is arguably the best on-screen fighter alive in both the East or the West, Li tries his best to distance himself from his film roles by tirelessly stressing that 'violence is not the only solution'; while shyness defines most of Li's screen characters, he always relates this trait to his 'real' personality as a shy man who devotes himself to his wife alone. As a consequence, in the eyes of his fans, Jet Li stands as an 'ordinary hero', a 'moral model' and a 'sex icon' (the last of these, mostly among female fans). This makes it possible to argue that Li's star image is built upon both consistency and contradiction between his on-screen and off-screen personalities. Through this very correspondence and conflict, such opposed terms as 'superhero/normal guy', 'shy man/sex idol', and 'fighter/preacher of non-violence' are perfectly reconciled in Li and help to constitute his multiple meanings for a new generation of North American Jet Li fans.

Furthermore, I would like to suggest that, if in the past film stars were mainly produced by the industry and the media, nowadays stars themselves and their fans are playing increasingly significant roles in star-making, as my research on *The Official Jet Li Website* evinces. This change could be largely attributed to the fact that the Internet is becoming the most powerful medium in contemporary life. The Internet (his official website in particular) provides Li with a new space, outside institutionally produced media, to construct his star image. Through essays, a personal blog and replies to fan mails, Li exposes his life and ideas to the public in the way he wants, thereby limiting industry intervention and media mediation. In this sense, the Internet empowers stars by giving them the opportunity to take more control over their own images.

Fans are empowered as well. The official website and other Internet sites offer fans access to the star's off-screen life to an extent not possible with previous channels of mass communication. They also encourage interplay between fans and the star as well as communication among fans. By publishing postings on the forum, writing mail to the star or participating in fan activities, fans gain a more visible existence in the formation and dissemination of the star image. In his book on the star system, Paul McDonald argues that the World Wide Web has changed the star system through 'decentring the production of star discourses' (2000: 114). Indeed, alongside the film industry and the media, and with the help of the Internet, the authorship of star discourses is opened up to the stars themselves as well as to their fans.

As seen in the above discussion, fans, aware of the artificiality of the star image and having a comprehensive knowledge of the star's on-screen and off-screen presence, can decide more independently the meanings of the star and are therefore more actively involved in star-making. This undoubtedly challenges the commercial and legal control of star identities on which the system has always depended (McDonald 2000). However, as McDonald insightfully points out elsewhere, 'Star discourse on the internet displays a continuing engagement with the stars as revered others and commercial identities' (2003: 43). In some ways, fan readings of Li as an 'ordinary hero', 'sex idol' and 'moral model' reveal that a new medium is still 'maintaining and perpetuating an old media realm of discourse' (ibid. 43). Nevertheless, without this vigorous Internet fandom, Li's image as a transnational Chinese star would not have been fully established.

Notes

1. This habit seems to have changed somewhat since Li announced the launch of the One Foundation at the end of 2006. He now appears on talk shows and press interviews much more frequently than before, mainly to promote the One Foundation.
2. For further discussion on this see my article 'Vulnerable Chinese stars: from *xizi* to film worker' in *Companion to Chinese Cinema* (Yu 2012).
3. A company based in Berkeley, California.
4. All postings quoted in this chapter were accessed in January 2007.

5. Jet Li, reply to Chill's letter, at the address above.
6. His co-star Xu Jinglei attests to Li's words by writing 'Jet Li is an actor who is the most hesitant person to perform romantic scenes that I have ever met. He made me feel very embarrassed as well' in her own blog. (Xu's blog, 2 March 2007, http://blog.sina.com.cn/xujinglei). Another of Li's female co-stars, Zhang Ziyi, reveals in an interview, 'Maybe Jet has a block or something, because he can't do love scenes in front of the camera' (Quoted in Eagan, 2004: 19).
7. This finding is supported by an interview with *AllHipHop Alternatives*. When the host tells Li that many women think he is sexy, Li shows his confusion: 'In Asia, a lot of actors and actresses are sexier than me. I don't know why, but in the States, suddenly Jet Li becomes sexy! I really don't know!' (quoted in Nand 2006).
8. Almost all publicity about Jet Li in recent years has centred on his One Foundation project. Reportedly, Li turned down several film roles in 2008 in order to devote himself to philanthropy.

Conclusion

This book has discussed how Jet Li films and his star image are received and interpreted by audiences in culturally and historically specific contexts. By tracing Li's changing meanings from a Chinese *wuxia* hero to a transnational kung fu star, it aims to reveal the ways in which star image is constructed and transformed within transcultural contexts in relation to the discourses of gender, sexuality, genre, race, nation and cultural identity. The present research is by no means an exhaustive examination of Jet Li's films or his audiences. Instead it looks at representative Jet Li films – the new *wuxia* films of the early 1990s, crossover English-language films made since 1998, and his first transnational Chinese blockbuster in the new century – as examples of Li's border-crossing career. However, this does not imply that Li's other films, such as his earlier *Shaolin Temple* films made in mainland China in the 1980s, or his action films made in Hong Kong between 1994 and 1998, do not deserve separate critical attention. Similarly, although the audience categories I have chosen to investigate in this book are representative in their own ways, they are certainly not the only audiences who could have been examined. My intention has been to use them as samples to look at a wider reception picture and to discuss a range of issues emerging from the cross-cultural reception of Li's star image.

As seen in the seven case studies above, Li's star persona, as perceived by different audiences, revolves around a range of diverse images, such as martial artist/actor; the heterosexual/the homosexual; father's son/mother's boy; charismatic villain/unattractive hero; sexless man/sexy idol; national image/symbol of spectacle; superhero/normal guy; fighter/preacher of non-violence. On the one hand, these seemingly contradictory images/representations point to the tensions and conflicts between film production and consumption, between critics and fans, and between the national and the transnational. On the other hand, I agree with Tim Bergfelder's comments (made with reference to the early transnational movie star Anna May Wong), that the fact that the star image is bound up in contradictions and conflicting cultural perceptions is 'not an obstacle, however, but part of the success of the image' (2004: 72). Indeed, while Li's meanings within these dichotomous categories have been continuously constructed, negotiated and modified by audiences from different cultural locations and historical eras, Li's enduring star appeal across cultural and national boundaries owes a good deal to a star persona capable of accommodating different and often conflicting interpretations. It is these diverse readings that construct the changing meanings of a transnational star and reveal the unstable and indefinite nature of transnational stardom.

What exactly, then, are Li's changing meanings? The Chinese reception of Li's new *wuxia* films undoubtedly apprehends Li as a 'hero', embodied in the elegant kung fu master Wong Fei-hung, the unruly, adventurous but ultimately patriarchal figure Ling Hucong and the comic 'mother's boy' Fong Sai-yuk. In the global responses to his transnational roles, however, Li has mainly been defined as a 'fighter' behind a range of masks, such as villain, killer, childlike man, asexual man or 'dead', 'soulless' hero. It thus becomes possible to suggest that in order to become a transnational star, Li's identity as a genuine martial artist has worked to upstage other aspects of his star persona. Yet, it would be too simplistic to describe Li's transnational star image as 'Orientalist', 'distorted' or 'catering to the West', as some audiences (mostly Chinese) tend to complain. Such claims first of all risk essentialising the star image which Li built up in his Chinese-language films. After all, *wuxia* hero, despite its layers of meanings, is only one among many labels attached to Li. Moreover, as the above case studies demonstrate, 'villain' (Chapter 5), 'childlike man' (Chapter 5), 'asexual male' (Chapter 6), and even 'dead hero' (Chapter 7), should not simply be viewed as negative images, but also as an ongoing refashioning of Li's star persona. The significant change in Li's star persona accompanying his career trajectory from a Hong Kong kung fu superstar to a transnational Chinese star may sometimes indicate loss and failure, but may also lead to opportunities and success, as Li's post-*Hero* career seems to suggest.

Li's transnational career since *Hero* (2002) has developed in intriguing ways. As discussed in Chapter 7, though he has made films in Western film studios since 1998, it was not until *Hero*, his first Chinese-language film since he transferred to the West and a sensational hit both in China and overseas, that Li's status as a transnational star was finally consolidated. Following the success of this film (in Asia in 2002 and in the West in 2004), Li started to travel between different film industries (mainland China/Hong Kong/Hollywood/France) to make films in both Chinese and English: for example, *Danny the Dog* (2005), which teams up Li and French producer Luc Besson again, four years after their first collaboration in *Kiss of the Dragon* (2001); *Fearless* (2006), made in Hong Kong and advertised as Li's last kung fu film; the star-studded war epic *The Warlords* (2007), directed by the acclaimed Hong Kong director Peter Chan; the long-awaited Hollywood blockbuster *The Forbidden Kingdom* (Rob Minkoof, 2008), in which Li co-stars with Jackie Chan; and a mainland China production *Ocean Heaven* (Xiao Lu Xue, 2010), in which Li plays a non-action role for the first time. Among the Jet Li films released after *Hero*, the critically and commercially successful *Fearless* and *The Warlords* deserve particular attention, not only because they, together with *Hero* and a few other films, inaugurated a trend of transnational Chinese martial art-house blockbusters and thus took the transnationalisation of Chinese cinema to a new stage of development, but also because they finally realised Li's triumphant return to the Chinese film industry, a goal many contemporary transnational stars strive to achieve, thus ushering in another golden age in Li's career.

Fearless was listed as the top Chinese-language film at the Hong Kong box office in 2006. Although the gross profit has not surpassed Li's previous *wuxia* films made in the 1990s, it was the first time that a Jet Li film had become Hong Kong's box office champion. *Fearless* secured third place at mainland China's box office and was the highest grossing Chinese-language film in Taipei in 2006. It also did well in North America. *The Warlords*, which remarkably grossed over RMB300 million from audiences in Greater China and South-East Asian countries, earned more money than any other Chinese-language film in 2007, and made director Peter Chan only the second Chinese director after Zhang Yimou to become a member of 'the RMB200 million club' at mainland China's box office.

Apart from their extraordinary commercial success, both films are critically acclaimed. After *Fearless* brought Li the first acting award of his career – Best Actor at the 2007 Hong Kong Film Critics Awards – as well as nominations for Best Actor at the Hong Kong Film Awards and China's Hundred Flowers Awards, he won Best Actor at the prestigious Hong Kong Film Awards in 2008 for his role in *The Warlords*. Li was the third kung fu star, after Hui Ying-Lung and Sammo Hung, to receive this award, and the first since 1989. These nominations and awards are significant given that Li has long been criticised for his 'lack of acting skills' and that kung fu stars in general are hardly ever given credit for their acting ability. Speaking highly of the director, the actors and the localised film-making which is characteristic of *The Warlords*, the Hong Kong critic Lie

Fu claims that the film is 'the most successful period martial arts film in the last twenty years' and 'the most successful example of Hong Kong film breaking into the Mainland market' (quoted in Liu, 19 December 2007). He comments that Li 'perfectly portrays a complex, half-villain character and subtly delivers the character's psychological conflict, thus completing the transformation from a star to an actor' (ibid.).

Lie is obviously thinking here of a star as somebody possessing fewer acting skills than an actor. His assertion is arguable, but it is suggestive, in terms of Li's changing meanings. The first case study of this book argues that, by foregrounding martial arts as a powerful tool with which to portray his character in *Once Upon a Time in China* (1991), Li started to develop a new approach to martial arts performance, namely, impersonation in fighting, thus completing the transformation from a martial arts performer to a star. It took sixteen years of continued effort after that for Li to syncretise martial arts and acting (not always with success) and in *The Warlords* he seems finally to do so, as implied in Lie's comments on Li's transformation from a star to an actor. Interestingly, of the three leading actors in *The Warlords*, Li has the least *wu xi* (fighting performance), though the other two (Andy Lau and Takeshi Kaneshiro) are not usually thought of as action/martial arts stars. *The Warlords*, together with *Danny the Dog* and *Fearless*, shows Li's constant intention to highlight fighting as acting and his new endeavour to place greater emphasis on his non-fighting performance.

From *Hero* in 2002 to *The Warlords* in 2007, Li was the highest earning star in a Chinese-language film, and is currently one of the highest paid Chinese stars in Hollywood (alongside Jackie Chan). These facts make Li's transnational film journey appear more prosperous, and less frustrating, than it was earlier in his crossover career. The same can be said of Jackie Chan, another transnational kung fu star. Like Li, Chan has shifted his focus back to the Hong Kong film industry in recent years but continues to make films in Hollywood. As Marchetti and Kam remark (2008), Chan has attained his American Dream of a Hollywood career while clinging to his 'brand-name' as Hong Kong celebrity. However, I would like to argue that the significance of transnational kung fu stars does not only depend on how successful their Hollywood/Western careers are. After all, according to Chris Holmlund, 'of the many foreign stars who have made or make a living in action, only Schwarzenegger ever really managed to cross over to big-budget Hollywood films' (2010: 106). It proves difficult for Li, as for Chan, to transcend 'the constraints placed on him as an Asian man' (Marchetti 2001: 154) in Hollywood. Luckily, for today's transnational stars who enjoy a high level of trans-border mobility, Hollywood is no longer the only goal and destination. A modest Hollywood presence can sometimes lead to a successful transnational career, as demonstrated in Li's case. The significance of transnational kung fu stars probably lies more in their irreplaceable role in transnationalising Chinese cinema: first, they increase global audiences' acceptance of Chinese stars, thus pioneering a road for future Chinese (action or non-action) stars' border-crossing careers; second, they help to bring Chinese-language films into mainstream cinema in the West.

Furthermore, Li's career establishes a model by which a non-Hollywood actor can become a transnational star, that is, in short, by being flexible but retaining one's global currency (in Li's case, martial arts skills). Li's flexibility has been manifested in several regards. The most visible one is his physical mobility; in his thirty-year career, Li has never stopped adapting to new film industries and cultural contexts, from mainland China to Hong Kong, from Hollywood to Europe. Being a real martial artist, a unique global brand, undoubtedly contributes to his ability to adapt to different film industries and audiences, although we should notice that in some ways it also limits his career development on the world stage. Under the surface of physical flexibility, however, it is Li's flexibility in performing diverse film roles as well as projecting different star images, that makes him unique and appealing to audiences across cultural and national boundaries. Despite the perception of action/martial arts stars as 'lacking in acting skills', Li shows a wide range of acting abilities by playing both the prestigious kung fu master and the comic teenage hero, both chaste romantic lead and troubled homosexual lover, both national hero and Oriental villain, both emotionless killer and thinker gripped by inner psychological struggles.

Li's ability to adapt to diverse screen images may benefit from his acting skills as much as his flexible attitude towards his career development and his star image. For example, in order to break into Western markets, Li accepted a villain role in his Hollywood debut and then took a series of stereotyped roles in Hollywood B action films. While a superstar in Asia, Li survives in the West at most as a second-rate star. This is why Li's Western performances have stirred much criticism, anger and disappointment, especially among Chinese audiences. However, what should not be ignored is that Li's English-language action films have kept him a notable presence on Western screens and have won him a solid fan base around the world. Li's box office appeal in the West, while not as remarkable as that in Asia before 1998, enabled him to return to the Chinese/Hong Kong film industry with great confidence and brought him opportunities to star in a number of big-budget Chinese-language films with renowned directors. Li's reputation as a reliable Hollywood action star then helped to bring these well-made Chinese blockbusters into Western theatres: they have not only performed better both critically and commercially than the films which Li has made in the West, but, perhaps for the first time, have brought him a global audience, from China, North America, Europe and other parts of the world. Despite the controversy and complaints accompanying his border-crossing career, Li has finally completed a successful transformation from a national star to a transnational star. All the compromises have proved to be part of the process of becoming a transnational star.

Li's flexible attitude is also manifested in his willingness not to cling to his identity as a real martial artist in his screen life. Unlike Bruce Lee and Jackie Chan, who place much emphasis on the authenticity of their on-screen fighting, Li sees fighting as a form of acting and has never refused the intervention of cinematic technology. As a result, he is probably less vulnerable in the face of some serious challenges posed to kung fu stars in recent years, for example, the heavy use of digital technology in martial arts/action films and the issue of ageing. I have argued in Chapter 2 that technology in Li's films is used to enhance rather than replace his physical performance. Below, I briefly discuss Li's transnational stardom in response to ageing.

Quite recently, the sustainability of the kung fu star has been put into doubt. Mary Farquhar asks of Jackie Chan, 'Can a 50-something Hong Kong-Hollywood star, whose image relies on extremes of actual bodily performance, keep going as a star?' (2010b: 192). In her article 'Celebrity, ageing and Jackie Chan: Middle-aged Asian in Transnational Action', Holmlund comments on Chan's recent Hollywood films: 'It may well look as if he is now dependent upon editing and CGI effects to "action-ise" his ageing body and (re)invigorate the celebrity he has achieved thanks to risk-taking, athletic acting' (2010: 104). Holmlund then concludes that 'to date, the right to age in action has been reserved for Anglo stars such as John Wayne, Clint Eastwood, Sean Connery and Harrison Ford. Significantly all . . . also work in drama. None is a physical performer on a par with Chan or Stallone' (ibid. 106). Leaving aside Holmlund's problematic categorisation of kung fu stars as physical performers only and Anglo action stars as competent in both action and drama, her conclusion cannot be applied to Li, not least because Li is nine years younger than Chan.

First of all, Li's fighting has always been mediated by cinematic technology such as wirework and special effects, so his ageing might not make as much difference as it does to Chan, whose star appeal rests largely on his stunt-based action. Indeed, from *Hero* to Li's two latest productions, *The Sorcerer and the White Snake* (Ching Siu-tung, 2011) and *The Flying Swords of Dragon Gate* (Tsui Hark, 2011) – in which Li reunites with his Hong Kong partners Ching Siu-tung and Tsui Hark, both well-known for their technology-heavy *wuxia* films – Li has played an important role in inaugurating another new trend of *wuxia* films characterised by big budgets, star-studded casts and substantial employment of CGI. It is remarkable that Li, in his late forties, is still favoured over many younger stars to play the leading role in these pan-Chinese *wuxia* blockbusters, despite the fact that his co-stars (usually non-action), with the help of CGI, can also easily look like martial arts masters on screen. This indicates that it is Li's global brand as a transnational kung fu star rather than his physical skills that has been highlighted as the main selling point of these films.

Second, with his successful portrayals of some less-action-defined and more dramatic roles in recent years (*Danny the Dog*, *The Warlord*), Li's action career seems to have taken a promising 'drama' turn, just like those of the Hollywood action stars mentioned by Holmlund. In his newly-released film *Ocean Heaven*, Li completely forsakes his action persona and does a fine job in playing a dying father who shows unfailing love and devotion for his autistic son. With his newly-gained flexibility across action and drama roles, Li probably does have the right to age.

Interestingly, while Li's title as a transnational star has certainly transferred to the kind of cultural capital that endows him with huge freedom in choosing film roles and enables him to maintain his superstardom in the Chinese/Hong Kong film industry, he continues to accept formulaic action roles in Hollywood action films such as *The Mummy: Tomb of the Dragon Emperor* (2008) and *The Expendables* (Sylvester Stallone, 2010). He plays a villain again in the former and plays only a supporting role to Sylvester Stallone in the latter, but both films had much bigger budgets than his previous English-language star vehicles. One may interpret this as Li's strategy to keep his Hollywood presence after he shifted his focus back to the Chinese/Hong Kong film industry, and this again attests to his flexible attitude towards his star persona. To sum up, Li's unique career trajectory points to the opportunities and the predicaments inherent in the process of transnationalising Chinese cinema and Chinese stars, and therefore reveals the complex nature of transnational stardom. The case study of Jet Li typifies the process of becoming a transnational star, and demonstrates that the ability to be flexible – the capacity to wear stardom like a mask and use it to one's own advantage – is essential to all forms of transnational stardom.

Bibliography

English-language sources

Abbas, Ackbar (1997), *Hong Kong: Culture and the Politics of Disappearance*, Minneapolis: University of Minnesota Press.
Allen, Robert C. and Douglas Gomery (1985), *Film History: Theory and Practice*, New York: Random House.
Anderson, Aaron (2001), 'Violent dances in martial arts films', *Jump Cut*, 44, pp. 1–11, 83.
Anderson, Benedict (1983), *Imagined Communities: Reflections on the Origin and Spread of Nationalism*, London: Verso.
Arroyo, José (2000), *Action/Spectacle: A Sight and Sound Reader*, London: BFI Publishing.
Austin, Guy (2003), *Stars in Modern French Films*, London: Arnold.
Babington, Bruce (ed.) (2001), *British Stars and stardom*, Manchester and New York: Manchester University Press.
Beale, Lewis (2005), 'Unleashed', *Film Journal International*, 108: 6, p. 37.
Benshoff, Harry M. (1997), *Monsters in the Closet: Homosexuality and the Horror Film*, Manchester: Manchester University Press.
Bergfelder, Tim (2004), 'Negotiating exoticism: Hollywood, Film Europe and the cultural reception of Anna May Wong', in Lucy Fisher and Marcia Landy (eds), *Stars: the Film Reader*, London and New York: Routledge, pp. 59–75.
Bernstein, Matthew (1997), 'Introduction', in Matthew Bernstein and Gaylyn Studlar (eds), *Visions of the East: Orientalism in Film*, New Brunswick, NJ: Rutgers University Press, pp. 1–18.
Berry, Chris (1994), 'A nation t(w/o): Chinese cinema(s) and nationhood(s)', in Wimal Dissanayake (ed.), *Colonialism and Nationalism in Asian Cinema*, Bloomington: Indiana University Press, pp. 42–64.
Berry, Chris (2003), '*Hero*', *Cinemaya*, 58, pp. 22–4.
Berry, Chris and Mary Farquhar (2006), *China On Screen: Cinema and Nation*, New York: Columbia University Press.
Bond, Matthew (2000), '*Romeo Must Die*', *Daily Telegraph*, 13 October 2000, p. 26.
Bordwell, David (1997), 'Aesthetics in action: kung fu, gunplay, and cinematic expressivity', in *Fifty Years of Electric Shadows*, Hong Kong: Urban Council of Hong Kong, pp. 81–9.

Bordwell, David (2000), *Planet Hong Kong: Popular Cinema and the Art of Entertainment*, Cambridge, MA: Harvard University Press.
Budd, Mike (1990), 'The Moment of Caligari', in Budd (ed.), *The Cabinet of Dr. Caligari: Texts, Contexts, Histories*, New Brunswick, NJ: Rutgers University Press, pp. 7–119.
Butler, Jeremy G. (ed.) (1991), *Star Text: Image and Performance in Film and Television*, Detroit: Wayne State University Press.
Butler, Judith (1990), *Gender Trouble: Feminism and the Subversion of Identity*, London and New York: Routledge.
Cha-jua, Sundiata K. (2008), 'Black audiences, blaxploitation and kung fu films, and challenges to while celluloid masculinity', in Poshek Fu (ed.), *China Forever: The Shaw Brothers and Diasporic Cinema*, Chicago and Urbana: University of Illinois Press, pp. 199–223.
Chan, Jachinson W. (2000), 'Bruce Lee's fictional models of masculinity', *Men and Masculinities*, 2: 4, pp. 371–87.
Chan, Jachinson W. (2001), *Chinese American Masculinities: From Fu Manchu to Bruce Lee*, London and New York: Routledge.
Chan, Kenneth (2009), *Remade in Hollywood: The Global Chinese Presence in Transnational Cinemas*, Hong Kong: Hong Kong University Press.
Chan, Stephen C. (2001), 'Figures of hope and the filmic imaginary of *jianghu* in contemporary Hong Kong cinema', *Cultural Studies*, 15: 3/4, pp. 486–514.
Chan, Stephen C. (2005), 'The fighting condition in Hong Kong cinema: Local icons and cultural antidotes for the global popular', in Meaghan Morris, Siu Leung Li, Stephen Chan Ching-kiu et al. (eds), *Hong Kong Connections: Transnational Imagination in Action Cinema*, Hong Kong, Durham and London: Hong Kong University Press and Duke University Press, pp. 63–80.
Cheng, Yu (1984), 'Anatomy of a legend', in Li Cheuk-to (ed.), *A Study of Hong Kong Cinema in the Seventies*, Hong Kong: Urban Council of Hong Kong, pp. 23–5.
Cheung, Esther M. K. and Jamie T. C. Ku (2004), 'Introduction: gender and sexualized bodies in Hong Kong cinema', in Esther M. K. Cheung and Chu Yiu-wai (eds), *Between Home and World: A Reader in Hong Kong Cinema*, Oxford: Oxford University Press, pp. 400–20.
Chin, Frank (1974), 'Introduction: fifty years of our whole voice', in Frank Chin, Jerry Paul Chan, Lawson Fusadinada and Shawn Wong (eds), *An Anthology of Asian American Writers*, Washington: Howard University Press, pp. i–lxiii.
Chow, Rey (1995), *Primitive Passions: Visuality, Sexuality, Ethnography, and Contemporary Chinese Cinema*, New York: Columbia University Press.
Chu, Rolanda (1994), '*Swordsman II* and *The East is Red*: The "Hong Kong film", entertainment, and gender,' *Bright Lights Film Journal*, 13, pp. 30–5, 46.
Chute, David (2001), 'The Asian evasion', *Premiere*, 14: 8, pp. 36, 38.
Ciecko, Anne T. (1997), 'Transnational action: John Woo, Hong Kong,

Hollywood', in Sheldon Hsiao-peng Lu (ed.), *Transnational Chinese Cinema: Identity, Nationhood, Gender*, Honolulu: University of Hawai'i Press, pp. 221–37.

Cohan, Steven (1997), *Masked Men: Masculinity and Movies in the Fifties*, Bloomington and Indianapolis: Indiana University Press.

Corliss, Richard (1998), 'Fighter Jet', *Time*, 12 October 1998, pp. 70, 72–3.

Corliss, Richard (2003), 'The tone is Black', *Time*, 31 March 2003.

Dai, Jinghua (2005), 'Order/Anti-order: representation of identity in Hong Kong action movies', in Meaghan Morris, Siu Leung Li, Stephen Chan Ching-kiu et al. (eds), *Hong Kong Connections: Transnational Imagination in Action Cinema*, Hong Kong, Durham and London: Hong Kong University Press and Duke University Press, pp. 81–94.

DeAngelis, Michael (2001), *Gay Fandom and Crossover Stardom: James Dean, Mel Gibson, and Keanu Reeves*, Durham and London: Duke University Press.

DeCordova, Richard (1991), 'The emergence of the star system in America', in Christine Gledhill (ed.), *Stardom: Industry of Desire*, London and New York: Routledge, pp. 17–29.

Desser, David (2000), 'The kung fu craze: Hong Kong cinema's first American reception', in Poshek Fu and David Desser (eds), *The Cinema of Hong Kong: History, Arts, Identity*, Cambridge: Cambridge University Press, pp. 19–43.

Desser, David (2005), 'Fists of legend: constructing Chinese identity in the Hong Kong cinema', in Sheldon H. Lu and Emilie Yueh-yu Yeh (eds), *Chinese-Language Film: Historiography, Poetics, Politics*, Honolulu: University of Hawai'i Press, pp. 280–97.

Dovey, Jon (2000), *Freakshow: First Person Media and Factual Television*, London: Pluto Press.

Dyer, Richard (1979), *Stars*, London: British Film Institute.

Dyer, Richard (1980), 'Stereotyping', in Dyer (ed.), *Gays and Films*, London: British Film Institute, pp. 27–39.

Dyer, Richard (1985), 'Male sexuality in the media', in Andy Metcalf and Martin Humphries (eds), *The Sexuality of Men*, London: Pluto Press, pp. 28–43.

Dyer, Richard (1986), *Heavenly Bodies: Film Stars and Society*, London: British Film Institute.

Eagan, Daniel (2004), 'Martial artist', *Film Journal International*, 107: 9, pp. 18–19, 2p, 1c.

Etherington, Daniel (2003), '*Cradle 2 the Grave*', *Sight and Sound*, 13: 5, p. 42.

Fair (2001), '*Kiss of the Dragon*', *Eve Voice*, 29 October 2001, p. 38.

Farquhar, Mary (2010a), 'Jet Li: "wushu master" in sport and film', in Louise Edwards and Elaine Jeffreys (eds), *Celebrity in China*, Hong Kong: Hong Kong University Press, pp. 103–24.

Farquhar, Mary (2010b), 'Jackie Chan: star work as pain and triumph', in Mary Farquahar and Yingjin Zhang, *Chinese Film Stars*, London and New York: Routledge, pp. 180–95.

Farquhar, Mary and Yingjin Zhang (2010), *Chinese Film Stars*, London and New York: Routledge.
Fde, Wendy (2005), '*Unleashed*', *Times*, 18 August 2005, T2, pp. 13.
Feng, Lin (2011), 'Glocalizing stardom: Internet publicity and the construction of Chow Yun-fat's transnational stardom', *Transnational Cinema*, 2: 1, pp. 73–91.
Ferrante, Anthony C. (2001), 'The one but not the only', *Fangoria*, 208, pp. 44–8, 80.
Fiske, John (1992), 'The cultural economy of fandom', in Lisa A. Lewis (ed.), *The Adoring Audience: Fan Culture and Popular Media*, New York: Routledge, pp. 37–42.
Floyd, Nigel (2000), '*Romeo Must Die*', *Time Out*, 11–18 October 2000, p. 81.
Fore, Steve (1997), 'Jackie Chan and the cultural dynamics of global entertainment', in Sheldon Hsiao-peng Lu (ed.), *Transnational Chinese Cinema: Identity, Nationhood, Gender*, Honolulu: University of Hawai'i Press, pp. 239–62.
Fore, Steve (2001), 'Life imitates entertainment: home and dislocation in the films of Jackie Chan', in Esther C. M. Yau (ed.), *At Full Speed: Hong Kong Cinema in a Borderless World*, Minneapolis: University of Minnesota Press, pp. 115–58.
Fore, Steve (2004), 'Home, migration, identity: Hong Kong film workers join the Chinese diaspora', in Esther M. K. Cheung and Chu Yiu-wai (eds), *Between Home and World: A Reader in Hong Kong Cinema*, Oxford: Oxford University Press, pp. 85–99.
Freer, Ian (2000), 'Joel Silver', *Empire*, 137, pp. 10–12, 15.
Fung, Richard (1991), 'Looking for my penis: the eroticized Asian in gay video porn', in Bad Object-Choices (ed.), *How Do I Look? Queer Film and Video*, Seattle: Bay Press, pp. 148–68.
Gallagher, Mark (1997), 'Masculinity in translation: Jackie Chan's transcultural star text', *The Velvet Light Trap*, 39, pp. 23–41.
Geraghty, Christine (2000), 'Re-examining stardom', in Christine Gledhill and Linda Williams (eds), *Reinventing Film Studies*, London: Arnold, pp. 183–200.
Grossman, Andrew (2000), 'The rise of homosexuality and the dawn of communism in Hong Kong film: 1993–1998', in Grossman (ed.), *Queer Asian Cinema: Shadows in the Shade*, New York: The Haworth Press, pp. 149–86.
Gunning, Tom (1990), 'The cinema of attractions: early film, its spectator and the avant-garde', in Thomas Elsaesser and Adam Barker (eds), *Early Film: Space, Frame, Narrative*, London: British Film Institute, pp. 56–62.
Haider, Arwa (2002), '*The One*', *Time Out*, 10–17 April 2002, p. 76.
Hansen, Miriam (1991), *Babel and Babylon: Spectatorship in American Silent Film*, Cambridge, MA: Harvard University Press.
Hayward, Susan (2003), *Simone Signoret: The Star as Cultural Sign*, New York and London: Continuum.
Hazelton, John (2001), 'Box office boost for the Jet Li career plan: *The One*', *Screen International*, 1332, p. 23.

Ho, Sam and Ho Wai-leng (2002), 'Tsui Hark on Tsui Hark: Three Hong Kong film archive interviews', in Sam Ho and Ho Wai-leng (eds), *The Swordsman and His Jiang Hu: Tsui Hark and Hong Kong Film*, Hong Kong: Hong Kong Film Archive, pp. 173–95.

Hollinger, Karen (2006), *The Actress: Hollywood Acting and the Female Stars*, New York and London: Routledge.

Holmlund, Chris (2010), 'Celebrity, ageing and Jackie Chan: middle-aged Asian in transnational action', *Celebrity Studies*, 1: 1, pp. 96–112.

Honeycutt, Kirk (2001), 'Li in game of "One" on One', *Hollywood Reporter – International Edition*, 370: 29, p. 18.

Hong Kong Film Archive (1999), *The Making of Martial Arts Films – As Told by Filmmakers and Stars*, Hong Kong: Provisional Urban Council.

Hoyle, Martin (2002), '*The One*' *Financial Times*, 11 April 2002, p. 16.

Huffer, Ian (2003), 'What interest does a fat Stallone have for an action fan? Male film audiences and the structuring of stardom', in Thomas Austin and Martin Barker (eds), *Contemporary Hollywood Stardom*, London: Arnold, pp. 155–66.

Huffer, Ian (2007), 'I wanted to be Rocky, but I also wanted to be his wife: heterosexuality and the (re)construction of gender in female film audiences' consumption of Sylvester Stallone', *Participations: Journal of Audience and Reception Studies*, 4: 2.

Hunt, Leon (1999), 'Once upon a time in China: kung fu from Bruce Lee to Jet Li', *Framework: The Journal of Cinema and Media*, 40, pp. 85–97.

Hunt, Leon (2003), *Kung Fu Cult Masters: From Bruce Lee to Crouching Tiger*, London: Wallflower Press.

Hunt, Leon (2004), 'The Hong Kong/Hollywood connection', in Yvonne Tasker (ed.), *Action and Adventure Cinema*, London: Routledge, pp. 269–83.

Hunt, Leon (2006), 'Introduction to "*wuxia* fictions: Chinese martial arts in film, literature and beyond"', *EnterText* 6: 1, http://arts.brunel.ac.uk/gate/entertext/issue_6_1.htm

Hunt, Leon (2008), 'Asiaphilia, asianisation and the gatekeeper auteur: Quentin Tarantino and Luc Besson', in Leon Hunt and Leung Wing-fai (eds), *East Asian Cinemas: Exploring Transnational Connections on Film*, London and New York: I. B. Tauris, pp. 220–36.

Hwang, Ange (1998), 'The irresistible: Hong Kong movie *Once Upon a Time in China* series: An extensive interview with director/producer Tsui Hark', *Asian Cinema*, 10: 1, pp. 10–23.

Jancovich, Mark (2001), 'Genre and the audience: genre classifications and cultural distinctions in the mediation of *The Silence of the Lambs*', in Jancovich (ed.), *Horror, The Film Reader*, London: Routledge, pp. 151–62.

Jancovich, Mark and Lucy Faire with Sarah Stubbings (2003), *The Place of the Audience: Cultural Geographies of Film Consumption*, London: British Film Institute.

Jensen, Jeff (2001), 'Chop talk', *Entertainment Weekly*, 604, p. 44.

Kaminsky, Stuart (1982), 'Kung fu film as ghetto myth', in Michael T. Marsden and John G. Nachbar (eds), *Movies as Artifacts: Cultural Criticism of Popular Films*, Chicago: Nelson-Hall, pp. 137–45.
Kim, James (2004), 'The legend of the white-and-yellow black man: global containment and triangulated racial desire in *Romeo Must Die*', *Camera Obscura*, 55: 19: 1, pp. 151–79.
Kimmel, Michael S. and Michael A. Messner (eds) (1995), *Men's Lives*, Boston: Allyn and Bacon.
King, Barry (1991), 'Articulating stardom', in Jeremy G. Butler (ed.), *Star Texts: Image and Performance in Film and Television*, Detroit: Wayne State University Press, pp. 125–54.
King, Geoff (2001), *Spectacular Narratives: Hollywood in the Age of the Blockbuster*, London and New York: I. B. Tauris.
Kirschling, Gregory (2005), '*Unleashed*', *Entertainment Weekly*, 820, p. 53.
Klinger, Barbara (1994), *Melodrama and Meaning: History, Culture and the Films of Douglas Sirk*, Bloomington: Indiana University Press.
Koehler, Robert (2001), '*The One*', *Film Review*, 29 October 2001, p. 27.
Koseluk, Chris and Chris Gennusa (2002), *Video Business*, 22: 8, p. 17.
Kraicer, Shelly (2003), '*Hero*', *Cinema Scope*, 14, p. 9.
Kuhn, Annette (1985), *The Power of the Image: Essays on Representation and Sexuality*, London: Routledge and Kegan Paul.
Larson, Wendy (1997), 'The concubine and the figure of history: Chen Kaige's *Farewell My Concubine*', in Sheldon Hsiao-peng Lu (ed.), *Transnational Chinese Cinema: Identity, Nationhood, Gender*, Honolulu: University of Hawai'i Press, pp. 331–46.
Lau, Jenny Kwok Wah (1998), 'Besides fists and blood: Hong Kong comedy and its master of the eighties', *Cinema Journal*, 37: 2, pp. 18–34.
Lau, Tai-muk (1999), 'Conflict and desire – dialogues between the Hong Kong martial arts genre and social issues in the past 40 years', in *The Making of Martial Arts Films – As Told by Filmmakers and Stars*, Hong Kong: Urban Council of Hong Kong, pp. 30–4.
Lee, Leo Ou-fan (1999), 'Hong Kong movies in Hollywood: An informal comment on Asian 'influences' in American popular culture', *The Harvard Asia Pacific Review*, 3: 1, pp. 30–4.
Leung, Helen Hok-sze (2004), 'Queerscapes in contemporary Hong Kong cinema', in Esther M. K. Cheung and Chu Yiu-wai (eds), *Between Home and World: A Reader in Hong Kong Cinema*, Oxford: Oxford University Press, pp. 459–83.
Leyland, Matthew (2001), '*Kiss of the Dragon*', *Sight and Sound*, 11: 10, p. 51.
Leyland, Matthew (2002), '*The One*', *Sight and Sound*, 12: 5, pp. 50–1.
Li Cheuk-to (1993), 'Tsui Hark and the Western interest in Hong Kong cinema', *Cinemaya*, 21, pp. 50–1.
Li, Cheuk-to (1994), 'The return of the father: Hong Kong new wave and its Chinese context in the 1980s', in Nick Browne, Paul G. Pickowicz, Vivian

Sobchack and Esther Yau (eds), *New Chinese Cinemas: Forms, Identities, Politics*, Cambridge: Cambridge University Press, pp. 160–79.

Lilley, Rozanna (1998), *Staging Hong Kong: Gender and Performance in Transition*, Surrey: Curzon Press.

Lin, Nien-tung (1981), 'The martial arts hero', in Lau Shing-hong and Leong Mo-ling (eds), *A Study of the Hong Kong Swordplay Film (1945–1980)*, Hong Kong: Hong Kong International Film Festival, pp. 7–16.

Lo, Kwai-cheung (1993), 'Once upon a time: Technology comes to presence in China', *Modern Chinese Literature*, 7, pp. 79–96.

Lo, Kwai-cheung (2001), 'Double negations: Hong Kong cultural identity in Hollywood's transnational representations', *Cultural Studies*, 15: 3/4, pp. 464–85.

Lo, Kwai-cheung (2004), 'Muscles and subjectivity: A short history of the masculine body in Hong Kong popular culture', in Lucy Fischer and Marcia Landy (eds), *Stars: The Film Reader*, New York and London: Routledge, pp. 115–26.

Lo, Kwai-cheung (2005), *Chinese Face/Off: The Transnational Popular Culture of Hong Kong*, Urbana and Chicago: University of Illinois Press.

Logan, Bey (1995), *Hong Kong Action Cinema*, London: Titan.

Louie, Kam (2002), *Theorising Chinese Masculinity: Society and Gender in China*, Cambridge: Cambridge University Press.

Lu, Sheldon Hsiao-peng (1997), 'Chinese cinema (1896–1996) and transnational film studies', in Lu (ed.), *Transnational Chinese Cinema: Identity, Nationhood, Gender*, Honolulu: University of Hawai'i Press, pp. 1–31.

Lu, Sheldon Hsiao-peng (2000), 'Soap opera in China: The transnational politics of visuality, sexuality, and masculinity', *Cinema Journal*, 40: 1, pp. 25–47.

Ma, Eric Kit-wai (2002), 'Translocal spatiality', *International Journal of Cultural Studies*, 5: 2, pp. 131–52.

Ma, Sheng-mei (2000), 'Yellow kung fu and black jokes', *Television New Media*, 1: 2, pp. 239–44.

Macaulay, Sean (2000), 'Is it a bird, is it a plane? Yes, it's Jet', *The Times*, 27 March 2000, section 2, pp. 22–3.

Magnan-Park, Aaron Han Joon (2007), 'The heroic flux in John Woo's trans-Pacific passage', in Gina Marchetti and Tan See Kam (eds), *Hong Kong Film, Hollywood and New Global Cinema: No Film is An Island*, London: Routledge, pp. 35–49.

Major, Wade (2000), 'The afterburner', in Stefan Hammond (ed.), *Hollywood East: Hong Kong Movies and the People Who Make Them*, Chicago: Contemporary Books Inc., pp. 149–75.

Marchetti, Gina (1993), *Romance and the 'Yellow Peril': Race, Sex, and Discursive Strategies in Hollywood Fiction*, Berkeley: University of California Press.

Marchetti, Gina (2001), 'Jackie Chan and the black connection', in Matthew Tinkcom and Amy Villarejo (eds), *Keyframes: Popular Cinema and Cultural Studies*, London and New York: Routledge, pp. 137–58.

Marchetti, Gina and Tan See Kam (2008), 'Hong Kong cinema and global

change', in Marchetti and Kam (eds), *Hong Kong Film, Hollywood and the New Global Cinema: No Film is an Island*, London and New York: Routledge, pp. 1–9.
Martin, Adrian (2005), 'At the edge of the cut: An encounter with the Hong Kong style in contemporary action cinema', in Meaghan Morris, Siu Leung Li, Stephen Chan Ching-kiu et al. (eds), *Hong Kong Connections: Transnational Imagination in Action Cinema*, Hong Kong, Durham and London: Hong Kong University Press and Duke University Press, pp. 175–88.
Mayne, Judith (1993), *Cinema and Spectatorship*, London and New York: Routledge.
McCarthy, Todd (2000), 'Li Jet-powers chopsocky for action-packed Gangsta ride', *Variety*, 20–26 March 2000, pp. 25, 33.
McDonald, Paul (1995), 'Star studies', in Joanne Hollows and Mark Jancovich (eds), *Approaches to Popular Film*, Manchester: Manchester University Press, pp. 79–97.
McDonald, Paul (1998), 'Reconceptualising stardom', A supplementary chapter for Richard Dyer, *Stars*, 2nd edn, London: British Film Institute, pp. 175–211.
McDonald, Paul (2000), *The Star System: Hollywood's Production of Popular Identities*, London: Wallflower Press.
McDonald, Paul (2003), 'Stars in the online universe: Promotion, nudity, reverence', in Thomas Austin and Martin Barker (eds), *Contemporary Hollywood Stardom*, London: Arnold, pp. 29–44.
Miyao, Daisuke (2007), *Sessue Hayakawa: Silent Cinema and Transnational Stardom*, Durham and London: Duke University Press.
Morris, Meaghan (2005), 'Introduction: Hong Kong connections', in Meaghan Morris, Siu Leung Li, Stephen Chan Ching-kiu et al. (eds), *Hong Kong Connections: Transnational Imagination in Action Cinema*, Hong Kong, Durham and London: Hong Kong University Press and Duke University Press, pp. 1–18.
Morris, Meaghan, Siu Leung Li, Stephen Chan Ching-kiu et al. (eds) (2005), *Hong Kong Connections: Transnational Imagination in Action*, Hong Kong, Durham and London: Hong Kong University Press and Duke University Press.
Moseley, Rachel (2002), *Growing Up With Audrey Hepburn*, Manchester: Manchester University Press.
Neale, Steve (1983), 'Masculinity as spectacle', *Screen*, 24: 6, pp. 2–16.
Negra, Diane (2001), *Off-White Hollywood: American Culture and Ethnic Female Stardom*, London and New York: Routledge.
Ng, Ho (1980), 'Kung-fu comedies: Tradition, structure, character', in *A Study of the Hong Kong Martial Arts Film (The Fourth Hong Kong International Film Festival)*, Hong Kong: Urban Council of Hong Kong, pp. 42–6.
Ng, Paul Chun-ming (1992), 'The image of overseas Chinese in American cinema', in *Overseas Chinese Figures in Cinema*, Hong Kong: Urban Council of Hong Kong, pp. 81–94.

O'Hehir, Andrew (1998), '*Lethal Weapon 4*', *Sight and Sound*, 8: 9, p. 46.
Pan, Esther (2000), 'Why Asian guys are on a roll', *Newsweek*, 135: 8, p. 50.
Pan, Lynn (1992), 'Chinese emigrés on screen', in *Overseas Chinese Figures in Cinema*, Hong Kong: Urban Council of Hong Kong, pp. 58–64.
Parish, James Robert (2002), *Jet Li: A Biography*, New York: Thunder's Mouth Press.
Park, JaeYoon (2009), 'Asian's beloved sassy girl: Jun Ji-Hyun's star image and her transnational stardom', *Jump Cut*, 51.
Perriam, Christopher (2003), *Stars and masculinities in Spanish cinema*, Oxford: Oxford University Press.
Phillips, Alastair and Ginette Vincendeau (2006), *Journeys of Desire: European Actors in Hollywood, A Critical Companion*, London: British Film Institute.
Ranaletta, Ray (1998), 'Lethal, deadly and . . . hot! – It's Jet Li', *Asian Cult Cinema*, 21, pp. 22–4.
Rawnsley, Gary D. and Ming-Yeh Rawnsley (eds) (2010), *Global Chinese Cinema: The Culture and Politics of Hero*, London and New York: Routledge.
Reid, Craig D. (1993–4), 'Fighting without fighting', *Film Quarterly*, 47: 2, pp. 30–5.
Reid, Craig D. (1994), 'An Evening with Jackie Chan', *Bright Lights*, 13, pp. 18–25.
Roberts, Shari (1993), 'The lady in the tutti frutti hat: Carmen Miranda, a spectacle of ethnicity', *Cinema Journal*, 32, pp. 3–23.
Rodriguez, Hector (1997), 'Hong Kong popular culture as an interpretive arena: The Huang Feihong film series', *Screen*, 38: 1, pp. 1–24.
Rooney, David (2003), 'Hip-hop vibe rocks chop-socky "Cradle"', *Variety*, 3–9 March 2003, pp. 41, 78.
Russell, Jamie (2005), '*Unleashed*', *Sight and Sound*, 15: 8, pp. 78–9.
Ryall, Tom (1998), 'Genre and Hollywood', in John Hill and Pamela Church Gibson (eds), *The Oxford Guide to Film Studies*, Oxford: Oxford University Press, pp. 327–41.
Ryan, Tony (1984), 'Bruce Lee and other stories', in *A Study of Hong Kong Cinema in the Seventies* (*The Eighth Hong Kong International Film Festival Catalogue*), Hong Kong: Urban Council of Hong Kong, pp. 26–9.
Rynning, Ronald (2000), 'The high life', *Film Review*, 599, pp. 82–4.
Said, Edward (1978), *Orientalism*, New York: Vintage.
Sandell, Jillian (1997), 'Reinventing masculinity: The spectacle of male intimacy in the films of John Woo', *Film Quarterly*, 49: 4, pp. 23–34.
Sardar, Ziauddin and Frances S. Saunders (2000), 'China syndrome', *New Statesman*, 129: 4487, p. 46.
Sarkar, Bhaskar (2001), 'Hong Kong hysteria: Martial arts tales from a mutating world', in Esther C. M. Yau (ed.), *At Full Speed: Hong Kong Cinema in a Borderless World*, Minneapolis: University of Minnesota Press, pp. 159–76.
Sek, Kei (1980), 'The development of "martial arts" in Hong Kong cinema', in

Lau Shing-hon (ed.), *A Study of the Hong Kong Martial Arts Film*, Hong Kong: Urban Council of Hong Kong, pp. 28–38.

Sek, Kei (1991), 'Achievement and crisis: Hong Kong cinema in the '80s', in *Hong Kong Cinema in the Eighties*, Hong Kong: Urban Council of Hong Kong, pp. 54–63.

Sek, Kei (1997), 'Hong Kong cinema from June 4 to 1997', in *Fifty Years of Electric Shadows*, Hong Kong: Urban Council of Hong Kong, pp. 120–5.

Shingler, Martin (2001), 'Interpreting *All About Eve*: A study in historical reception', in Melvyn Stokes and Richard Maltby (eds), *Hollywood Spectatorship: Changing Perceptions of Cinema Audiences*, London: British Film Institute, pp. 46–62.

Shohat, Ella and Robert Stam (1994), *Unthinking Eurocentrism: Multiculturalism and the Media*, London and New York: Routledge.

Shu, Yuan (2003), 'Reading the kung fu film in an American context: From Bruce Lee to Jackie Chan', *Journal of Popular Film and Television*, 31: 2, pp. 50–9.

Sieglohr, Ulrike (ed.) (2000), *Heroines Without Heroes: Reconstructing Female and National Identities in European Cinema (1945–51)*, London and New York: Cassell.

Som, Rituparna (2001), '*Kiss of the Dragon*', *Asian Age*, 12 November 2001, p. 17.

Stacey, Jackie (1994), *Star Gazing: Hollywood Cinema and Female Spectatorship*, London and New York: Routledge.

Staiger, Janet (1986), 'The handmaiden of villainy: Methods and problems in studying the historical reception of a film', *Wide Angle*, 8: 1, pp. 19–27.

Staiger, Janet (1992), *Interpreting Films: Studies in the Historical Reception of American Cinema*, Princeton: Princeton University Press.

Staiger, Janet (2000), *Perverse Spectators: The Practices of Film Reception*, New York and London: New York University Press.

Stoila, Tytti (ed.) (2009), *Stellar Encounters: Stardom in Popular European Cinema*, London: John Libbey Publishing.

Stokes, Lisa Odham and Michael Hoover (1999), *City on Fire: Hong Kong Cinema*, London and New York: Verso.

Stringer, Julian (2003a), 'Scrambling Hollywood: Asian stars/Asian American star cultures', in Thomas Austin and Martin Barker (eds), *Contemporary Hollywood Stardom*, London: Arnold, pp. 229–42.

Stringer, Julian (2003b), 'Talking about Jet Li: Transnational Chinese movie stardom and Asian American internet reception', in Gary D. Rawnsley and Ming-Yeh T. Rawnsley (eds), *Political Communications in Greater China: The Construction and Reflection of Identity*, London: Routledge Curzon, pp. 275–90.

Studlar, Gaylyn (1996), *This Mad Masquerade: Stardom and Masculinity in the Jazz Age*, New York: Columbia University Press.

Tasker, Yvonne (1993), *Spectacular Bodies: Gender, Genre and the Action Cinema*, London and New York: Routledge.

Tasker, Yvonne (1997), 'Fists of fury: Discourses of race and masculinity in the martial arts cinema', in Harry Stecopoulos and Michael Uebel (eds), *Race and the Subject of Masculinities*, Durham: Duke University Press, pp. 315–36.

Tasker, Yvonne (2004), 'Introduction: Action and adventure cinema', in Tasker (ed.), *Action and Adventure Cinema*, London and New York: Routledge, pp. 1–13.

Teo, Stephen (1992), 'The true way of the dragon: the films of Bruce Lee', in *Overseas Chinese Figures in Cinema*, Hong Kong: Urban Council of Hong Kong, pp. 70–80.

Teo, Stephen (1997), *Hong Kong Cinema: The Extra Dimensions*, London: British Film Institute.

Teo, Stephen (2005), 'Wuxia redux: *Crouching Tiger, Hidden Dragon* as a model of late transnational production', in Meaghan Morris, Siu Leung Li, Stephen Chan Ching-kiu et al. (eds), *Hong Kong Connections: Transnational Imagination in Action Cinema*, Hong Kong, Durham and London: Hong Kong University Press and Duke University Press, pp. 191–204.

Teo, Stephen (2009), *Chinese Martial Arts Cinema: The Wuxia Tradition*. Edinburgh: Edinburgh University Press.

The Making of Martial Arts Films – As Told by Filmmakers and Stars (1999), Hong Kong: Urban Council of Hong Kong.

Tian, Yan (1984), 'The fallen idol – Zhang Che in retrospect', in *A Study of Hong Kong Cinema in the Seventies*, Hong Kong: Urban Council of Hong Kong, pp. 44–6.

Tookey, Christopher (2001), 'Jet gets his kicks, but what about us?' *Daily Mail*, 1 November 2001, p. 48.

Vincendeau, Ginette (2000), *Stars and stardom in French Cinema*, London: Continuum Publishing Co.

Wang, Yuejin (1991), '*Red Sorghum*: Mixing memory and desire', in Chris Berry (ed.), *Perspectives on Chinese Cinema*, London: British Film Institute, pp. 80–103.

Willemen, Paul (2005), 'Action Cinema, labour power and the video market', in Meaghan Morris, Siu Leung Li, Stephen Chan Ching-kiu et al. (eds), *Hong Kong Connections: Transnational Imagination in Action Cinema*, Hong Kong, Durham and London: Hong Kong University Press and Duke University Press, pp. 223–48.

Williams, Linda (1991), 'Film bodies: Gender, genre and excess', *Film Quarterly*, 44: 4, pp. 2–13.

Williams, Tony (2000), 'Under "Western eyes": The personal Odyssey of Huang Fei-Hong in *Once Upon a Time in China*', *Cinema Journal*, 40: 1, pp. 3–24.

Williams, Tony (2003), 'Transnational stardom: The case of Maggie Cheung Man-yuk', *Asian Cinema*, 14: 2, pp. 180–96.

Willis, Andy (2004), 'Cynthia Rothrock: From the ghetto of exploitation', in Willis (ed.), *Film Stars: Hollywood and Beyond*, Manchester: Manchester University Press, pp. 174–88.

Xing, Jun (1998), *Asian America Through the Lens: History, Representations and Identity*, Walnut Creek, CA and London: AltaMira Press.
Xu, Gary G. (2006), *Sinascape: Contemporary Chinese Cinema*, Lanham, MD: Rowan and Littlefield Publishers.
Yau, Esther Ching-mei (1989), 'Cultural and economic dislocations: Filmic phantasies of Chinese women in the 1980s', *Wide Angle*, 11: 2, pp. 6–21.
Yau, Esther Ching-mei (1994), 'Border crossing: Mainland China's presence in Hong Kong cinema', in Nick Browne, Paul G. Pickowicz, Vivian Sobchack and Esther Yau (eds), *New Chinese Cinemas*, Cambridge: Cambridge University Press, pp. 180–201.
Yau, Esther Ching-mei (1997), 'Ecology and late colonial Hong Kong cinema: Imaginations in time', in *Fifty Years of Electric Shadows,* Hong Kong: Urban Council of Hong Kong, pp. 107–13.
Yu, Sabrina Q. (2012), 'Vulnerable Chinese stars: From *xizi* to film worker', in Yingjin Zhang (ed.), *A Companion to Chinese Cinema*, Hoboken, NJ: Wiley-Blackwell, pp. 218–38 (forthcoming).
Yung, Sai-shing (2005), 'Moving body: The interactions between Chinese opera and action cinema', in Meaghan Morris, Siu Leung Li, Stephen Chan Ching-kiu et al. (eds), *Hong Kong Connections: Transnational Imagination in Action Cinema*, Durham and London: Duke University Press, pp. 21–34.
Zhang, Che (1999), 'Creating the martial arts film and the Hong Kong cinema style', in *The Making of Martial Arts Films – As Told by Filmmakers and Stars*, Hong Kong: Urban Council of Hong Kong, pp. 16–24.
Zhang, Xudong (1998), 'Nationalism, mass culture, and intellectual strategies in post-Tianamen China', *Social Text*, 16: 2, pp. 109–40.
Zhang, Yingjin (2004), *Chinese National Cinema*, New York and London: Routledge.
Zimmerman, Paul (2005), '*Unleashed*', *Cinefantastique*, 37: 4, p. 56.

Chinese-language sources

A, Lisi (1993), '*Fong Sai-yuk* de wufa chu wei' (The mediocrity of *Fong Sai-yuk*), *City Entertainment*, 365, p. 104.
Chen, Pingyuan (1992), *Qiangu Wenren Xiake Meng: Wuxia Xiaoshuo Leixing Yanjiu (The xiake dream of Chinese literati for centuries: genre studies of wuxia novels)*, Beijing: Beijing University Press.
China Film Year Book 1994 (1994), Beijing: China Film Press.
Dazhong Dianying (Popular Cinema) (2005), 'Jet Li fan sites collection', 664, p. 31.
Deng, Tuzi (1993), 'Shi nian ren shi zai fanshen: Li Lianjie yu *Fang Shiyu*' (Jet Li and *Fong Sai-yuk*), *City Entertainment*, 362, pp. 39–40.
Guo, Yuelian (2003), 'Lun *Yingxiong* yu xin lishi zhuyi' (*Hero* and the new historicism), *Diaying wenxue* (Film literature), 3, pp. 7–9.
Hai, Yin (2003), 'Chenfu yu hengxing tianxia de baquan de wei yingxiong'

(Pseudo-hero submits to hegemony*)*, *Dianying wenxue* (Film literature), 3, pp. 12–13.

Hong, Xiu (2004), '*Yingxiong*: lishi yu xianshi de shuangchong huangmiu' (*Hero*: double absurdity of history and reality'), *Kexue zhongguoren* (*Scientific Chinese*), 3, p. 49.

Huang, Shixian (2003), '*Yingxiong* de shichang kaixuan ji qi wenhua beilun' (*Hero*'s commercial success and cultural dilemma), *Dangdai dianying* (Contemporary cinema), 2, pp. 19–22.

Jia, Leilei (1999), 'Zhongguo leixing dianying' (Chinese genre films), *Dianying yishu* (Film art), 3, p. 11.

Jia, Leilei (2003a), '*Yingxiong* dui baoli de xiaojie yu qianghua' (Deconstruction and reinforcement of violence in *Hero*), *Dianying yishu* (*Film Art)*, 2, pp. 19–23, 30.

Jia, Leilei (2003b), 'Zhongguo *wuxia* jingshen – moluo? taowang?' (Chinese *wuxia* spirit: downfall or desertion?), *Zhongguo wenyjia* (*Culture and art of China*), 4, pp. 20–1.

Jia, Leilei (2005), *Zhongguo Wuxia Dianying Shi* (Chinese *wuxia* film history), Beijing: Culture and Art Publishing House.

Jin, Junhai (1995), 'Jiushi niandai xin *wuxia* dian ying manlun' (New *wuxia* films in the 1990s), *Hangzhou shifan xueyuan yuanbao* (Journal of Hangzhou Normal University), 6, pp. 56–9.

Kang, Xueying (1991), 'Yi hua jie mu, zhang guan li dai' (The artistry of remaking), *City Entertainment*, 325, p. 67.

Kuai Bao (1995), 'Shanghai *nü* yingmi dixue yi shi chiqing' (Shanghai female fan self-harms to show her adoration of Jet Li), 28 March 1995, p. 38.

Kuang, Youhua (1992), 'Lian fengliu de beihou; jie *Dongfang Bubai* qi de xing' (Behind the romance: talk about *Swordsman II*), *City Entertainment*, 349, pp. 104–5.

Lang, Tian (1992), '*Dongfang Bubai* de baoli meixue' (Aesthetics of violence in *Swordsman II*), *City Entertainment*, 349, p. 106.

Law Kar, Ng Ho and Cheuk Pak Tong et al. (eds) (1997), *Xianggang dianying leixing lun* (*Generic studies in Hong Kong cinema*), Hong Kong: Oxford University Press, pp. 85–8.

Lie, Fu (1997), 'Xu Ke "*Wong Fei-hung*" xilie yanjiu' (A study of Tsui Hark's *Wong Fei-hung* series), *Dangdai dianying* (Contemporary cinema), 3, pp. 97–101.

Luo, Weiming (1991), 'Dai congdou shoushi jiu shanhe' (Tsui Hark's *Wong Fei-hung*), *City Entertainment*, 324, pp. 38–9.

Ming Bao (1994), 'Li Lianjie de sange mimi: Jiating, jinqian he aiqing" (Jet Li's three secrets: family, money and romance), 3 October 1994, D5.

Ng, Ho (1997), 'Huang Feihong zhi yingxiong sanbian' (The three heroic transformations of Wong Fei-hung), in Law Kar, Ng Ho and Cheuk Pak Tong (eds), *Xianggang dianying leixing lun* (*Generic studies in Hong Kong cinema*), Hong Kong: Oxford University Press, pp. 85–8.

Shang, Ke and Gao Jian (2002), 'Duihua: yibu yangbanxi' (Dialogue: a model-drama?), *Qin dianying* (New cinema), 10, pp. 16–18.
Shang, Ke and Gao Jian (2003), '*Yingxiong* bei lun' (The dilemma of *Hero*), *Qin dianying* (New cinema), 11, p. 28.
Shi, Wenhong (1992), 'Xifang dianying zhong huaren de dingxinghua wenti' (Chinese stereotypes in Western cinema), in *Overseas Chinese Figures in Cinema*, Hong Kong: Urban Council of Hong Kong, pp. 10–14.
Wang, Dong (2003), 'Yishu shi benneng de fankang' (Art is instinctive resistance), *Xin dianying* (New cinema), 11, p. 26.
Wang, Xiaodong, Pang Ling and Song Qiang (1999), *Quanqiuhua Yinying Xia de Zhongguo Zhi Lu* (*China's road under the shadow of globalisation*), Beijing: Chinese Social Science Press.
Wang, Zhiqiang (1994), '1993 quanguo dianying shichang pingshu' (Review of the 1993 film market), in *China Film Year Book 1994*, Beijing: China Film Press, pp. 202–4.
Wenhui (1994a), 'Yinmu tanqing diandao weizhi, Li Lianjie wei xian chuwen' (Understated screen romance, Li Lianjie's first kiss yet to come), 22 July 1994.
Wenhui (1994b), 'Li Lianjie xingge haixiu, pai qinre xi nan touru' (Shy Li Lianjie finds filming love scenes difficult), 16 September 1994.
Wu, Yanzhen (1991), 'Xu ke gaizao Huang Feihong' (Tsui Hark reinvents Wong Fei-hung), *City Entertainment*, 317, pp. 35–7.
Xiao Zi (1984), 'Ban shi ban fei' (Tittle-tattle), *Dianying* (Film), 106, p. 5.
Yang, Xiaowen (1991), 'Li Lianjie yan zhong de Huang Feihong' (Wong Fei-hung in the eyes of Jet Li'), *City Entertainment*, 323, pp. 23–6.
Yang, Xiaowen (1993), 'Gongshi xia de renao fanrong' (Prospering under stereotyping), *City Entertainment*, 364, p. 106.
Zeng, Jingbiao (2003), '*Yingxiong*: yige jiti zhizao de shenhua' (*Hero*: a collectively created myth), *Dianying wenxie* (Film Literature), 3, p. 10.
Zhang, Hongqiu (2003), '*Yingxiong,* queshi minzu wenhua' (*Hero,* a lack of national culture), *Zhongguo wenyijia* (*Culture and art of China*), 4, p. 23.
Zhang, Kerong (2005), *Huaren Zongheng Tianxia: Li An* (The world is not enough: Ang Lee), Beijing: Contemporary Press.
Zhang, Ying (2003), '*Yingxiong: Xili yu huihuang*' (*Hero*: parody and glory), *Dianying wenxue* (Film literature), 3, pp. 14–15.
Zhang, Yiwu (2003), '*Yingxiong: xin shiji de yinyu*' (*Hero*, the metaphor of the new century), *Dangdai dianying* (Contemporary cinema), 2, pp. 11–15.
Zhang, Zhicheng (1991), '*Huang Feihong* wuda changmian chaofan rusheng' (Wonderful fight scenes in *Once Upon a Time in China*), *City Entertainment*, 323, pp. 62–3.
Zheng, Xiaoping (2004), '*Dianying Yingxiong de meixue jiazhi yu minzu guojia zhishang guan*' (Aesthetic value of the movie *Hero* and the view of the nation-state as supreme), *Tansuo yu zhengming* (Exploration and free views), 3, pp. 21–3.
Zhou, Xing (2003), 'Lakai zhongguo dianying de shiji yingxiong wenhua damu:

da pian *Yingxiong* wu lun' (The curtain goes up on Chinese cinema's hero culture in the new century: Five arguments about *Hero*), *Dianying xinzuo* (New films), 2, pp. 32–5.

Web sources

A., Marc (2002), Fan letter to Jet Li, *The Official Jet Li Website*, 12 August 2002, http://www.jetli.com/jet/index.php?l=en&s=work&ss=questions&p=x&date=020812 (accessed January 2007)

Angel (2001), Fan letter to Jet Li, *The Official Jet Li Website*, 13 October 2001, http://www.jetli.com/jet/index.php?l=en&s=life&ss=questions&p=x&date=011013_0217 (accessed January 2007)

Bahrom1 (2001), 'Somewhat disappointing', *IMDb*, 27 March 2001, http://www.imdb.com/title/tt0165929/usercomments?start=90 (accessed October 2006)

BBC News (2007), 'Jet Li breaks film salary record', 26 November 2007, http://news.bbc.co.uk/2/hi/entertainment/7112639.stm (accessed January 2008)

Bell, Josh (2004), 'Once upon a time in China: *Hero* finds beauty in violence', 26 August 2004, http://www.lasvegasweekly.com/content/fileadmin/oldsite/2004/08/26/screen.html (accessed October 2007)

Berardinelli, James (2004), '*Hero*', *Reelviews*, http://www.reelviews.net/movies/h/hero.html (accessed October 2007)

Blew12 (2001), 'I like the movie', *IMDb*, 16 December 2001, http://www.imdb.com/title/tt0165929/usercomments?start=60 (accessed October 2006)

BlueNeon-2 (2000), 'Ugh', *IMDb*, 7 April 2000, http://www.imdb.com/title/tt0165929/usercomments?start=190 (accessed October 2006)

Bob-45 (2001), 'Entertaining carnage', *IMDb*, 23 July 2001, http://www.imdb.com/title/tt0271027/reviews?start=150 (accessed October 2006)

Brenner, Jules (2004), '*Hero*', *Film Critic*, 30 August 2004, http://www.film-critic.com/reviews/2002/hero/ (accessed October 2007)

Callanvass (2005), 'Entertaining enough action/sci-fi film', *IMDb*, 25 May 2005, http://www.imdb.com/title/tt0267804/reviews?start=40 (accessed October 2006)

Callanvass (2006), 'Jet Li's best film in my opinion', *IMDb*, 28 February 2006, http://www.imdb.com/title/tt0342258/reviews?filter=chrono;filter=chrono;start=90 (accessed October 2006)

Ccthemovieman-1 (2006), 'Not your normal martial arts fare', *IMDb*, 15 July 2006, http://www.imdb.com/title/tt0271027/usercomments (accessed October 2006)

Charlie_062497 (2001), 'I love this movie!!', *IMDb*, 5 December 2001, http://www.imdb.com/title/tt0271027/reviews?start=100 (accessed October 2006)

Cills (2000), 'Okay movie', *IMDb*, 29 March 2000, http://www.imdb.com/title/tt0165929/usercomments?start=210 (accessed October 2006)

Clark, Bill (2004), '*Hero*', *From the balcony*, 23 December 2004, http://www.fromthebalcony.com/reviews.php?id=35 (accessed October 2007)

Cooper, Jackie K (2004), 'Hero', 30 August 2004, http://www.jackiekcooper.com/MovieReviews/MovieArchive/Hero.htm (accessed October 2007)

Deepcheck (2000), 'A fun film with lots of laughs and a disjointed plot', *IMDb*, 28 March 2000, http://www.imdb.com/title/tt0165929/usercomments?start=210 (accessed October 2006)

Dragonfly Dreams (2001), Fan letter to Jet Li, *The Official Jet Li Website*, 13 October 2001, http://www.jetli.com/jet/index.php?s=life&ss=questions&p=x&date=011013_0113 (accessed January 2007)

Frost, Jonny (2001), 'Brutal adult action fare', *IMDb*, 25 August 2001, http://www.imdb.com/title/tt0271027/reviews?start=130 (accessed October 2006)

Gambino1-1 (2005), 'Great movie!', *IMDb*, 22 October 2005, http://www.imdb.com/title/tt0342258/reviews?start=90 (accessed October 2006)

Gatsby2244 (2005), 'Very violent, very good', *IMDb*, 24 April 2005, http://www.imdb.com/title/tt0271027/reviews?start=50 (accessed October 2006) (accessed October 2006)

Gilchrist, Todd (2004), 'Hero', 30 August 2004, http://www.filmstew.com/ShowArticle.aspx?ContentID=9543 (accessed October 2007)

Gillespie, Eleanor Ringel (2004), 'Hero', http://www.accessatlanta.com/movies/content/shared/movies/reviews/H/hero.html (accessed October 2007)

Hahn, Lorraine (2003), 'Jet Li interview transcript', *CNN*, 29 January 2003, http://edition.cnn.com/2003/WORLD/asiapcf/01/29/talkasia.li.script/index.html (accessed October 2007)

Hanke, Ken (2004), 'Hero', *Mountain Xpress*, 1 September 2004. http://www.mountainxcom/movies/h/hero.php (accessed October 2007)

Huskey, Cassaundra (2002), Fan letter to Jet Li, *The Official Jet Li Website*, 3 April 2002, http://www.jetli.com/jet/index.php?l=en&s=work&ss=questions&p=x&date=020403 (accessed January 2007)

IMDb, 'What is the Internet Movie Database?', http://imdb.com/help/show_leaf?about (accessed October 2006)

Imperial, Chill (2000), Fan letter to Jet Li, *The Official Jet Li Website*, 10 November 2000, http://www.jetli.com/jet/index.php?s=life&ss=questions&p=x&date=001110 (accessed January 2007)

Jiangliqings (2001), 'An action thriller that features Li's return to form', *IMDb*, 23 September 2001, http://www.imdb.com/title/tt0271027/reviews?start=120 (accessed October 2006)

Knight, Tim (2004), 'Hero', *Reelview*, http://www.reel.com/movie.asp?MID=137889&Tab=reviews&buy=open&CID=13#tabs (accessed October 2007)

Kyrat (2005), 'Best of Jet Li's non-Hong Kong releases', *IMDb*, 31 May 2005, http://www.imdb.com/title/tt0342258/reviews?start=160 (accessed October 2006)

L'Apprenti (2001), 'One, or none???', *IMDb*, 23 November 2001, http://www.imdb.com/title/tt0267804/usercomments?start=150 (accessed October 2006)

Li, Jet (1999), 'Greetings', *The Official Jet Li Website*, http://www.jetli.com/jet/index.php?l=en&s=mind&ss=essays&p=1 (accessed January 2007)

Li, Jet (1999), 'To my fans', *The Official Jet Li Website*, 17 June 1999, http://www.jetli.com/jet/index.php?l=en&s=mind&ss=essays&p=2 (accessed January 2007)

Li, Jet, '*Shaolin Temple*', *The Official Jet Li Website*, http://www.jetli.com/jet/index.php?l=en&s=work&ss=essays&p=1 (accessed January 2007)

Li, Jet, '*Swordsman II*', *The Official Jet Li Website*, http://www.jetli.com/jet/index.php?l=en&s=work&ss=essays&p=11 (accessed January 2007)

Li, Jet, '*Crouching Tiger, Hidden Dragon*', *The Official Jet Li Website*, http://www.jetli.com/jet/index.php?l=en&s=work&ss=essays&p=cthd (accessed January 2007)

Li-1 (2003), 'A lot of people seem to like this movie', *IMDb*, 5 April 2003, http://www.imdb.com/title/tt0165929/usercomments?start=290 (accessed October 2006)

Liu, Jiayi (2007), '*Toumingzhuang*: Gangpian beishang zui chenggong de yici shengchan huodong' (*The Warlords*: the most successful example of Hong Kong films breaking into Mainland market'), *Dongfang zhaobao* (Eastern morning newspaper), 19 December 2007, http://ent.qq.com/a/20071219/000061.htm (accessed January 2008)

Lowerison, Jean (2004), '*Hero*', *San Diego Metropolitan*, http://sandiegometro.com/reel/index.php?reelID=723 (accessed October 2007)

Lowry, Peter (2004), '*Hero*', 22 August 2004, http://www.filmthreat.com/index.php?section=reviews&Id=6405 (accessed October 2007)

McGranaghan, Mike (2004), '*Hero*', *The Aisle Seat*, http://www.geocities.com/gamut_mag/heroqt.htm (accessed October 2007)

Meyer, Carla (2004), '*Hero*', *San Francisco Chronicle*, 27 August 2004, http://www.sfgate.com/cgi-bin/article.cgi?f=/c/a/2004/08/27/DDG478DLQJ27.DTL (accessed October 2007)

Misterkim-2 (2000), 'Cinema criticism 101', *IMDb*, 25 March 2000, http://www.imdb.com/title/tt0165929/reviews?start=230 (accessed October 2006)

Mohsen, Sherif (2001), 'Excellent but needs more romance', *IMDb*, 4 August 2001, http://www.imdb.com/title/tt0165929/usercomments?start=70 (accessed October 2006)

Morrissette, Mélanie (2002), 'Choreography: the unknown and ignored', *Offscreen*, 31 August 2002, http://www.horschamp.qc.ca/new_offscreen/choreography.html (accessed August 2007)

Movielover-9 (2002), 'Nice standard for action but that's about it', *IMDb*, 24 February 2002, http://www.imdb.com/title/tt0271027/usercomments?start=80 (accessed October 2006)

Nand, Ashlene (2006), 'Jet Li: enter the wu', *AllHipHop Alternatives*, http://www.allhiphop.com/Alternatives/?ID=387 http://allhiphop.com/2006/09/22/jet-li-enter-the-wu/ (accessed November 2011)

Ogle, Connie (2004), 'Breathtaking martial arts action makes surprising turns', *Miami Herald*, http://ae.miami.com/entertainment/ui/miami/movie.html?id=165025&reviewId=15927c (accessed October 2007)

Pollard, Mark (2004), 'Jet Li and the essence of a "Hero"', *Hong Kong Cinema*, 15 August 2004, http://www.hkcinema.co.uk/ (accessed October 2007)
Rizzo, Frank (2005), *IMDb*, 12 September 2005, http://www.imdb.com/title/tt0165929/usercomments?start=280 (accessed October 2006)
Robotman-1 (2001), 'The form of lightning', *IMDb*, 7 August 2001, http://www.imdb.com/title/tt0271027/reviews?start=140 (accessed October 2006)
Rotten Tomatoes, 'About Rotten Tomatoes', http://uk.rottentomatoes.com/pages/about (accessed October 2007)
Rotten Tomatoes, '*Hero*', http://uk.rottentomatoes.com/m/hero/ (accessed October 2007)
Ryan, Tony (2005), 'Jet's best "modern day" actioner', *IMDb*, 5 August 2005, http://www.imdb.com/title/tt0342258/reviews?start=140 (accessed October 2006)
sexcnessim (2005), 'What more could you ask for?', *IMDb*, 20 September 2005, http://www.imdb.com/title/tt0342258/usercomments?start=20 (accessed October 2006)
Shadows-8 (2000), 'Impressive beginning to Jet Li's leading role', *IMDb*, 31 March 2000, http://www.imdb.com/title/tt0165929/usercomments?start=200 (accessed October 2006)
Skubrick-5 (2000), 'My thoughts', *IMDb*, 18 December 2000, mhttp://www.imdb.com/title/tt0165929/usercomments?start=100 (accessed October 2006)
Stanley, Larry (2005), 'Sometimes you should bite the hand', *IMDb*, 14 May 2005, http://www.imdb.com/title/tt0342258/reviews?start=190 (accessed October 2006)
Tai, Wilson (2001), 'I underestimated this solid film', *IMDb*, 10 July 2001, http://www.imdb.com/title/tt0271027/usercomments?start=170 (accessed October 2006)
Tavernetti, Susan (2004), '*Hero*', *Palo Alto Weekly*, 27 August 2004, http://paloaltoonline.com/movies/moviescreener.php?id=002019&type=long (accessed October 2007)
Thome, Simon (2005), 'Entertaining, not more not less!', *IMDb*, 27 March 2005, http://www.imdb.com/title/tt0165929/reviews?start=280 (accessed October 2006)
Wei, Junzi (2002), 'Tan xin wuxia dianying' (Discussion of the new *wuxia* cinema), http://www.xici.net/d8477718.htm (accessed November 2011)

Visual sources

Cause: The Birth of Hero, documentary, directed by Gan Lu. China, 2002.
Cinema Hong Kong: Sword Fighting, documentary, directed by Ian Taylor. USA/Hong Kong, 2003.
Lu Yu youyue: Li Lianjie – Wo de sijia gushi (Interview with Lu Yu: Li Lianjie – My private story), Phoenix Television. Hong Kong, 2007.
Yang ± Yin: Gender in Chinese Cinema, documentary, directed by Stanley Kwan. UK/Hong Kong, 1997.

Index

A Lisi, 87, 98
Abbas, Ackbar, 40, 49
action genre, 11, 14, 16–18, 65–6, 136, 142, 179
    action cinema, 11–14, 16–17, 117, 128, 136, 142–3, 177
    action comedies, 11–13, 15, 141, 147
    Hong Kong action, 11–16, 18, 21, 26, 42, 54, 119
action hero, 8, 11, 108, 121–3, 140, 142, 147
adaptation, 14, 67
Advocate/preacher of non-violence, 29, 179, 180–2, 185
aesthetics of violence, 11; *see also* John Woo
Ageing, 190
All about Eve, 26
American dream, 173, 188
Anderson, Benedict, 159
Anderson, Aaron, 12, 15
anti-Japanese, 9, 146
anti-stereotyping, 106–9, 125; *see also* re-stereotyping; stereotyping
anti-violence, 179, 182
anticolonialism, 11, 147
appeal studies, 12
Around the World in 80 Days, 108
Ashes of Time, 16, 41, 43
Asian as child, 115, 122–3
Asian boy sidekick, 121
Asian-American, 9, 113–14, 127, 130
Asianisation, 13, 146–7
Asiaphilia, 117
Asiaphobia, 117
audiences/reception studies, 22, 25–7
    audience studies, 22, 24–6
    fan discourse, 25, 29, 70–1, 74, 114, 181

historical reception studies, 24–5, 27
Internet fandom, 167, 183
spectatorship theory, 23
Aunt Thirteen, 43, 51, 78, 138; *see also Once Upon a Time in China*
authenticity, 44, 47–9, 52–3, 55, 57–60, 62, 171–2, 190

Banderas, Antonio, 3
Benshoff, Harry, 77, 80
Bergfelder, Tim, 185
Bergman, Ingrid, 3, 24,
Besson, Luc, 5, 13, 110, 183
Binoche, Juliette, 2
black connection, 12
Black Mask, 6, 105
blockbuster, 5, 11, 13–14, 110, 149, 163, 185, 187, 190–1
body genre, 15–16
body size, 114–15, 122
Bodyguard from Beijing, The, 6, 105, 148
Bond, James, 40, 137
Bordwell, David, 11–12, 15–16, 42, 50–1, 54, 56, 58
Born to Defense, 5, 148
Bride with White Hair, The, 35, 41, 43
Bridget Jones's Diary, 2
Broken Blossoms, 107
Budd, Mike, 94
Buddhist, 167, 170, 179, 180–2
Butler, Jeremy G., 24
Butterfly Murders, The, 15, 39

Cause, 150–2, 159, 164
Chan, Charlie, 106, 128
Chan, Gordon, 8, 37–8
Chan, Jachinson, 129

INDEX

Chan, Jackie, 3–4, 9–12, 15, 17–19, 20, 33, 47–8, 59–60, 62–3, 65, 85, 94, 105, 107–8, 119, 120, 122–3, 130, 137, 146–8, 162, 172–3, 176, 187–8, 190
   Clown-like Chinese male, 109, 123
   see also action genre: comedies; kung fu comedy/comedies; outtakes
Chan, Peter, 4–5, 77, 187
Chan, Stephen, 8
changing meanings of Jet Li, 27, 45, 185–6, 188
characterisation, 15, 87, 108, 119, 121, 148, 158, 162
Charlie's Angels, 13
Chen Baisheng, 49–50
Chen Kaige, 19, 83
Chen Pinyuan, 160
Chen Zhen, 35, 38, 105
Cheng Huan, 106–7, 128
Cheung, Leslie, 41, 52, 78
Chiang, David, 59
childlike man, 122, 124–5, 132, 186
China's Road under the Shadow of Globalisation, 160
Chinese Communist Party (CCP), 84, 96, 100
Chinese intellectuals, 153, 159–61
Chinese masculinity, 10, 17–21, 58, 99, 107, 127, 136–7, 144, 161
   asexual/sexless Chinese male/men, 28, 128, 130–1, 135–6, 138, 144
   feminisation of Chinese men, 18–19
   wu masculinity, 20, 137
Chineseness, 34, 146–8, 163, 165
Ching Siu-tung, 6, 34–9, 41, 67, 105, 190–1
chopsocky, 10, 13–14, 16, 21, 163
choreography, 52, 157–8, 163
   choreographer, 13, 15, 58–9, 71, 119
   wirework, 13, 39, 41, 48, 52, 55–7, 190
Chow, Rey, 116, 123
Chow, Stephen, 37, 41, 94
Chow Yun-fat, 20, 29n, 118, 120, 129, 137
Chu, Rolanda, 68, 72, 74
cinema of attractions, 163
cinema of spectacle, 162–3

cinematic technology/techniques, 28, 40–1, 44, 47, 49, 52–3, 55–7, 60, 62–3, 172, 190
City Entertainment, 27–8, 49–53, 55, 60, 63, 87, 89
clichés, 10, 13, 21, 107, 113, 131, 136, 172
   memory, 25–6, 28, 45, 88–90, 94, 96, 98–9, 158, 160
comparative reading, 26
compensatory fantasy, 178
compulsory viewing, 88, 95
computer-generated imagery (CGI), 48, 190–1
Corliss, Richard, 111, 117, 119–20
country bumpkins, 7
Cradle 2 The Grave, 110, 113, 120, 148, 158, 163,
cross-cultural/transcultural reception, 29, 106, 130, 150, 152, 164, 185
cross-dressing, 36, 41–2, 68, 74–7, 80
Crouching Tiger, Hidden Dragon, 11, 14, 16, 33, 163, 175
Cruz, Penelope, 2
cultural hegemony, 2, 138
Cultural Revolution, The, 7, 61, 158, 160
Cyber-fu, 13

Dai Jinghua, 80
Danny the Dog (*Unleashed*), 5, 110, 113–15, 121–2, 131–2, 134–5, 139–42, 148, 179, 187–8, 191
Dazhong dianying, 71
Decisive Engagement 1–3, The, 96
DeCordova, Richard, 168
depoliticised male hero, 99
desexualised Chinese men *see* Chinese masculinity: asexual/sexless Chinese male/men
desinicisation, 96, 147
Desser, David, 12, 14, 123, 146–7
Di Long, 17, 59
Dingding, 71
Dingding Studio, 71, 73–80, 81, 89, 169
Dr. Wai in the Scripture With No Words, 105
Donner, Richard, 5, 111
Dovey, Jon, 173
Dragon Fight, 5

Drunken Master, 50, 85
Dyer, Richard, 1, 22, 106, 128, 136, 144, 167–8, 174, 180

East is Red, The, 41–2
Eastern Productions, 6, 83
Eat Drink Man Woman, 84
Enter the Dragon, 107, 123, 129, 147
Expendables, The, 191

family man, 175, 178
Farquhar, Mary, 1, 9, 17, 20–1, 85, 149, 190
Father and Son, 84
Father Knows Best, 84
father-son relationship, 83–6, 92, 100
father's son, 28, 84, 86, 99–100, 185; *see also* father-son relationship
Fearless, 5–6, 178–9, 187–8
fighting machine, 16, 60, 112–15, 120, 124, 132–3, 180
film émigré, 3, 9
Fiske, John, 178
Fist of Fury, 45n
Fist of Legend, 8, 38, 41
Flirting Scholar, 37
Flying Swords of Dragon Gate, The, 190–1
Fong Sai-yuk and Miu Chui-fa, 86
Fong Sai-yuk II, 6, 62, 86, 91
Fong Sai-yuk, 6, 16, 26, 28, 33, 36, 38, 41, 44–5, 62, 83–100 passim
Forbidden Kingdom, The, 5, 187
Fore, Steve, 3, 8, 119, 147
Four Weddings and a Funeral, 2
Freeman, Morgan, 121, 133, 140
Fu Manchu, 106–7, 116–17, 128
Fu Sheng, 17, 105
Fung, Richard, 129

Garbo, Greta, 3
gay film, 43, 66–7
gender-bending, 28, 36, 41–4, 65–6, 68, 71, 74, 78, 80
gender-blurring *see* gender-bending
gender confusion, 28, 67–8, 75, 77; *see also* gender trouble
gender trouble, 65–6, 73–4, 83
Geraghty, Christine, 167–8

globalisation, 21, 130, 132, 160–1
Golden Bauhinia Awards, 49
Golden Swallow, The, 17
Gong Li, 118

Hansen, Miriam, 23
hard body, 18, 61, 108
He's a Woman, She's a Man, 77
Heavenly Bodies, 180
Hepburn, Audrey, 23
Hero, 4–6, 11, 14, 28–9, 33, 120, 148–65 passim, 179, 186–8, 190
High Risk, 105
Hitman, 105
Hollinger, Karen, 22
Holmlund, Chris, 11, 188, 190–1
Holy Weapon, 41, 43
homosexuality, 42–3, 65, 77
 decriminalisation of homosexuality, 77
 gay ideology/politics, 65–6, 77–8
 homophobia, 69, 77
 homosexual undertone/implication, 66, 75, 80
Hong Kong Connections, 12
Hong Kong Film Awards, 49, 125, 187,
Hong Kong Film Critics Awards, 187
Hong Kong New Wave, 15, 49
horizon of expectation, 136, 162
Horsemen, 118
Hou Hsiao-hsien, 83
Hu-Du-Men, 77
Hu, King, 11, 15, 34, 58
Huang Qiuyan, 79
Huang Shixian, 154
Huffer, Ian, 24
Hui Ying-hung, 187
Hung, Sammo, 15, 39, 59, 65, 85, 147, 187
Hunt, Leon, 9, 11, 13, 34–5, 41, 48–9, 54–5, 58, 65, 79, 85, 87–8, 100, 110, 117, 120, 130, 132, 147, 162–3, 167

impact studies, 12
impersonation in fighting, 60, 62–3, 188; *see also* personification in fighting
Indiana Jones and the Temple of Doom, 121
internationalisation, 11, 16
Internet Movie Database, The (IMDb), 28, 131–44 passim, 169

interracial male-female buddy narrative, 142
interracial politics, 135, 138
interracial romance, 130, 134–6, 144; *see also* miscegenation
Intimates, 77

Jancovich, Mark, 24
Jeet Kune Do, 62
Jet Li Official Website, The, 29, 169–82 passim
Ji Chunhua, 6
Jia Leilie, 35, 57, 154–5
Jin Yong, 14, 35, 67, 76, 160
ju pian, 95
Jue Yuan, 51, 97–8, 100, 155
June 4 Syndrome, 89
Jungle Book, 121
Justice, My Foot, 37

Kaminsky, Stuart, 12, 122
Kang Xueying, 51–2
Kelly, Gene, 4, 162
Kidman, Nicole, 2
kinaesthetic artistry, 12; *see also* David Bordwell
King of Beggars, 37
King of Qin, 149, 152–4, 160
Kiss of the Dragon, 5–6, 110, 112, 131–2, 134, 139–41, 148, 158, 171, 187
Klinger, Barbara, 27
Kuai Bao, 177
Kuhn, Annette, 74–6, 81
kung fu comedy/comedies, 11, 33, 50, 60, 83, 85, 95–6; *see also* action genre: action comedies
kung fu craze, 4, 12, 59, 118
Kung Fu Cult Masters, 11
Kung fu kid, 51–2, 63
Kwan Tak-hing, 37, 50–1, 58, 105

lack of chemistry, 130, 134, 144, 174
Lan Yu, 73
Lang Tian, 69
Larson, Wendy, 19
Last Emperor, The, 107
Last Hero in China, 38
Lau Kar-leung, 58–9

Lau Tai-muk, 59
Lee, Ang, 11, 14, 16, 33, 83–4, 163
Lee, Bruce, 4, 9–12, 17–20, 33–4, 40, 47–9, 57, 59–63, 65, 105, 107–8, 118, 122–3, 128–30, 137, 142, 146–7, 172, 190
Lee, Leo Ou-fan, 129
leitmotif films, 95–6
Lethal Weapon 4, 4, 5, 110–11, 117–18, 124, 149, 153, 162, 171
Li Zhi, 79
liang xiang, 54
Lie Fu, 43, 188
Lin, Brigitte, 41–2, 52, 68, 70–4, 76, 78–80
Ling Hucong, 35, 38, 42, 44, 62, 68–81 passim, 83, 93, 105, 155, 186
Lo, Kwai-cheung, 2, 11, 18, 40, 59, 107, 120, 148
Logan, Bey, 47
Loon Sheng, 58
Louie, Kam, 20, 136–8, 143–4
Luo Weiming, 60

MacDowell, Andie, 2
Major, Wade, 9, 50, 63, 79, 86
male bonding, 65–6, 73, 83
Mao Zedong and His Son, 96
Marchetti, Gina, 11–12, 18, 116–17, 125, 147, 188
martial arts champion, 6, 9, 44, 49, 120, 172–3
martial art-house films/blockbusters, 5, 11, 14, 33, 163, 187
Martrix, The, 13, 150
martyrdom complex, 17–18; *see also* Zhang, Che
masquerade, 28, 98–100
Master, The, 5
master-disciple relationship, 83, 85
Mayne, Judith, 24, 168
McDonald, Paul, 22, 26, 61, 168, 183
Memoirs of a Geisha, 118
Ming Bao, 167
miscegenation, 138
misogyny, 69
mixed methodology, 22, 25–6
mo-lei-tau, 36–7, 44

moral model, 29, 182–3
Moseley, Rachel, 23–4
mother-son relationship, 86, 92
mother's boy, 28, 83, 86–8, 91–3,
    98–100, 185–6; *see also* mother-son
    relationship
Mr. Nice Guy, 147
multiculturalism, 147
Mummy, Tomb of the Dragon Emperor, The,
    118, 191
My Father is a Hero, 105

Nameless, 149–50, 154–5, 157–8, 160–1,
    164
national identity, 11, 20, 29, 116, 145, 147,
    165
national treasure, 7
nationalism, 59, 96, 123, 146–8, 151,
    159–61
Negra, Diane, 1–2
New Dragon Gate Inn, 36, 43
New Legend of Shaolin, The, 45n
Ng Chun-ming, 106
Ng Ho, 37–8, 85
1997 handover, 7, 15, 36, 77, 89, 98
97 Syndrome films, 47, 89
normal guy, 29, 171–4, 178, 182, 185
nostalgia, 39, 44, 48, 97–8

Ocean Heaven, 187, 191
Ocean's Eleven, 121
Ocean's Thirteen, 121
Ocean's Twelve, 121
Oedipus complex, 92, 99
Official Jet Li Website, The, 29, 169–83
    passim
Once Upon a Time in China (OUATIC),
    5–6, 8, 15, 28, 33, 35–8, 43–5, 47–64
    passim, 83, 87–8, 93, 138, 149, 174,
    188
Once Upon a Time in China II, 45n
Once Upon a Time in China III, 86
One, The, 110–11, 113, 118, 131–2, 134,
    141, 148–9, 158
One Foundation, The, 179–82
Orientalism, 109, 116, 125
    Orientalist construction, 18, 112,
    123

Orientalist discourse, 116, 124
Orientalist imagination, 115, 117, 124
outtakes, 18, 130; *see also* Jackie Chan

Pan, Lynn, 106, 109
pan-Chinese film, 6, 11, 148, 191
pan-Chinese identity, 146, 148
Parish, James Robert, 5, 9
parody, 36, 42, 44, 85, 91
pause/burst/pause, 12, 54; *see also* David
    Bordwell
Peking opera, 15, 54, 57–8
People's Republic of China (PRC), 5, 7,
    152, 165, 167
performativity of martial arts, 15, 52, 57,
    62–3; *see also* authenticity
personification in fighting, 62; *see also*
    impersonation in fighting
philanthropy/charity, 167, 179, 181–2
physical intimacy, 128–9, 134–6, 138, 144,
    175
Pirates of the Caribbean: At World's End,
    118
Pushing Hands, 84

Qin Shaobo, 121

racial politics, 11–12, 107, 123, 147
remasculinisation of Chinese men, 10,
    17–21
re-stereotyping, 107–8; *see also* anti-
    stereotyping; stereotyping
rhetoric of hardness, 18; *see also* hard
    body
rhetoric of castration, 84
romantic hero films, 17, 66; *see also* John
    Woo
Romeo Must Die, 110, 112, 119, 122,
    131–2, 134–5, 138–41, 148, 163, 171
Rotten Tomatoes, 155–6, 161, 169
Royal Tramp II, 36–7
Royal Tramp, 37
Rumble in the Bronx, 119, 147
Rush Hour 2, 2, 108, 118
Rush Hour, 12, 147

Sarkar, Bhaskar, 36, 39, 41, 45
Scar Literature, 158, 160

Seagal, Stephen, 113, 172
Sek Kei, 35–6, 41–2, 44, 58, 137
Sense and Sensibility, 16
sex idol/icon, 29, 174, 176, 182–3, 185
Sexiest Foreign Man, 177
Shang Ke, 153–5
Shaolin Temple (as a film), 4–7, 44–5, 47, 49, 51, 97, 100, 130, 149, 158, 160, 171, 177, 185
Shaolin Temple (as a site), 4, 146, 181
Shaolin Temple II: Kids from Shaolin, 49
Shaw Brothers, 58–9, 71
Shen Bian, 95
Shi Wenhong, 107
shifu, 84–5
Shingler, Martin, 26
Shohat, Ella and Robert Stam, 124
Shower, 84
Shu, Yuan, 12, 18, 107, 146–7
Silver, Joel, 5, 110, 119, 135, 141
slow motion, 12, 56
Smiling, Proud Wanderer, The, 14, 67
Snake in the Eagle's Shadow, 85
socialist stardom, 167
Sorcerer and the White Snake, The, 190
special effects, 39–41, 44, 48–9, 55–6, 59, 119, 190
Stacey, Jackie, 23–4, 90
Staiger, Janet, 23, 25
Stallone, Sylvester, 24, 190–1
star bodies, 11, 61
star vehicles, 123–4, 191
star-as-ordinary, 174; *see also* normal guy
star-as-special, 174
star-making, 3, 168–9, 179, 183
Stars/stardom
　Hollywood stars/stardom, 1–4
　international star/stars, 1, 2, 9
　national stardom, 1, 4
　transnational kung fu stardom, 1, 4, 9–11, 16, 19, 21–2, 33, 106, 119, 122–3, 145–6, 185, 188–9, 191
　transnational stardom, 1–4, 8, 10, 22, 186, 190–1
　transnational star/stars, 1–4, 8–9, 22, 29, 108, 116, 118, 129, 135, 145, 150, 164–5, 179, 186–91

stereotype, 7–9, 68, 70, 106–10, 116–18, 120–2, 127–9, 135, 137, 144, 189
stereotyping, 106–7, 109–10, 116–18, 120, 125; *see also* anti-stereotyping; re-stereotyping
Stoke, Lisa Odham and Michael Hoover, 36, 38–9, 42, 70
Story of Wong Fei-hung, The, 50
Stringer, Julian, 8, 9, 113, 127
superhero-next-door, 174
Sword, The, 15
swordplay films, 11, 15, 34, 58
Swordsman, 14, 34, 67
Swordsman II, 6, 15, 28, 33, 38, 41–2, 44–5, 62, 64, 65–81 passim, 83, 93, 155, 175
symbolic femininity, 19; *see also* Wendy Larson

Tai Chi Master, 38, 105
Tam, Patrick, 15
Tang, Billy Hin-sing, 5
Tarantino, Quentin, 13, 163
Tasker, Yvonne, 11, 13, 18, 108, 117, 128–9, 147
technologised masculinity, 40
Teo, Stephen, 11, 18, 33–4, 36, 40–2, 66, 68, 70, 84, 86, 107, 123, 129, 147
Three Kingdoms, The, 66
Three Swordsmen, The, 42
Tiananmen Square protests/incident, 36, 89, 95, 99, 160–1
tianxia/all under heaven, 150, 153–5, 161
transnational action, 10, 33, 190
transnational identity, 29, 149–50, 165
transnationalisation, 6–7, 9, 11, 16, 21, 153, 187
Tsui Hark, 5–6, 14–15, 34–5, 38–40, 47–52, 54, 56, 63, 67, 71–3, 88, 175, 191
Two Heroes, 86

underdog, 50, 123–4

View behind, 75–7
View with, 75–7

Wachowski, Andy, 13
Wachowski, Lana, 13
Wang Dulu, 14
Wang Yichuang, 160
Wang Yu, 12, 17, 59
Wang Yuejin, 19
War, 118, 179
Warlords, The, 4–6, 9, 118, 125, 175, 179, 187–8
Water Margin, The, 66
Wedding Banquet, The, 84
wen-wu, 20, 136
Wenhui, 174
Western gaze, 8
Western paradigms, 20–2
Williams, Linda, 15
Williams, Tony, 47
Wing Chun, 43, 59
Winslet, Kate, 2
wire-fu, 162
Wong, Anna May, 186
Wong Fei-hung, 35, 37–8, 43, 50–63 passim, 65, 78–9, 81, 83, 85, 93, 95, 97, 100, 105, 122, 138, 148, 174, 186
Wong Jing, 35–8, 41, 105
Wong Kar-wai, 15–16
Woo, John, 11, 15, 17–18, 20, 66
Wu Dang, 95
Wu Lin Zhi, 95
Wu Jing, 6
wuda, 91
wushu, 7, 54, 170, 174, 181
wuxia
    jianghu, 38, 68, 84
    wu, 20, 34, 137, 179
    wuxia complex, 160
    wuxia novels, 14, 35, 160

xia, 34, 150, 154
xiake, 34, 36, 38–9, 149, 155
xianü, 43, 65, 75, 83
xiayi, 34, 38

Xiake Dream of Chinese Literati for Centuries, The, 160
Xiao Zi, 7, 177
Xing, Jun, 8, 110, 120

Yang ± Yin: Gender in Chinese Cinema, 58, 66–7, 78, 83
Yang, Edward, 83
Yang Xiaowen, 52, 88, 98
yanggang, 17–18, 43, 58, 65; see also Zhang, Che
Yau, Esther, 40, 84
Yellow Peril, 109, 115–17, 120, 124
Yu, Ronny, 3, 35
Yu, Sabrina Qiong, 1, 183n
Yuen Biao, 59
Yuen, Corey, 6, 15, 39, 105, 124
Yuen Woo-ping, 15, 35, 38–9, 43, 50, 62, 71, 85

Zellweger, Renée, 10
Zhang Che, 17, 34, 40, 43, 58–9, 65–6, 86
Zhang Xudong, 159
Zhang Yimou, 5, 16, 20, 120, 148–52, 155, 157–9, 165, 195
Zhang, Yingjin, 21, 37
Zhang Zhicheng, 51
Zhang Ziyi, 118
Zhao Wenzhuo, 6
Zheng Peipei, 59
Zheng Xiaotian, 158

EU representative:
Easy Access System Europe
Mustamäe tee 50, 10621 Tallinn, Estonia
Gpsr.requests@easproject.com

www.ingramcontent.com/pod-product-compliance
Lightning Source LLC
Chambersburg PA
CBHW051057230426
43667CB00013B/2342